Rhinegold Study Guides

A Student's Guide to A2 Music

for the **OCR** Specification
2007 onwards

by

Paul Terry and David Bowman

R·

Rhinegold Publishing Ltd
241 Shaftesbury Avenue
London WC2H 8TF
Telephone: 020 7333 1720
Fax: 020 7333 1765
www.rhinegold.co.uk

Rhinegold Music Study Guides
(series editor: Paul Terry)

A Student's Guide to GCSE Music for the OCR Specification
Listening Tests for Students (Books 1 and 2): OCR GCSE Music Specification

A Student's Guide to AS Music for the OCR Specification
A Student's Guide to A2 Music for the OCR Specification
Listening Tests for Students: OCR AS Music Specification
Listening Tests for Students: OCR A2 Music Specification

Similar books have been produced for the AQA and Edexcel Music Specifications. Also available are:

A Student's Guide to AS/A2 Music Technology for the Edexcel AS and A2 Specification
AS/A2 Listening Tests for Music Technology
A Student's Guide to GCSE Music for the WJEC Specification (separate English and Welsh language versions)

The following books are designed to support all GCSE and GCE music courses:

A Student's Guide to Composing (Book 1 for GCSE and Book 2 for A-level Music)
A Student's Guide to Harmony and Counterpoint (for AS and A2 Music)

Other Rhinegold Study Guides

Students' Guides to AS and A2 Drama and Theatre Studies for the AQA and Edexcel Specifications
Students' Guides to AS and A2 Performance Studies for the OCR Specification
Students' Guides to AS and A2 Religious Studies for the AQA, Edexcel and OCR Specifications

Rhinegold Publishing also publishes Classical Music, Classroom Music, Early Music Today, Music Teacher,
Opera Now, Piano, The Singer, British and International Music Yearbook, British Performing Arts Yearbook,
Music Education Yearbook, Rhinegold Dictionary of Music in Sound.

First published 2002 in Great Britain by
Rhinegold Publishing Limited
241 Shaftesbury Avenue
London WC2H 8TF
Telephone: 020 7333 1720
Fax: 020 7333 1765
www.rhinegold.co.uk
Reprinted 2003. Revised edition 2006

You should always check the current requirements of the examination, since these may change.
Copies of the OCR Specification may be obtained from Oxford, Cambridge and RSA Examinations at
OCR Publications, PO Box 5050, Annesley, Nottingham NG15 0DL
Telephone 0870 770 6622, Facsimile 0870 770 6621.
See also the OCR website at http://www.ocr.org.uk/

A Student's Guide to A2 Music for the OCR Specification
British Library Cataloguing in Publication Data.
A catalogue record for this book is available from the British Library.
ISBN 1-904226-94-9
Printed in Great Britain by WPG Ltd

*La musique exprime ce qui ne peut être dit
et sur quoi il est impossible de rester silencieux.*

*Music expresses that which can not be said
and on which it is impossible to be silent.*

Victor Hugo (1864)

Contents

The authors

David Bowman and Paul Terry have written many books in support of A-level music, including three *Student Guides to AS Music*, three *Student Guides to A2 Music* (all published by Rhinegold) and three books published by Schott: *Aural Matters* (1993), *Aural Matters in Practice* (1994) and *Listening Matters* (2003).

Paul Terry was director of music at the City of London Freemen's School for 15 years and later taught at Kingston Polytechnic. He currently works as a music editor, engraver and publisher. Paul has been a music examiner for nearly 30 years and has been engaged as a consultant by several examination boards. He also served as a member of the Secondary Examinations Council and its successor the Schools Examinations and Assessment Council. He was chief examiner for the Oxford and Cambridge Schools Examinations Board (now part of OCR) and he was a chief examiner for London Examinations (now part of Edexcel).

In addition to the books listed above, Paul is co-author with William Lloyd of *Music in Sequence* (1991), and its companion volumes *Classics in Sequence* (1992) and *Rock in Sequence* (1996), and also *Rehearse, Direct and Play: A Student's Guide to Group Music-Making* (1993), all of which are published by Musonix Publishing.

David Bowman was for 20 years director of music at Ampleforth College where he still teaches. He was a chief examiner for the University of London Schools Examination Board (now Edexcel) from 1982 to 1998. He now spends more time with his family, horses and dogs.

In addition to the titles listed above, David's publications include the *London Anthology of Music* (University of London Schools Examinations Board, 1986), *Sound Matters* (co-authored with Bruce Cole, Schott, 1989), *Analysis Matters* (Rhinegold, Volume 1 1997, Volume 2 1998) and numerous analytical articles for *Music Teacher*. He is a contributor to the *Collins Classical Music Encyclopedia* (2000) edited by Stanley Sadie and is the author of the *Rhinegold Dictionary of Music in Sound*.

Acknowledgements

The authors would like to thank Veronica Jamset, formerly chief examiner in music to OCR, for her advice during the preparation of this book, and Dr Lucien Jenkins of Rhinegold Publishing for so much help and encouragement. Nevertheless if any errors have been made it is only right to state that these are the responsibility of the authors.

Recordings

Details of CD recordings are believed to be correct at the time of publication. However recording companies frequently delete CDs and then rerelease the recordings in different compilations with new catalogue numbers and, just occasionally, a reduction in price! In case of difficulty, good local dealers should be able to locate recordings from the information we have given.

Introduction

This book is intended to assist students preparing for the OCR A2 examination in music. Like other books in the *Rhinegold Study Guides* series its purpose is to supplement, but not supplant, the work of teachers.

The full Advanced GCE in Music is made up of six units, three AS and three A2. This book deals only with the latter. The AS units are discussed in a separate *Rhinegold Study Guide* (see *right*).

The A2 course is underpinned by two areas of study – 'tonality', which is a continuation of your AS work on the same subject, and 'words and music', which counter-balances the AS emphasis on 'instrumental techniques'. There is a summary of the entire A2 specification on the next page.

In this book we have included many suggestions and tips which we hope will help you do well in performing and composing, but the main emphasis is on preparation for Unit 2555 (*Historical and Analytical Studies*) and especially for the prescribed historical topic that forms the second part of this unit.

There are five such topics (listed on page 33) of which you have to study one. Each deals with the relationship between words and music at various points in history. We have written a chapter on each topic, dealing with the main genres, techniques and styles that you will need to know, illustrated by examples mainly from easily accessible works. OCR does not set specific works for this paper, so there is no need to limit your study to the pieces we have suggested. However in our discussions we have tried to cover all of the principal issues outlined in the specification.

The questions during the course of these chapters will help you check your understanding of the context, style and technical features of the music – they are not intended to be representative of actual exam questions. If you have difficulty with these questions, you will generally find the right answers by rereading the preceding pages. The sample questions at the ends of the chapters on historical topics are more demanding and should preferably be worked under exam conditions. For examples of the questions that are likely to be encountered in the exam, you should be guided by the specimen and (when available) past papers produced by OCR.

We have included explanations of the main technical terms you are likely to encounter in studying vocal music. If you need further help with these, or with other terminology you encounter during the course, we recommend you consult the **Rhinegold Dictionary of Music in Sound**. This comprehensive resource not only gives detailed explanations of a wide range of musical concepts, but it also illustrates them using a large number of examples on a set of accompanying CDs, thus enabling you to hear directly how theoretical concepts are realised in the actual sounds of music.

The details of the specification are correct at the time of going to press, but you and your teachers should always check current requirements for the examination with OCR as these may change.

A Student's Guide to AS Music for the OCR Specification by Veronica Jamset, Chris Batchelor and Paul Terry. *Rhinegold Publishing Ltd.* ISBN: 1-904226-63-9.

Rhinegold Dictionary of Music in Sound by David Bowman. *Rhinegold Publishing Ltd.* ISBN 0-946890-87-0.

A2 Music: an overview

There are three units, each of which accounts for one third of the marks for A2 Music:

Unit 2553 **Performing: Interpretation** Section A accounts for 65% of the marks for this unit, and Section B accounts for the remaining 35%.	There are two parts to this unit: **Section A – Recital** You will have to perform a programme of music of between 12 and 15 minutes in length. This will be assessed by a visiting examiner, and you may have an audience present if you wish. You can perform as a soloist, as a member of an ensemble, or as an accompanist. **Section B – Performance Investigation** You will have to prepare your own written comparison of two or three recordings of a single work (or small group of works) for the instrument (or voice) that you offered in Section A. The work(s) should be related to the music you presented in your recital. Your written report, with examples on cassette, must be given to the visiting examiner on the day of your recital.
Unit 2554 **Composing 2** Each of the options you choose accounts for 50% of the marks for this unit. The coursework will be assessed by an external examiner.	There are four options in this unit, of which you must choose two – one of your choices must be either 1 or 2. **1 – Vocal Composition.** You will have to write a vocal composition to a detailed brief that will be set by OCR. The brief will include two texts, one of which you must set to music. **2 – Film Storyboard.** You will have to compose music for a set of short film scenes, the details of which will be set by OCR. **3 – Stylistic Techniques.** You will have to produce a portfolio of eight to ten exercises in one of a range of prescribed styles. **4 – Free composition.** A composition of your own choice.
Unit 2555 **Historical and Analytical Studies** Section A accounts for 45% of the marks for this paper (30% for the first piece and 15% for the second). You can play the CD for Section A as many times as you wish, but bear in mind that you will need to allow sufficient time to answer the two essay questions. Section B accounts for 35% of the marks for this paper, and Section C accounts for the remaining 20% of marks.	This unit has three parts, all of which will be assessed by means of a single 2½-hour written paper in three sections. **Section A – Aural Extracts** You will be given recordings of two pieces of music. The first will be vocal music from the period 1900–45, and you will also have a score of the piece (with some passages omitted). You will be asked about how the text is set, how tonality is relevant to the piece and how recording techniques are used. Some questions may require you to add pitches, rhythms, chords and performance directions to the score. The second piece, for which you will not have a score, may come from any music other than that set for Section B, and will test your general aural awareness. **Section B – Prescribed Historical Topics** You have to prepare one of five prescribed historical topics and answer one question (from a choice of three) about it. **Section C – Synoptic Essay** You will have to answer one question (from a choice of five) on a general musical subject, showing that you can make critical judgements about music, and that you can perceive connections between the various types of music you have studied.

Performing: Interpretation

Section A: Recital

The recital accounts for 65% of the marks for the performing unit. You will need to plan a programme that lasts between 12 and 15 minutes. You can have an audience present if you find this helpful – it could be just a small group of friends and fellow students – or you can choose to perform privately to the visiting examiner (which will probably make the occasion feel more like an exam). You can perform as an instrumentalist or as a singer, so when we use the term 'instrument' below you can take it to include the voice.

You can perform as a soloist (with accompaniment where required), or as a member of a small ensemble, or you can choose to play as an accompanist to someone else. If you perform as a member of a small ensemble you must play or sing a part that is not doubled by other instruments or voices.

Note that you cannot combine these roles. For instance, you are not allowed to include both solo and ensemble items in a recital.

You will probably choose to perform on the same instrument that you offered for AS Music, but it can be a different one if you wish. However the A2 recital must all be presented on one instrument – you are not, for example, allowed to play some pieces on the flute and some on the piano, even if you play both instruments to the same standard.

Choosing the right music is vitally important. The pieces should allow you to show technical, expressive and interpretative skills as a performer as well as an understanding of the music you perform. As we said in the AS Guide, remember that some styles of music, particularly technical studies and some types of pop music, may focus on only a limited range of techniques and not really give you much of a chance to show what you can do as a musician.

Planning your programme

The music you select should be typical of the repertoire of your instrument and should show the instrument to its best advantage. For instance flautists might play music from the French flute repertoire or horn players might select movements from Mozart's famous horn concertos.

Whatever you choose, the programme must have a sense of unity. You may be able to achieve this by performing a single piece in several movements, providing it meets the minimum time length. If you choose to perform several short pieces they should be related in some way. For instance singers might present a programme of songs by the American songwriters Irving Berlin and Cole Porter, or pianists might choose to play a group of romantic character pieces by, say, Mendelssohn, Schumann and Borodin. This need for a sense of focus in the programme applies equally to ensemble performance or accompanying.

You can perform single movements taken from longer works, but avoid presenting a succession of slow movements. It is acceptable to omit repeats and curtail long sections that are written for just the accompaniment (eg in a concerto movement) but it is not really acceptable to cut passages because you find them too difficult.

The technical difficulty of the music you offer also needs careful consideration. Easy pieces played musically are much more likely to attract high marks than difficult pieces marred by hesitations and breakdowns. In order to be able to achieve the highest marks the pieces need to be of grade 6 standard or higher (if you do not take graded exams your teacher will help explain what this means). However there is no need to struggle to reach this standard (and risk a potential disaster if it proves too difficult) since you will be given credit for what you can do with the music you offer.

The most important matter in planning the A2 recital programme is the requirement to undertake a Performance Investigation for the second part of this unit. This will involve making a comparative study of recordings of music related to the pieces you have played in your recital and it must be ready to hand to the examiner on the day of the recital. This will need very careful thought since, if you plan your investigation around a piece that you subsequently have to withdraw because it is not ready, it may prove impossible to find replacement music that still relates to your written work. If this should happen you could then be faced with having to locate and write about recordings of a different piece at very short notice.

To avoid a last-minute panic of this kind, it is essential to base your investigation on music related to some item in your recital programme that you *know* you will be able to manage – hoping it might be ready on the day is too great a risk to take!

Final preparations   Having chosen and studied the programme with your teacher and practised the pieces to a standard that you feel is acceptable, it is essential that you try out the music under performance conditions – if possible not to anyone who has heard you working on the music week by week, but to someone who is able to hear your performance for the first time. This could be a visiting relative, your fellow students, or a different teacher at your school or college. A small slip or two in performance should not concern you greatly, but if you find you are often hesitating in difficult passages or that the piece completely if unexpectedly breaks down then it is a sign that you may have chosen something which is too difficult. This means that you will need to decide if the work is suitable or whether it would be better to make a more realistic choice.

If the music is intended to have an accompaniment (as will be the case in most music apart from that for piano and other chordal instruments) then it is important that it should be played with accompaniment otherwise it will sound very incomplete. Try to work with an accompanist who can rehearse with you regularly, or at least on several occasions before the recital. Even the most accomplished accompanist will not be able to let you sound your best if the first time you perform together is at the final recital. Similarly, if you have chosen ensemble playing, you will need to rehearse regularly with the group – we have given some advice on ensemble performance on pages 11–13 of the AS Guide.

In planning the run-up to the recital always allow several more weeks than you think you need. Illness may curtail practice time, other commitments may prevent rehearsals with accompanists or the arrival date of the visiting examiner may be much sooner than you anticipated. It will save a lot of worry if you ensure that your performance investigation is finished well before the exam date – remember that it has to be handed to the visiting examiner on the day of the recital. The last thing you will want is to have to find time to complete your written work during the last few days of precious practice time.

As we wrote in the AS Guide, it is important to have a run-through of the music in the venue in which you will be performing. If it is a large hall you will probably find that you need to project the sound and exaggerate the contrasts much more than when practising at home. Conversely if you are playing a loud instrument (brass or electric guitar, for example) in a small room you will almost certainly need to limit the louder dynamics. Decide where you are going to sit or stand and check that the lighting is adequate but not dazzling. If you have an accompanist make sure that you have good eye contact without having to stand with your back to the examiner. If the piano is an upright one it may take some experimentation to find the best position.

If you need a music stand, make sure it is suitable and that you know how to adjust it. If your music is printed on thin paper or requires a page turn, check that it won't be likely to fall off the music stand in mid-performance. This can be a particular problem with well-worn sheet music that has been crumpled up in an instrument case!

Singers need to consider where to look when performing – staring the examiner in the eye can be a bit unnerving for both of you, so it is usually better to focus on a point above the examiner's head. Pianists should make sure that the piano stool is the right height (and if and how it can be adjusted) and should also check the pedal action of the instrument, as well as the keyboard touch.

If the recital is to be given to an audience you should also spend a few minutes practising walking on and off stage, and deciding how you will react to applause. The audience will be disappointed if you shamble on at the start and rush off at the end. Audiences need plenty of time to show their appreciation: a hurried nod in their direction as you exit will appear clumsy, if not downright rude. If there is no printed programme, you can create a friendly start by announcing the pieces you are going to perform – and if you are playing to a lone examiner this will help break the ice.

Finally, remember that the examiner will need copies of the pieces you are to perform – this needs to be organised in advance.

Section B: Performance investigation

The Performance Investigation accounts for the remaining 35% of marks for this unit. You are required to make a comparison of interpretations of a single work (or small group of short pieces) for the instrument on which you performed in Section A. The work you choose must have a clear relationship to the main focus of your recital for Section A. It could be the same piece, or it might be a more difficult piece by the same composer, or you might choose a work in similar style and genre but by a different composer.

Remember that you must concentrate on the role and performance of *your* instrument in the recordings you choose and not on the accompaniment or other instruments in the case of an ensemble work.

Your investigation must be based on two (or at most, three) recordings of the chosen work. These should be compared in a written report of no more than 2,500 words. It is essential that the points you make in your account are substantiated by references to clearly identified examples recorded on an accompanying cassette tape. You may also want to include notated examples within the text, but the examiner will not require a score of the complete work.

Selecting recordings

If you choose to investigate performances of a well-known work from the standard repertoire for your instrument you are likely to be able to choose from many recordings. This may well give you the scope to choose two highly contrasted interpretations, making the task of comparison that bit easier.

For instance, there are currently more than a dozen recordings of Mozart's Piano Sonata in A, K331 (the one with the famous 'Turkish rondo' finale). The 1985 recording by Mitsuko Uchida for Philips is highly regarded for its subtlety of playing and attention to detail, as well as for the technical quality of the recording. The slightly older interpretation by András Schiff for Decca is outstanding, but is more romantic and colourful in approach. This recording was made at a live performance, which perhaps accounts for the real sense of spontaneity in his playing, and the recording (while not as technically clean as Uchida's CD) was made in a warmer acoustic. The famous 1971 recording by Alfred Brendel (also on Philips) was made by one of the world's greatest pianists at the height of his powers. His customary attention to every detail of articulation produces insights into the work that are markedly different to either of the other two pianists we have mentioned. Although now issued on CD, the original recording predates the digital age, and some people find the analogue sound more realistic and convincing than digital recordings. The recording by Ronald Brautigam (for BIS) is played on a fortepiano (a modern copy of an 18th-century instrument) rather than on the type of piano we normally hear today. The sound is altogether different – more intimate and more agile – and Brautigam takes the Rondo alla Turca considerably more slowly than most performers (he clearly noticed that Mozart marked it only *Allegretto*).

This last recording raises the point that choosing older music, particularly from the 18th century or earlier, will often provide the opportunity to compare a recording of a work played on a modern instrument with one played on a period instrument. For instance a flute sonata by Bach played by William Bennett on a modern flute may be compared with Stephen Preston's recording of the same sonata played on a baroque one-keyed flute. Or a performance of one of Mozart's horn concertos played on a modern horn (eg by Dennis Brain) could be compared with one played on a handhorn (eg by Timothy Brown).

Comparisons of this sort may also enable you to compare a modern style of performance with one that takes a historically-informed approach to matters of rhythm, ornamentation and so forth. While this can be a fruitful approach, enabling you to explore changing attitudes to performance, there is ample scope for more straightforward comparisons, such as those that could be made between the first three recordings of the Mozart piano sonata mentioned earlier. In the case of music that is normally totally rearranged when performed by a different artist (as often occurs in pop music and jazz) you can choose to compare a cover version with the original, or a studio recording with a recording of a live performance.

So far so good, but how do you research the type of information about recordings that we have outlined above? There are several options, and it would be a good idea to explore them all:

✦ a good starting point is your instrumental (or singing) teacher – having decided on the piece you wish to investigate, discuss with your teacher (and your A-level teacher) the recordings and artists they like and dislike – and why

✦ find out what other players of your instrument think about different performers

✦ search out any relevant material in the CD collections of your school and local public library

✦ listen out for performances that feature your instrument on radio stations such as Classic FM and BBC Radio 3

✦ look out for *The Penguin Guide to Compact Discs* – it contains helpful evaluations of thousands of classical recordings

✦ read record reviews in the broadsheet newspapers and in music magazines such as *Gramophone* and the *BBC Music Magazine*

✦ go to the website http://www.gramophone.co.uk/cdreviews.asp to gain free access to more than 23,000 expert reviews that have appeared in *Gramophone* magazine

✦ make a point of listening to at least part of *CD Review* on BBC Radio 3, Saturday mornings between 9am and noon.

Reading and listening to professional reviews of the sort mentioned in the last four points above will help you get a feel for the type of approach that is needed, although most printed reviews tend to be rather shorter and less detailed than the type of investigation you will need to undertake. If you are working in a jazz idiom, some of the resources listed on page 71 of the AS Guide will be helpful. If you are working in a pop-music idiom, a special note of caution is needed. In the world of commercial pop music, reviews are more often about personalities than the music itself (eg 'John's return from the USA has been accompanied by rumours of a new girl-friend and increasing disagreement with the rest of the group'). This is definitely *not* the approach to adopt in your A2 submission – you need to write in detail about the performances, not the lives of the performers, whatever the style of music, using your ears as a guide.

The Internet can be a particularly useful resource, although it needs to be used with caution. For instance www.amazon.co.uk is not only a good place to check prices and availablity of recordings, but it also includes short audio samples from some CDs, enabling you to make a quick audition of recordings that you think may be of interest for this part of the course. But beware, the same website allows 'reviews' to be submitted from any member of the public

Research tips

Detailed Radio 3 listings can be found on the web at http://www.bbc.co.uk/radio3/ and in the *Radio Times*.

and some of these may be naive or misleading, and so would not be a good example to follow in your own work.

Initial comparisons

There may well be some obvious contrasts between the recordings you choose. A quick glance at the track playing times shown on the CD display will reveal if there are clear differences in speed, although this may mask more subtle variations of tempo that you will need to explore later. There may also be differences in instrumentation of the sort that can occur if one performer decides to play a baroque keyboard work on the piano while another prefers the harpsichord or clavichord. Similarly, a madrigal might be sung by soloists (one voice per part) or by a small vocal group (say, four voices per part) – or perhaps even by a choir. In the case of earlier music there may also be differences in key and/or tuning if one performance is reflecting as exactly as possible the way the work would have been heard by its composer.

There are likely to be clear differences in timbre, not only due to performing techniques but also, for instance, because one pianist has preferred a brightly-toned piano while another has played on a more sweetly-toned instrument, or one clarinettist has decided to use a harder reed than another.

There are also likely to be marked contrasts in the technical nature of the recordings. Some CDs are engineered to give the impression of very close 'presence' so that the performers appear to be only a couple of metres in front of the listener. This can often sound very exciting, but it can also be unrealistic. Exaggeration of the stereo field can make a piano keyboard seem to be several metres wide, and close recording can draw unwanted attention to the mechanics of performing, such as the noise of key mechanisms, or the breathing of the players. Other recordings are designed to create a more natural soundfield, as though the listener is sitting some distance away in a hall. Here the acoustics of the recording venue will be more obvious and, unless closely controlled by the engineer, can lead to recordings in which there is a muddying of the sound and perhaps even unwanted resonance that exaggerates certain parts of the frequency range.

There is also likely to be a difference between digital and analogue recordings. Some people feel that modern digital recordings can sound clinical in their precision, while older recordings that were made on analogue tape and then transferred to CD can seem warmer, any imperfections in the original helping to create a more natural overall effect.

Detailed listening

You will need to be critical and questioning when comparing recordings. Begin by trying to identify the main focus of the piece. What is the music trying to convey? The answer may be relatively easy if there is a clue in the title. For instance if an instrumental piece is called *Song without words* you might consider how the performances succeed in sounding like a song. Is most of the attention on presenting a *cantabile* melody, with a mainly supportive accompaniment? Does the melody have 'breathing points' like a song and does the performer phrase it like a singer? Does the technical balance of the recording reflect the prominence of the melodic line? Music with a more abstract title, such as a concerto or fugue, needs a bit more research. What is the essential nature of a fugue? It is about the interplay of simultaneous independent melodic lines and the changing relationship of motifs within those lines. So such a piece needs great clarity in execution. Not only must the performer's articulation make these simultaneous melodies clear and distinct in character, but it should also help the listener to understand the music by subtly drawing attention to entries of the melodic material, even if they are hidden in inner parts. You should expect any half-decent performer to give sympathetic attention to fugal devices such as *stretto* (in which the composer creates a climactic effect by writing parts that enter in closer imitation than at the start of the fugue), but your job is to analyse *how* the performer conveys this excitement to the listener – is it by means of a *crescendo* (perhaps not notated by the composer), for example, or is it by bringing out the entries of the subject particularly clearly so that the cumulative effect of the *stretto* is more obvious?

Similarly, if you choose to write about performances of a sonata-form movement, first make sure you understand what sonata form is all about. You should recall from your AS studies that it is essentially a dramatic form. In the first section (exposition) the composer sets up a contrast between two keys, each of which is often (but not always) associated with its own set of distinctive themes. In a central argument (the development) the conflict is widened to embrace a greater range of tonal centres and at the same time the melodic material is presented in new ways, often pared down and presented in close, dramatic juxtaposition. Finally the tonal tension reaches a climax which is resolved by a recapitulation in which the contrasting keys of the exposition, and the tonal instability of the development, resolve into a single, main tonal centre.

This is musical architecture. It is not the same as the architecture of a building, the main outlines of which we may be able to perceive in an instant (although even a building takes time to explore if we are to appreciate it from all angles, inside and out). It is the architecture of time – the type of construction that might be found in a good play or poem, with areas of novelty, challenge, uncertainty, familiarity, tension and release.

This may seem very strange. We are discussing performance and yet referring all the time to things we study in music history. But this is what A2 music is all about – making clear that whatever we learn, as listeners, composers or performers, has one single purpose: the greater understanding of music. Thus we should reasonably expect a performer of a sonata-form movement to make clear to the listener the architecture designed by its composer – and this is a very good place to start in the case of a sonata-form movement.

The philosophy is important, but let's finish this section by turning to a short and practical example of music that you may have played and that you might wish to investigate for this unit – a bourrée by Handel. What are the main characteristics of this type of music? If we consult any music dictionary we learn that a bourrée is a baroque binary-form dance in moderate to fast duple time, with phrases that start on the last half-beat of the bar. So, do the performances 'dance'?

Musical character

Do they both sound like a springy duple metre, or does one of them have a boring sense of four plodding beats per bar? Does the performer phrase the dance to bring out or to disguise the regularity of its phrase lengths? How is articulation used? Are notes mainly legato, mainly staccato or does the performer stress the up-beats with a slur? (See the example below.) If we investigate further we learn that baroque music was often ornamented by the performer, especially when a section is repeated. How is ornamentation used in the performances in question? Are the repeats also differentiated in some other way, such as by using a quieter dynamic? If there is a figured-bass accompaniment, how is it realised – elaborately or simply? And is it played by just one instrument (eg harpsichord) or has a bass instrument (eg cello) also been used? Consider tempo – do the two interpretations adopt similar speeds? Is the tempo constant and forward-looking, or does either performer relax the speed at cadences and perhaps slow-up noticeably at the end?

Music examples In working on detailed points of this sort, music examples can add considerable weight to your arguments. For example after close listening you may be able to point out that the phrase notated as (a) is articulated as (b) by one performer and (c) by another:

The next example shows at (a) the opening of Chopin's Nocturne in E minor, Op. 72, No. 1. Below the score the diagrams indicate how two different pianists, (b) and (c), have interpreted this music.

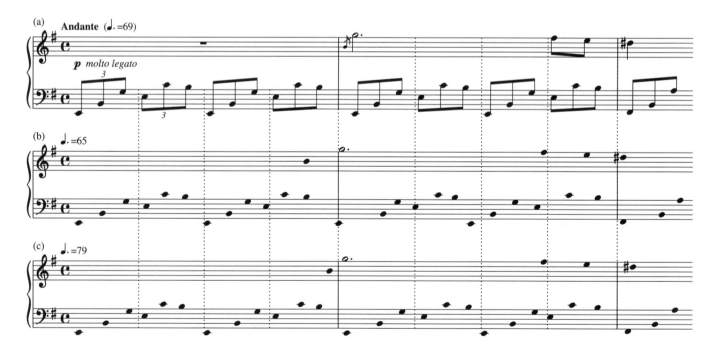

You could also use computer tools such as *Musician's CD Player for Windows* to slow down music without changing its pitch: see http://www.ronimusic.com/muscdpl.htm

This vividly illustrates different ways in which rubato can be applied to romantic music – notice the extreme lengthening of the grace note in (b), the anticipation of the start of bar 2, and the expressive broadening of the first beat of each bar. Such analysis needs great concentration, but a bar or two is enough to make the point. It is also relatively easy if you use technology to make a sample of the bars and then analyse the results graphically.

It is a good idea to begin with a brief discussion of the context of the music concerned. This doesn't mean writing out the composer's biography or providing lists of the composer's other works. Keep to the work under investigation and concentrate on those aspects that are most clearly related to performing, such as:

✦ the circumstances under which the music would originally have been heard in performance

✦ differences between the type of instrument(s) available at the time of composition and those used today, and how these might result in different approaches to performance

✦ relevant performing conventions, such as the ways in which a figured bass might be realised, or ornamentation improvised, or rhythm modified (eg by using rubato, double-dotting, accented hemiola patterns, swung quavers in jazz and so on).

You should also discuss how the character of the piece may govern the overall approach in any performance – the moonlit night of a nocturne, with its need for romantic rubato, or the crystal clarity of a fugue, with its need for clear independence of fingerwork.

Most of the report should consist of a close comparison of the performances you have chosen. Concentrate on matters of real significance and avoid long discussion of trivial similarities or differences. Remember that it is vital to justify your points by referring to the cassette of examples that you will have to prepare, and by including short examples of notation in the report where appropriate. Avoid comments such as 'he copes well with the very fast passages' as these are likely to appear patronising – professional performers should, after all, be capable of playing difficult music! Try to maintain an objective approach and when there are aspects of a performance that you like (or dislike) be precise in explaining why. Remember, too, that your report should refer to the technical quality of the recordings – matters such as the feeling of presence with the performers, the type of ambience, the degree of resonance and the use of the stereo soundfield. At the end of the report remember to give precise details of the resources you have used (recordings, scores, reviews, books, websites etc).

If you use a score to help you make the comparisons, make sure it is a reliable one that shows possible alternative readings and that indicates those things (such as tempi, phrasing and articulation) that have been added by a modern editor. Otherwise you may be misled into thinking that performers have made mistakes, when in fact they have simply used a different edition from yours.

The examiners award marks in the following six categories for your performance investigation:

✦ the quality of your aural perception

✦ your ability to identify and discuss matters of significance

✦ your ability to support arguments by means of apt examples

✦ your use of analysis and investigative techniques, and your use of an appropriate technical vocabulary

✦ your research into the nature and context of the music

✦ your skill in communicating your findings clearly, with correct use of language and proper acknowledgement of sources.

Composing 2

Note that the two options you choose must include either option 1 or option 2.

You have to complete two of the following four options, each of which accounts for 50% of the marks for this unit. Your portfolio of coursework will need to reach the external examiner by 15 May in your examination year. Your teacher will advise you of the deadlines required, but clearly it will be important to complete the bulk of the work by the end of the spring term.

Option 1: Vocal composition

You will have to write a vocal composition to a detailed brief that will be set by OCR. The brief will include a choice of two texts, from which you must select one for your piece.

The brief will also prescribe the resources to be used and again you are likely to have a choice. The specimen paper indicates the two main alternatives:

1. **Either** a song for solo voice with accompaniment for:

   ✦ a solo polyphonic instrument (such as piano, organ or guitar)

   ✦ or a group of at least four instruments (such as a chamber ensemble or rhythm section)

   ✦ or a sequenced and synthesised backing track produced by using music technology.

2. **Or** a work for unaccompanied voices in no fewer than four parts.

If you compare these options it should be clear that all the parts, not just the main vocal line, are expected to have melodic and/or rhythmic interest of their own. This is underlined by the use of the term 'polyphonic' in the first option. An accompaniment that consists merely of chord symbols for guitar or piano is unlikely to do as well as one in which the accompaniment has been worked out in sufficient detail to create a real interplay with the main vocal melody.

In the chapter on Words and Music (page 25) we have outlined some technical features about vocal composition, but first we need to consider the basics of how to go about about setting a text to music. As an example, we will use the poem 'Windy Nights' by Robert Louis Stevenson (1850–94):

> Whenever the moon and stars are set,
>   Whenever the wind is high,
> All night long in the dark and wet,
>   A man goes riding by.
> Late in the night when the fires are out,
> Why does he gallop and gallop about?
>
> Whenever the trees are crying aloud,
>   And ships are tossed at sea,
> By, on the highway, low and loud,
>   By at the gallop goes he.
> By at the gallop he goes, and then
> By he comes back at the gallop again.

There are some interesting images to explore in this poem, but first we must consider the mechanics of setting a text to music. You hardly need to be reminded that music has rhythm – but so does poetry. Music can modify the rhythm of spoken text but it cannot totally contradict it – the two must work together if the result is to be intelligible. Our first job is therefore to decide where the natural accents occur in the poem – in other words, to work out its scansion. The easiest way to do this is to speak the words aloud, underlining the syllables that attract a natural stress:

> When<u>ev</u>er the <u>moon</u> and <u>stars</u> are <u>set</u>,
>   When<u>ev</u>er the <u>wind</u> is <u>high</u>,
> <u>All</u> night <u>long</u> in the <u>dark</u> and <u>wet</u>,
>   A <u>man</u> goes <u>rid</u>ing <u>by</u>.
> <u>Late</u> in the <u>night</u> when the <u>fires</u> are <u>out</u>,
> <u>Why</u> does he <u>gal</u>lop and <u>gal</u>lop a<u>bout</u>?

You may feel that the last line would be more expressive if the second syllable was accented – 'Why <u>does</u> he gallop' – and this is indeed the sort of subtlety that could add interest to your setting, but it is something to consider later. For now it should be clear that the stresses divide the text into patterns (known as 'feet' in poetry) of either two or three syllables.

These patterns offer a template for a musical rhythm – our music will reinforce the rhythm of the words if the underlined words are given a musical stress by being placed in accented parts of the bar (such as the first and third beats in $\frac{4}{4}$ time). The poem starts with an unaccented syllable, so the vocal part must start in a weak part of the bar (a device known as an anacrusis). The first part of this bar will probably become the end of an introduction:

When - e - ver the moon and   stars are   set, When - e - ver the wind is   high,   All night   long   in the dark ...

But if you carry on like this you will bore your audience (and your examiner) to tears before the end of the first verse! The musical and verbal stresses all match, but the music now imposes such a tight and predictable rhythm that the poetry sounds stilted.

The secret is to realise that the scansion of a poem offers nothing more than a *template* for a musical rhythm. There are infinite ways in which to interpret this template, and the compositional decisions you make at this point can lift your piece from a dull theory exercise into a living piece of music. Here are just a few possibilities, all of which conform to our original template. The first keeps to our $\frac{4}{4}$ model but its syncopation on 'whenever' adds much more life. Notes on less important syllables (eg 'and') are shorter, allowing a new semiquaver pattern to appear for 'in the'. It introduces a short melisma on 'wind' (and who could then resist a scalic ascent to 'high'?) and it then provides a vital breathing point for the singer by means of a rest. Notice how the word 'long' receives its accent – not because it starts on a strong beat, but because it is syncopated (and this also makes the note for 'long' the longest note so far):

When - e - ver   the moon   and   stars are   set, When - e - ver the wind ____ is   high,   All night long ____   in the dark...

Locating the correct positions for stressed syllables is vitally important if the word-setting is not to sound confused. The very meaning of words is enshrined in the way they are accented. For instance a <u>de</u>fect is a flaw, while to de<u>fect</u> means to desert a country or a cause.

But the most important thing to realise is that a poem's scansion does not force you into using any one particular metre. All of the following examples continue to follow the principle that word and music accents should coincide, but all offer different approaches to the setting of these words:

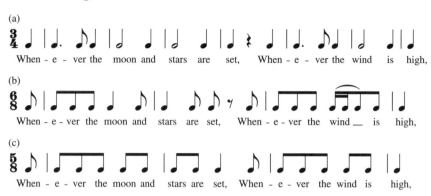

Which should you use? Well, example (a) suggests that you may have decided that 'moon' is the first keyword in the poem. It could well lead to an elegant setting in which this word is highlighted by an approach of a yearning upward leap of a 6th, eg:

On page 94 we discuss Schubert's setting of Goethe's *Erlkönig* – an altogether more dramatic account of a horse-ride through a wild night, with a tragic conclusion. Study how Schubert's use of a persistent figure in the accompaniment not only reflects the wild gallop but also underpins the urgency of the drama and enhances the tension of the words.

However, would such a lilting waltz-like approach suit the mood of the poem? The images of a high wind, the trees 'crying aloud' and the 'ships tossed at sea' suggest a much more urgent treatment. The poem has a strong, insistent rhythm, enhanced by the use of hard monosyllables (wind, dark, wet, night) for key words, and by the frequent repetitions of 'gallop'. Whether you think the rider of the night is a literal image or a child's imaginative response to the sound of branches banging against a bedroom window during a storm, the style of the poem suggests a strongly rhythmic setting.

We have already indicated that too much rhythmic repetition will lead to a very dull vocal point. But we could use the image of galloping to create a motif for the accompaniment. The use of a short, highly rhythmic motif will also make it easier to adapt this accompaniment figure to different harmonies and keys throughout the song. Here is just one possible approach:

The final line of verse 1 ('Why does he gallop and gallop about?') is a clear point of climax and deserves special treatment. One solution would be to set the word 'Why' to a high note, and perhaps emphasise the theme of galloping by some appropriate repetition:

In a choral setting, these repetitions could be very effective if set in close imitation between the parts.

If you choose to write a song with accompaniment, don't double the vocal-part by the piano (or other instrument) throughout as it can sound very dull – although short sections in which the piano doubles the voice in a different octave can provide a welcome change of texture.

Make sure you use the full vocal range, placing important high notes on key words in the text. Singers will be appreciative if high notes are set to an open vowel sound that is easy to sing such as 'ah', but this is often not possible with English-language texts.

Remember that singers must have breathing places. The necessary rests will provide a good opportunity for the accompaniment to emerge with a short motif of its own. In *a cappella* choral settings changes of texture (eg to just the three upper parts, or to just tenors and basses) can help provide the necessary breaks for singers. Whatever type of setting you choose, try to ensure that all the parts have interest of their own – if the lower voices merely copy the rhythms of the melody, or the piano part consists of endless minims and semibreves, your work is unlikely to score high marks.

Underlay

Underlay refers to the way that syllables are written under notes. Many candidates (and some computer programs) seem to have trouble getting this right. The basic principles are quite simple and well worth learning. There are two main conventions:

✦ Spaced hyphens are used to split multisyllabic words into their separate syllables, eg ho - li - day

✦ An extension line is used when a monosyllabic word or the last syllable of a multisyllabic word is extended by a tied note or by additional notes sung to the same syllable, eg love. _____

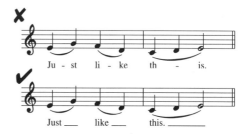

One of the most common mistakes is to split up single syllables with hyphens, as in the first example *right*. All of these words are single syllables and, because each is set to two or more notes, they follow our second rule above – they require extension lines, as shown in the second example *right*. Notice that punctuation is written before extension lines. It is also conventional to slur notes that are sung to the same syllable.

When hyphenating text, split words between consonants whenever possible: eg mag - net, dis - mal. If there is only one central consonant, split the word before that consonant: eg o - pen, de - mon. When there are no central consonants hyphenate between the vowels: eg cha - os, flu - id. But never split diphthongs (compound vowels that are pronounced together): eg 'point' should always be written as a single word and never hyphenated as 'po - int'.

Take care over syllables that are frequently elided (run together) in ordinary speech – eg you may need to decide whether you want his-to-ry or his-t'ry, or if you prefer gov-ern-ment to gov'-ment. Notice how an apostrophe is used if you want to show an elision in an English text.

Submitting your work

It is important to try out your work in performance as it proceeds, so that you can discover any miscalculations or areas that need improvement and make the necessary changes before preparing the final score. Music software is of only limited help in vocal composition – the sounds available are not sufficiently realistic or flexible, and the technology will not complain if you forget to include breathing points or if you write successions of impossibly taxing high notes. Therefore it is important that you leave yourself enough time to try out the work with some real singers if you are going to produce a really successful setting.

The music must be fully notated. If you compose an *a cappella* choral setting, write it in open score, as shown *left* (the tenor part uses the 'vocal tenor clef' – basically the same as the treble clef, but the small figure *8* indicates that the notes are sung an octave lower than written). If you opt to compose a song, write the vocal part on a separate stave and don't try to combine it with the right-hand of the piano part. In all cases vocal music tends to need much more generous spacing than instrumental music if the words are not to appear cramped. Use manuscript paper with widely-spaced staves, or set your music software to use wide inter-stave spacing, and don't attempt to fit in too many bars per system.

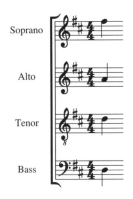

Use the following checklist to ensure that you haven't missed any essential points in your score:

✦ Is there a title and an initial tempo marking?

✦ Have you remembered the time signature?

✦ Are the staves labelled with the correct instruments and/or voices?

✦ Do all the staves have the correct key signature?

✦ Have all dynamics, articulation and other essential performing directions been included?

✦ Are phrase marks and slurs clear? They should always begin and end on specific notes – not on barlines or between notes.

✦ Does every bar have the correct number of beats? Checking is tedious but essential if you are to avoid this common fault.

✦ Have you numbered the bars for easy reference?

✦ Are there any blank bars? If a part is not playing or singing it should be given whole-bar rests.

✦ Are all the pages numbered and in their correct order?

With the composition you must submit all preparatory notes and drafts, and a **full commentary** which describes and explains the decisions you have made about the style of the music, and the techniques you have used. Outline your research and identify the pieces you have studied as models for your own work. If you have used music technology, include details of the sounds, equipment and processes you have employed.

Finally, remember that you should also submit a **recording** of the completed assignment.

Option 2: Film storyboard

If you choose this option, you will have to compose music to a very detailed specification set by OCR. This is very similar to the type of commission received by composers working in fields such as film and television music, advertising music, music for corporate videos and music for computer-game consoles. Storyboards often include sketches or photographs to illustrate the video images, but you are likely to find that the requirements are expressed in written instructions that include

+ the types of scene to be accompanied
+ the types of music to be composed for each scene
+ precise timings that you are expected to meet.

The total duration of music will not exceed five minutes. The assignment may be composed for any electro-acoustic, synthesised or purely acoustic medium.

You must submit a recording of the completed assignment, either in its intended instrumentation, or as a piano reduction, or as a synthesised/sequenced demonstration. Along with your recording you must submit either a full score or a full commentary on the methods of mixing and producing the final recording. If you decide to offer the latter, it will be your commentary and recording that will be assessed (including, for the latter, the use of appropriate sound levels, balance, stereo imaging, equalisation, reverberation or other effects, and use of a full frequency spectrum).

The requirements of film often dictate that music cues are short, although the opening title music and any scenes requiring musical illustration (battles, storms, love scenes and so on) provide an opportunity for more extended composing. Listen carefully to how music is used in a variety of films. Often musical motifs are used to identify particular characters, scenes or events. These motifs can then be used later to remind the audience of previous events without the picture or dialogue necessarily needing to refer to them explicitly. This technique is related to the leitmotif of late-romantic music (see page 105), although there is little opportunity for the large-scale development of such motifs as those found in the operas of Wagner.

Music in films

Film music is often used to heighten a dramatic situation, and it can involve the audience in the plot in a more intimate way than even the characters themselves. In Alfred Hitchcock's famous film *Psycho*, when the bank-worker Marion innocently takes a shower, the spine-chilling score (by Bernard Herrmann) alerts the audience to a danger of which she is totally oblivious, his music anticipating the fatal stabbing of the knife through the shower curtain and thus heightening its impact.

At the other extreme, music is often used in cartoon films to add colour to comic sequences. The cartoons of Walt Disney led to a new type of score in which music was synchronised very precisely with almost every event in the action. For example sliding down a drainpipe might be accompanied by a descending xylophone scale and the dazed bump when the character hits the ground by a 'wah-wah-wah' from muted trumpets. This technique, known as mickey-mousing (after Disney's famous animated character), was also widely used in comedy films. Listen carefully to other ways in which music is used in films and television programmes. These include:

✦ illustrative music, such as Walton's thrilling depiction of the Battle of Agincourt in *Henry V*

✦ evocative music to suggest a place, such as the use of the Austrian zither in *The Third Man*, which is set in Vienna

✦ pastiche (music written in an old style) to evoke a specific historical period, as in David Munrow's music for TV's *Six Wives of Henry VIII*, or a more general bygone age, as in Eric Idle's television theme music for *One Foot in the Grave*

✦ dramatic music to enhance tension, as in the capture of the humans by the apes in Jerry Goldsmith's *Planet of the Apes*

✦ romantic music to increase the emotional impact of love scenes, as in Francis Lai's score for *Love Story*

✦ comic music, as in Auric's scores for the Ealing comedies (such as *Passport to Pimlico*) and most cartoons

✦ music to enhance emotional impact as in *Scott of the Antarctic* where the bleak score by Vaughan Williams accompanies the explorers' final doomed attempt to return to base, portraying in music the mens' emotional states in a way that could not easily be expressed by pictures or dialogue in the film

✦ theme music to identify a product – particularly common in television series, where the 'signature tune' provides a signal that another episode of something familiar is about to start

✦ bridge passages that link one scene with the next by under-pinning the visual transition with musical continuity

✦ diegetic (or 'featured') music – that is music which is part of the action on screen, such as that heard when a character switches on the radio or walks past some buskers in the street.

This last point should remind us that most film music is non-diegetic. It is something that is presumed not to be heard by the characters – it is music intended for the observer, enhancing the audience's understanding and perception of events. Music thus forms an intimate bond between the film and the viewer, as well as serving the more mundane purpose of filling the silence that is a normal part of many film scenes.

Practice exercises

One of the main problems you will face in this option is writing music to very specific timings. For the actual assignment you will probably be required to compose a continuous piece of music, lasting up to five minutes, that matches the descriptions and cues you will be given. But for practice purposes it may be better to start with a relatively short exercise, such as the following:

Compose a new suite of music for the long-running Channel 4 television programme *Countdown*. It must include the following items, all of which should be musically related:

Length	Description	Type of music
22 seconds	Opening title music.	Lively and up-beat.
30 seconds	Music to cover the 30 seconds of silence while contestants answer a question.	A quiet but distinctive pulse at exactly one-second intervals, with a crescendo in the last seven seconds to indicate that time is up.
10 seconds	Lead in (and return from) an advertising break.	Must refer to the opening title music in an abbreviated form.
25 seconds	End title music.	Based on the opening title music.

The actual assignment is likely to show the precise timings at which changes should occur in a long musical sequence. The following exercise is loosely based on the famous western, *The Magnificient Seven*. The timings, which are given in minutes and seconds, represent the start of each section.

Timing	Description of scene	Type of music cue
0:00	A typical cowboy scene: a barren area with the rocky mountains in the distance.	Opening title music, broad and expansive. Drums are heard as the main title appears.
0:31	Three Mexican farmers are seen riding on horseback.	More sense of movement, with rhythms and instrumentation to suggest Mexican folk music.
0:52	A cut to two seated Mexicans who are preparing sweetcorn.	The opening theme briefly returns but is interrupted by an ominous melody.
1:03	The evil Calvera rides into the village with his group of men.	A dark, threatening theme to identify Calvera.
1:16	Calvera demands that the farmers supply him with food.	Very sparse musical activity – mysterious single notes.
1:32	One of the villagers runs up to threaten Calvera and is shot.	A sudden and violent crescendo.
1:38	The villager's wife runs to her dying husband.	High strings underline the poignancy of the moment.
1:54	Calvera and his men leave, saying they will be back.	Calvera's theme returns, followed by its rhythm (only) being echoed by drums as he rides away.
2:13	The farmers discuss what to do.	A sad theme, heard on a variety of solo instruments.
2:43	An old man tells them that they must buy guns.	The theme becomes more sinister and is heard on brass.
2:58	Three of the farmers are seen riding into a town.	A development of the music heard at cue 0:31. The music stops as the horses stop.
3:17	A burial cannot take place – nobody will help because the dead man is a Red Indian.	Again, very sparse musical activity, similar but not identical to that heard at cue 1:16.
3:44	Two strangers appear and agree to drive the hearse.	The opening title theme is heard in a more muted arrangement.
4:02	As they head for the burial ground an angry crowd follows them, jeering 'Indian lovers'.	A quiet but sinister funeral march gathers in intensity as the tension mounts.
4:27	They are shot at, but shoot back.	A big crescendo leads to a passage of loud solo drumming during the shooting.
4:33	Men are called to help and the burial continues, after which everyone heads back to town.	The funeral music returns, subtly merging into the main title theme for the end of the sequence.
5:00	End of sequence.	

Option 3: Stylistic techniques

The work for this option is essentially a continuation of the study you began for the first part of the AS unit, Composing 1. However there are some differences. For A2 you are required to submit eight to ten exercises, whereas AS required a minimum of six. And while the AS exercises could be as little as eight bars in length, at A2 you are expected to complete longer exercises.

But the main difference is that OCR more precisely specifies the styles that should be used at A2. Your exercises must be based on **one** of the following stylistic categories:

+ two-part counterpoint of the late 16th century
+ two-part baroque keyboard counterpoint
+ chorale treatments in the style of J. S. Bach
+ string quartets in the classical style
+ keyboard accompaniments in an early romantic style
+ 20th-century musical theatre.

For all styles, except 16th-century, you must submit exercises in both major and minor keys. Your portfolio must consist of legible working copies of your exercises, along with initial sketches and drafts. It is not necessary to write-out final 'fair copies', providing your own work can easily be distinguished from your teacher's corrections and comments. However the examiners will expect to see how your workings of the exercises progressed, so it is essential to include initial drafts.

All of your exercises must be dated and must state the composer and title of the work from which the extract has been taken. You are allowed to use music technology for the notation of exercises.

Details about working exercises of this sort are beyond the scope of the current book, but the following sources provide useful information and exercises for some of the categories:

A Student's Guide to Harmony and Counterpoint by Hugh Benham. *Rhinegold Publishing.* ISBN: 1-904226-31-0.

Harmony in Practice by Anna Butterworth. *The Associated Board of the Royal Schools of Music*, 1999. ISBN: 1-85472-833-4.

Modal Counterpoint, Renaissance Style by Peter Schubert. *Oxford University Press.* ISBN: 0-19-510912-0.

Option 4: Free composition

For this option you have to compose a piece of not more than five minutes in length. It can be for any combination of instruments and/or voices, and in any style – although it shouldn't be in the same style as the other option you choose for this unit.

Think carefully about what is meant by a score 'appropriate to the style of the music'. Detailed graphic scores are often used in experimental electronic music, but songs from musicals are more likely to appear in full score. In pop and jazz, main patterns and structures should be fully notated and templates for improvisation must be given.

You must submit a recording of the work. This could be of a fully-scored performance, or of a reduction for piano, or of a synthesised and sequenced demonstration version. You must also submit a score in a form appropriate to the style of the music and a commentary of the sort outlined at the foot of page 20. Use the checklist on that page to help ensure that your score doesn't contain easily avoidable mistakes.

Words and music

Before discussing the details of the final unit, it will be useful to understand some of the terminology and theory that is particularly relevant to writing and studying vocal music.

Vocal ranges and voice names

You will already be familiar with the four main types of voice – soprano, alto, tenor and bass. The typical compass of each is shown *right* – these limits are usually suitable for amateur singers, but professional soloists will generally be able to produce notes well outside of these ranges.

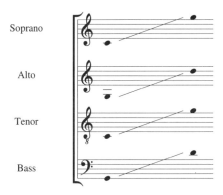

A mezzo-soprano voice is between soprano and alto in range, and a baritone voice is between tenor and bass in range.

The word 'register' refers to specific parts of a range. For instance you might describe a particular bass singer as having a rich and vibrant low register. Another useful term is 'tessitura'. This Italian word refers to the *average* range of a part. For example you might describe a song as having a high tessitura.

Church music was, and often still is, sung by all-male choirs. In such cases the uppermost part is sung by boys, and is usually described as treble rather than soprano. Alto parts in church music are also often sung by boys in continental Europe, but in English-speaking countries such parts are usually sung by men (male altos) using a high falsetto register.

Falsetto is a style of singing in which just the edges of the vocal cords are used to produce a range of very high, pure notes.

The male alto (or countertenor) voice is not only heard in church music. In addition to a large repertoire of music from before the 19th century it has been used in modern opera, and pop singers such as the Bee Gees have made a feature of falsetto singing.

You may also come across the term contralto, which nowadays is generally used exclusively to refer to female altos.

Soloists, particularly in opera, often indicate their specialities by the use of additional terms. For instance a coloratura soprano will specialise in roles that use *coloratura* (extravagant ornamentation, often in an exceptionally high register), while a lyric soprano or lyric tenor will have a light-toned voice. A *Heldentenor* ('heroic tenor') will have the stamina needed for heroic parts in German opera, while a basso profundo will specialise in roles that require a very low range.

All of these vocal categories can be heard on the Cardiff Singer of the World website: www.bbc.co.uk/wales/cardiffsinger05/generic/guide_singingvoice.shtml

Types of vocal music and vocal ensemble

Vocal music includes a wide range of different genres, from solo song to church music and opera.

A genre is a category or group, such as the solo song or the madrigal.

Church music is simply music designed for performance in church. The term sacred music includes not only church music but also works of a religious nature intended for performance in the home or concert hall. The opposite of sacred is secular (ie non-religious) and so secular vocal music encompasses a broad range of genres from pop songs to opera.

The body of singers who perform church music is always known as a choir, but the term chorus is preferred in opera and other types of secular music (and the type of music that they sing is usually referred to as a chorus as well). A small choir, particularly one that performs secular music, is often called a chamber choir.

The Italian term *a cappella* means 'in the church style', but it is nowadays freely used to mean any unaccompanied singing.

Music for a small number of solo singers is usually described in the same way as instrumental music (eg duet, trio, quartet, quintet, sextet etc).

The word song usually refers to a piece for one singer. Aria, the Italian word for song, suggests a formal type of song, as do the related words air and ayre. We will discuss examples of these and other vocal genres later in the book.

An opera is a dramatic fusion of words, music, spectacle and sometimes dancing. Operas are often substantial works, incorporating a number of the genres we have already mentioned, such as arias, duets and choruses. The term operetta (little opera) came to be used in the 19th century for short, popular operas with tuneful music and spoken dialogue (such as the operettas by Gilbert and Sullivan). In the USA the term musical comedy was preferred, and this is now shortened to just 'musical', retaining its meaning as a stage work that features music in a popular style.

The term libretto (Italian for booklet) refers to the complete text of an opera (including any spoken dialogue). In a musical this is often simply called the book. Words of songs, which are often in rhyming verse, are known as the lyrics.

Music theatre refers to compositions that involve some sort of dramatic presentation, but not necessarily fully staged and acted like an opera or musical.

Church music

Many of the main Christian churches, including Roman Catholic, Orthodox, Anglican and Lutheran, place much importance on the use of a liturgy – a set pattern for church services that prescribes the precise words to be included.

The principal liturgy of the Roman Catholic church is the Mass (known as the service of Holy Communion in Anglican churches). The words of these (and similar liturgical services) include unchanging texts, known as the Ordinary, and texts that vary according to the current season or festival (such as Easter or Christmas) being celebrated, known as the Proper. Church music written for either of these sets of texts, Ordinary or Proper, is known as liturgical church music. Other church music (such as the Anglican anthem or hymn) for which composers can choose their own words, is known as non-liturgical church music.

The Mass is a whole service containing readings, prayers and other set texts, culminating in the sharing of bread and wine. When musicians refer to a setting of the Mass they mean the music for the Ordinary – the five texts printed in bold in this table:

Ordinary	Proper
	Introit
Kyrie Eleison	
Gloria in excelsis Deo	
	Collect (prayer)
	Epistle (bible reading)
	Gradual
	Gospel (bible reading)
Credo in unum Deum	
	Offertory
	Prayers
Sanctus and Benedictus	
Prayers	
Agnus Dei	
	Communion
	Prayers
Dismissal	

Some changes to this basic layout occur at different times of the year and for special purposes, such as a Requiem Mass (a Mass for the dead).

In a concert performance you will normally hear the five movements of a Mass sung in succession, but you can see from the table above that in a liturgical performance most of the sections are separated by other parts of the service.

The texts shown above in italics are often chanted to plainsong, but they too are sometimes set to more elaborate music in a type of church music known as a motet.

Masses and motets are not the only types of liturgical church music. For instance, the text of the Magnificat, which forms a central focus in the evening service of vespers (evensong in Anglican churches) has often been set to music.

For centuries the Mass was said or sung in Latin (although the short text of the Kyrie is Greek) – when translated into the local language of the people, it is said to be in the vernacular.

Later in this book we shall encounter other types of sacred music, such as the oratorio, which are essentially concert works and are not performed as part of a church service. Some large-scale settings of the Mass and the Requiem Mass, such as Britten's *War Requiem*, are also intended for concert rather than liturgical performance.

Writing vocal music

We have already discussed the importance of scanning a lyric to establish its accentuation, and of correctly hyphenating the text when fitting it to a melody. Choral music is sometimes written in short score, in which the soprano and alto parts share a single treble stave (with note tails in opposite directions) and tenor and bass parts share a single bass stave (again with tails in opposite directions) – see Example 5 on page 42. This style suits hymn-like music in which all the parts move in the same rhythm, although it tends to encourage writing tenor parts that are too low. For your own *a cappella* compositions it is better to use the type of open score shown on page 20. Take care over the vertical alignment of parts within each bar – notes that occur on the same subdivisions of the bar must be precisely aligned in all the parts. Keeping a good open spacing, with not too many bars per system, will help achieve this.

In older scores you will often see vocal parts printed with tails on every short note sung to a separate syllable, using beams only when several notes are sung to the same syllable – as in (a) below. This can be confusing to read, and modern practice is to beam notes in the same way as instrumental music, as in (b) below.

Bach: Cantata No. 51

Translation: Praise God in all lands.

The type of ornamental melisma shown in the first bar of this example is often known as a roulade when it occurs in 18th-century vocal music.

This example illustrates two main types of word setting. It begins with a melisma (a group of notes all sung to one syllable) but at the end of bar 2 Bach sets each syllable to a separate note. In many styles of vocal music it is common to find melismatic and syllabic word-setting in close proximity, as here, and this is a good way of maintaining variety in vocal melodies.

The above melody also shows two different types of melodic movement. The ascent in bar 1, from a low G to the G an octave higher at the start of bar 2, consists entirely of movement between adjacent notes of the scale. This is known as conjunct or stepwise movement. Disjunct motion (movement by leaps) is seen in the final three semiquavers of the extract. Once again, most melodies freely combine both types of motion in order to maintain variety.

Vocal textures and techniques

Vocal textures are described in the same way as any other musical texture. A monophonic texture is shown in the start of the unaccompanied plainsong hymn in Example 1 (page 36). Example 39 (page 93) illustrates a song with a homophonic texture, while Example 7 (page 46) shows a polyphonic texture. An antiphonal texture can be seen in Example 16 (page 56) while the type of thin, polarised texture that characterises much baroque music can be seen in Example 20 (page 62). The type of texture known as 'melody and accompaniment', and that is characteristic of many simpler kinds of romantic music, can be seen in Example 42 (page 95). One type of texture (or at least an addition to a musical texture) that occurs only in vocal music is the descant – a countermelody sung by trebles or sopranos above the main melody of a hymn tune.

Finally here are some Italian terms used frequently by singers. Sliding between notes is known as *portamento*. Singing in a style resembling natural speech is called *parlando*. *Mezza voce* ('half voice') indicates reducing the volume, usually for dramatic effect. *Sotto voce* ('under the voice') means singing in a very hushed style, like a stage whisper. *Vibrato* refers to small but rapid undulations in pitch and is used to warm vocal tone, particularly on long notes.

Historical and analytical studies

There are three sections in this unit, all of which are assessed in a single 2½-hour written paper:

✦ section A (Aural Extracts) consists of questions on two recorded passages of music

✦ section B (Prescribed Historical Topics) contains a choice of questions about the historical topic you have studied – you have to write an essay that answers one of these questions

✦ section C (Synoptic Essay) consists of five questions about continuity and change in various musical traditions – again you have to write an essay in answer to one of these questions.

Section A carries 45% of the marks for this unit, section B is worth 35% and section C is weighted at 20%.

Aural extracts

You will be given a CD of two extracts (or complete short pieces) of music. You can play the CD as many times as you wish, but you need to allow sufficient time to answer the two essay questions in the rest of the paper. The questions on the first recording are worth 30 marks, while those on the second recording carry 15 marks – this difference should also help you allocate your time in the most sensible way.

The first recording will be of vocal music from the period 1900–1945 and will be up to three minutes in length. You will be given a score of the piece, with some passages omitted, and a translation if the text is not in English. The tasks required may include:

✦ adding notation to the score (eg a melody, rhythm, bass, chords or performance markings)

✦ identifying chords, keys, cadences and modulations

✦ identifying structures and compositional techniques

✦ identifying voice types and performing techniques

✦ recognising common effects of recording techniques

✦ understanding word-setting techniques, including the use of word-painting and the expressive use of texture

✦ writing a short commentary to describe, compare, analyse or respond to various points about the music.

The questions focus on the relationship between text and music, and the composer's use of a tonal (or non-tonal) musical language. Some questions may ask you to identify how the interpretation on the recording differs from the score (eg by adjusting the tempo or varying the printed dynamics or articulation to suit the needs of the text) and to suggest reasons why these changes have been made. You may also be asked to compare the music with other pieces of 20th-century vocal music that you know. Your answers should refer to specific events in the music whenever appropriate and they should show that you can use technical terms correctly.

Useful practice material for Section A of this paper can be found in **Listening Tests for Students (OCR A2 Music Specification)** by Veronica Jamset, *Rhinegold Publishing Ltd.* ISBN: 1-904226-47-7 (book plus CD).

It is important to remember that this is a listening test. You are not expected to learn facts about all the possible different types of 20th-century vocal music. Listen to a good range of music but try to concentrate on identifying musical detail and recognising how musical techniques are employed in the setting of words. The first three books listed in the margin of page 33 all come with CDs and include a number of extracts from 20th-century vocal music.

Don't forget that technical terminology can help to convey a point clearly and concisely, but it needs to be used accurately. It will only confuse the issue if you say that a texture is 'harmonic' when you mean that it is 'homophonic', or if you say that the final phrase is an 'imitation' of the opening phrase, when it is actually a restatement. If in doubt it is better to use plain English to express exactly what you hear: eg 'all the voice parts sing in the same rhythm' or 'the last phrase is a repeat of the opening melody'.

A good way to start preparation for this part of the exam is to work without a score at all. Just use your ears, as any listener does. Let's use the song 'Summertime' from Gershwin's folk-opera *Porgy and Bess* as an example. It is a theatrical interpretation of a lullaby sung by a black mother in the hot, deep south of the USA. Here are the lyrics, with the lines numbered for ease of reference:

1   Summertime an' the living is easy,
2   Fish are jumpin' an' the cotton is high.
3   Oh yo' daddy's rich an' yo' ma is good-lookin',
4   So hush, little baby, don' yo' cry.
5   One of these mornin's you goin' to rise up singin',
6   Then you'll spread yo' wings an' you'll take the sky.
7   But till that mornin' there's a-nothin' can harm you
8   With Daddy an' Mommy standin' by.

How does Gershwin create the mood of a lullaby?
Is the tempo slow or fast? Is there any use of rubato?
Is the articulation staccato or legato?
Is the accompaniment loud or quiet?
Is the accompaniment supportive or elaborate?
Is the main melody sung by one voice or many voices?
Do most phrases rise in pitch or fall in pitch?
How does the introduction suggest a mood of repose?

How does Gershwin suggest the repetitious nature of a lullaby?
What do you notice about the melody in lines 1, 2 and 3?
Name the falling interval heard at the start of these three lines.
Where did you *first* hear this interval?
Compare the music for lines 5–8 with that for lines 1–4.

What influences from African-American music do you hear?
Can you locate any blue notes in the accompaniment?
On what type of scale is most of the melody based?
Where does the soloist use portamento?
Is the rhythm 'straight' or is it gently swung?
Where do you first hear a syncopated rhythm?

How can you tell this song comes from an opera?
What plays the accompaniment?
What is added to the accompaniment in lines 5–8?

Here are some similar exercises you could undertake, based on recordings of well-known early 20th-century works that should be available in most music departments and libraries.

Listen to the opening section of Vaughan Williams' *Serenade to Music* and comment on the ways in which the composer conveys a sense of soft stillness and sweet harmony. Include in your answer a reference to how the long instrumental introduction relates to the vocal setting that follows. Here is the text:

1   How sweet the moonlight sleeps upon this bank!
2   Here will we sit, and let the sounds of music
3   Creep in our ears: soft stillness and the night
4   Become the touches of sweet harmony.

Listen to the central section (identified by the text below) of the oratorio *Belshazzar's Feast* by William Walton. Comment on how the composer expresses the horror of the disembodied hand that wrote the prophecy of the fall of Babylon and contrast this with the way in which Walton captures the mood of rejoicing that followed the blasphemous King Belshazzar's death.

1   And in that same hour, as they feasted,
2   Came forth fingers of a man's hand
3   And the King saw the part of the hand that wrote.
4   And this was the writing that was written:
5   *Mene, Mene, Tekel Upharsin* – 'Thou art weighed in the
6   balance and found wanting'. In that night was
7   Belshazzar the King slain and his Kingdom divided.
8   Then sing aloud to God our strength:
9   Make a joyful noise unto the God of Jacob.
10   Take a psalm, bring hither the timbrel,
11   Blow up the trumpet in the new moon,
12   Blow up the trumpet in Zion
13   For Babylon the Great is fallen. Alleluia!

Listen to the fifth movement (Dirge) of Britten's *Serenade for Tenor, Horn and Strings*. Explain how Britten combines repetition with increasing complexity of texture, tonality and instrumentation to create a long climactic effect, culminating in the last verse. The six verses of the 15th-century text describe the soul's journey through purgatory and the consequence of leading an uncharitable life:

A more detailed aural test on this movement can be found in *Aural Matters* (Bowman and Terry) page 151.

1   This ae nighte, this ae nighte,
        Every nighte and alle,
    Fire and fleet and candle-lighte,
        And Christe receive thy saule.

2   When thou from hence away art past,
        Every nighte and alle,
    To Whinnymuir thou com'st at last;
        And Christe receive thy saule.

3   If ever thou gav'st hos'n and shoon,
        Every nighte and alle,
    Sit thee down and put them on;
        And Christe receive thy saule.

4   If hos'n and shoon thou ne'er gav'st nane,
        Every nighte and alle,
    The whinnies shall prick thee to the bare bane;
        And Christe receive thy saule.

5   From Whinnymuir when thou may'st pass,
        Every nighte and alle,
    To Brig o' Dread thou com'st at last;
        And Christe receive thy saule.

6   From Brig o' Dread when thou may'st pass,
        Every nighte and alle,
    To Purgatory fire thou com'st at last;
        And Christe receive thy saule.

An extended extract from another movement of *Pierrot Lunaire* appears in RDMS (see margin note opposite) C34.

Listen to *Der kranke Mond* (The Sick Moon) from Schoenberg's *Pierrot Lunaire*. Describe the techniques used by Schoenberg to convey the intensity of this text (refer to fragmentation, unusual performance techniques and extremes of expression). Here is the German text, with an English transliteration:

1 Du nächtig todeskranker Mond
   Dort auf des Himmels schwarzem Pfühl,
   Dein Blick, so fiebernd übergross,
   Bannt mich wie fremde Melodie.

   You sombre death-stricken moon
   lying on heaven's dusky pillow,
   your stare, so wide-eyed, feverish,
   enchants me like a far-off melody.

2 An unstillbarem Liebesleid
   Stirbst du, an Sehnsucht, tief erstickt,
   Du nächtig todeskranker Mond
   Dort auf des Himmels schwarzem Pfühl.

   You die of the insatiable pain of love,
   choking, suffocated in longing.
   O sombre deathly-stricken moon
   lying on heaven's dusky pillow.

3 Den Liebsten, der im Sinnenrausch
   Gedankenlos zur Liebsten geht,
   Belustigt deiner Strahlen Spiel –
   Dein bleiches, qualgebornes Blut,
   Du nächtig todeskranker Mond!

   The hot-blooded lover who heedlessly
   steals away to meet his love,
   rejoices in your play of light –
   your pallid, pain-begotten blood.
   O sombre death-stricken moon.

You may be surprised to learn that *Pierrot Lunaire* is the earliest of the five pieces we have mentioned in this section. It was written in 1912. *Belshazzar's Feast* appeared in 1931 and *Porgy and Bess* in 1935. Vaughan Williams' *Serenade to Music* sounds almost romantic in style but dates from 1938, while Britten's *Serenade for Tenor, Horn and Strings* was written in 1943. Such wide diversity of styles within a short period is characteristic of 20th-century music.

Aural extract 2

The second extract, for which you will not be given a score, will be up to two minutes in length. It may come from any type of music from any period or tradition – except that it will not be directly related to any of the Prescribed Historical Topics listed opposite.

The intention is to test your general aural awareness when dealing with unfamiliar music. Accordingly, the questions will focus on what can be heard in the recording, and are unlikely to involve detailed historical knowledge. The specimen paper indicates the type of tasks that may arise, such as:

✦ identifying the structure of the music by using letters (A, B etc) to show different sections and numbers (A1, A2 etc) to show varied repeats

✦ commenting on how the sections are varied (eg by alterations in rhythm, melody, harmony, instrumentation, length etc)

✦ describing features such as the texture or accompaniment

✦ commenting on compositional devices in the work

✦ relating your comments to other styles or genres with which you are familiar.

Many of the exercises in *Aural Matters* and *Aural Matters in Practice* (detailed in the margin of the next page) will provide you with practice materials for these types of question.

Prescribed historical topics

For section B of the paper in Historical and Analytical Studies you have to prepare **one** of the following five topics, each of which concentrates on the relationship between words and music (or music and drama) at a time of change.

Topic 1: 1550–1620.   *See page 34.*
Areas of principal focus: the influence of the Council of Trent, the English Reformation, *Prima Prattica* and *Seconda Prattica*.

Topic 2: 1685–1765.   *See page 58.*
Principal focus: reactions against *Opera Seria*.

Topic 3: 1815–1885.   *See page 85.*
Principal focus: aspects of romanticism.

Topic 4: 1945 to the present day.   *See page 108.*
Principal focus: integration of music and drama.

Topic 5: 1945 to the present day.   *See page 132.*
Principal focus: aspects of solo song.

OCR does not set specific works for this paper. The pieces we have suggested in this guide exemplify the main points you need to know for your chosen topic but you may well study different examples in class, in which case this book can be used as a source of supplementary material. Remember that it is best to get to know a limited number of works well – you will not be expected to have studied every genre of music from the period in question. We have given details of CDs that we recommend – other recordings of the works are also available in most cases. Useful additional material related to the examples we discuss can be found in the collections listed *right*, several of which include recordings. Studying music from a score is useful, but it is no substitute for getting to know the *sound* of the works you study in real detail. Remember, you will not have access to scores in the exam.

Aural Matters by David Bowman and Paul Terry. *Schott and Co Ltd*, 1993. ISBN: 0-946535-22-1. With two CDs of examples. **Aural Matters in Practice** by David Bowman and Paul Terry. *Schott and Co Ltd*, 1994. ISBN: 0-946535-23-X. With CD of examples.

Rhinegold Dictionary of Music in Sound [RDMS] by David Bowman. *Rhinegold Publishing Ltd*, 2002. ISBN 0-946890-87-0. With three CDs of examples.

Historical Anthology of Music [HAM], two volumes, edited by Archibald T. Davison and Willi Apel. *Harvard University Press*, 1949–1950/1974. ISBN: 0-674-39300-7 and 0-674-39301-5

The examination

In the exam there will be three questions on your chosen topic, of which you must answer one. We have included some sample questions for you to practise at the end of each of the chapters on the topics. We suggest that you allow 45 minutes for your answer. Don't forget that marks are awarded for accurate spelling, punctuation and grammar in this question. Attention to the following points will help achieve a good result:

✦ Begin by immediately addressing the question – don't waste time trying to set the scene with background information.

✦ Avoid information that is not relevant to the question – it will not impress the examiner, even if it is correct.

✦ Support your points by referring to specific examples of music.

✦ Avoid repetition. You won't get extra marks for making the same point twice, even if you clothe it in different language.

✦ Keep to factual information rather than personal opinion.

Topic 1: 1550–1620

Three movements profoundly affected the whole fabric of society in this period of unprecedented change, and helped determine the styles and genres of vocal music of the age:

✦ the early 16th-century protestant reformation
✦ the catholic counter-reformation
✦ the rise of humanism – a rebirth (or renaissance) of belief in the dignity and potential of the individual.

The need for reform

By 1500 most of western Europe had been Christian for centuries. There was one church, Roman Catholic (with services in Latin), and one spiritual leader, the pope. The church had a monopoly on education, through its monasteries, schools and universities, and dominated many spheres of life, from politics to art, architecture and music. But the enormous wealth and influence of the church had led to many corrupt practices and its seat of power in Rome seemed remote, especially to people living in northern Europe.

There was a growing awareness of the need for widespread reform – of music as of much else in the church. Concern was expressed about the incorporation of popular secular tunes in sacred music, the increasing use of complex imitative counterpoint that obscured the words, and an indulgence in melismatic writing for purely musical effect. The renowned Dutch scholar Erasmus (who taught at Cambridge University for a time) wrote:

> We have brought into our churches an artificial and theatrical music, a confused, disorderly chattering of voices … The church rings with the noise of trumpets, pipes and dulcimers; and human voices strive to bear their part with them. Amorous and lascivious melodies are heard such as elsewhere accompany only the dances of courtesans and clowns. Men run to church as to a theatre, to have their ears tickled. And for this end organ-makers are hired with great salaries, and a company of boys, who waste all their time in learning this gibble-gabble. Pray now compute how many poor people, in great extremity, might be maintained by the salaries of those singers.

The challenge to the church in this last sentence is typical of the humanist views of scholars such as Erasmus. Humanism was one of the most powerful forces behind reform. By emphasising the importance of the individual it challenged the medieval tradition that the hierarchies of church and state were given by God and could not be changed. The power behind humanism was a new understanding of the civilisation of ancient Greece and Rome. On the one hand this led to the creation of many new schools, colleges, hospitals, and almshouses for the relief of the poor and needy. On the other, it also led to a rebirth (renaissance) of secular arts and sciences culminating in a terrific flowering of the visual arts, vernacular literature and music in the 16th century.

The reformation

In 1517 a Roman Catholic priest called Martin Luther (1483–1546) nailed to the door of the Castle Church at Wittenberg in Germany 95 theses against the corrupt practices of his church. It was his intention to reform the church from within, but the inflexible attitude of Rome forced him to adopt a more intransigent stance against continuing corruption and what he saw as false doctrine. There seemed to be no common ground with Rome and so during the 1530s Luther and his followers in Germany (and in other northern European countries) established their own churches that were independent of Rome. They rejected the authority of the pope and instead emphasised the authority of the bible and a humanist belief in the importance of individual faith, stressing the right of ordinary people to take a full part in church services. This is the movement known as the reformation.

The church in England also declared itself independent of the pope in the 1530s – the immediate reasons were political, although an underlying desire for protestant reform soon emerged here too. Lutherans and Anglicans retained or adapted many features of catholic worship, including the use of specialist choirs, organs and elaborate music in their principal churches, although both made provision for ordinary people to take an active musical part in church services for the first time. Other protestant movements (such as the Calvinists, who originated in Switzerland) took a harder line and believed that music should be restricted to unaccompanied congregational singing. By the mid 16th century it was clear that attempts to reform the church had led to its division. Europe had split into a protestant north and catholic south.

Protestant ■
Catholic ▨

Protestant and Catholic Europe, *c.* 1560

The counter-reformation and the Council of Trent

The catholic church responded to this division by instituting its own reforms that sought to revitalise catholicism with a new sense of spirituality – a movement known as the counter-reformation. The pope convened the Council of Trent, named after the small city of Trento in the foothills of the Italian Dolomites – a location close to the centres of reformist zeal in Switzerland and Germany, but near enough to the solidly catholic states of Italy to be regarded as neutral territory. It was here that bishops and theologians from all catholic countries met on several occasions between 1545 and 1563 to seek ways to abolish corrupt practices within the church and to establish dogmatic definitions of the catholic faith. Despite internal conflict the council was largely successful in both aims and, partly through the proselytising zeal of new religious orders such as the Jesuits, the catholic church managed to reclaim some of the ground it had initially lost to the protestant reformation.

Debate about church music took up only a small part of the agenda of the Council of Trent but it was a subject of such serious concern that the bishops considered banning polyphonic music altogether. Fortunately the clear part-writing of special prayers set to music by Jacobus de Kerle and sung at the Council in 1561 impressed the bishops so much that this extreme measure was not implemented. Nor were proposals to ban the use of instruments in church music agreed. Instead it was merely decreed that 'nothing profane' should be introduced into the Mass; that singing should not 'give empty pleasure to the ear' and that church music should be composed so that 'the words be clearly understood by all'. These statements now seem rather bland, but they encouraged a more devotional type of church music, based on the style already being used in Rome by composers such as Palestrina (*c*1525–1594), with its emphasis on simplicity, restraint and elegance of musical line.

An old story claims that the future of polyphonic church music was saved when the Council heard Palestrina's beautiful *Missa Papae Marcelli* (Mass for Pope Marcellus). This is unlikely to be true, for the Council of Trent had virtually finished its work by the time the Mass was written, but it is clear that the purity of Palestrina's style became a model for many of his contemporaries.

Latin church music

The Mass

Palestrina had been entrusted with the task of revising Gregorian chant – the plainsong that had been sung for hundreds of years in church services. So it is not surprising that his style owes much to the melodic contours of plainsong. This is evident in every one of his 104 masses, but it is particularly clear in his paraphrase masses. In these he takes a traditional plainsong chant and moulds phrases from it in such a way that they become suitable subjects for imitative counterpoint. This paraphrase technique is evident in Palestrina's *Missa Iste confessor*, written at an unknown date before 1590. *Missa* is Latin for Mass, and *Iste confessor* is the plainsong hymn on which the work is based. Here is the beginning of this medieval hymn:

Example 1
Iste confessor (plainsong). Translation: The saintly confessor of the Lord …

The complete melody of this hymn and the second Kyrie from Palestrina's Mass can be found in RDMS, A49–51.

Like most plainsong melodies it has a small range, it is mostly conjunct with just a few small leaps (no more than a 3rd in this phrase) and it is modal, using the scale G–A–B–C–D–E–F–G (the mixolydian mode). If you look at the soprano part in Example 2 you will see that it begins with the first six pitches of the plainsong phrase *above* then veers off into a freely composed short melisma on the second syllable of *eleison*. This is true of the second soprano phrase, but the melismatic part now rises higher to form one of those beautifully poised arch shapes for which Palestrina is so famous. All of the other parts begin with five or six pitches of the plainsong, but their continuations are subtly varied.

Example 2 Palestrina, Kyrie I from *Missa Iste confessor*

Translation: Lord have mercy upon us.

Study each part in turn and you will find that, like the plainsong, it moves mainly by step or by 3rds. Only very rarely does a part leap more than this, and when it does it returns gracefully within the leap (the only exception being the descent to the final of the mode in the last two bars of the bass part). The really significant differences between Palestrina's melodies and the plainsong phrase are his precise rhythms (necessary in writing polyphony) and the introduction of a few F♯s that indicate a transition from pure modality to G-major tonality.

The sharps in the soprano part are printed above the notes to which they refer. This indicates *musica ficta*, accidentals that the editor thinks singers would have added in conformance with 16th-century performance practice. In the other parts we make no distinction between sharps in the original manuscripts and those we have added ourselves. In the alto part words have not been underlaid after the first phrase, and no words are given for the tenor part at all. This is because word underlay was often incomplete in settings of such common texts as the Kyrie. As with *musica ficta* the singers were so familiar with what was expected that they could add the syllables of the text in accordance with contemporary convention. This throws light on a very important point about text and music in Palestrina's style. Why doesn't he make more use of what may seem to be an impassioned leap of an octave in the alto part of bar 5 in this setting of words which are a plea for mercy? The answer is that Palestrina was often quite unconcerned about word painting. What he tried to do was to provide a type of polyphony that, like plainsong, and in accordance with The Council of Trent's decree on music, allowed the text to speak for itself.

Example 2 is shown as a 'short score' in which the four parts have been condensed on to two staves. In Palestrina's time each voice part was normally printed in a separate book – the illustration *right* shows the cantus (soprano) of the opening Kyrie from his *Missa Papae Marcelli* as it was printed in the 16th century. Notice that the text is not precisely underlaid and that barlines are not used. Also there are no indications of tempo, dynamics, articulation or phrasing. Decisions on these matters would have been taken by the performers. If you do see such markings (and regular barlines) in scores of renaissance music, they will be suggestions that have been added by a modern editor. When you listen to music of this era you may hear it sung in a lower key than printed. This is because the evidence of pipes from surviving organs of the period suggests that pitch in the 16th century was at least a tone lower than it is now (eg a renaissance C probably approximates to a modern B♭).

Throughout the adult life of William Byrd (1543–1623), and for long after, England was staunchly protestant. Laws were passed that required everyone to go to a Church of England service at least once a month while attendance at a catholic Mass was made illegal and could result in a fine or even imprisonment. Although Byrd was a musician in Queen Elizabeth I's Chapel Royal, and wrote music for Anglican worship, he (like many others of his generation) remained a catholic and wrote some of his finest church music for performance at private, mainly secret, Roman Catholic services. He said of the Latin texts that he set:

> There is a certain hidden power ... in the underlying thoughts of the words so that, as one meditates on [them] ... the right notes ... suggest themselves quite spontaneously.

This approach to the setting of sacred texts is totally different from Palestrina's cool detachment. Here we have a composer as deeply committed to his faith as Palestrina, but one who, in his subjective responses to sacred texts, displays a clear sense of renaissance humanism. This is most evident in Byrd's startlingly original set-

Further listening

Palestrina's Mass based on the plainsong hymn *Aeterna Christi munera* and his *Missa Papae Marcelli* are sung by the Oxford Camerata on CD 8.550573 (Naxos).

The motet

tings of items from the Proper of the Mass (ie those texts that apply only to specific seasons or feasts in the church calendar). *Sacerdotes Domini* (Example 3 printed opposite, first published in 1605) is a motet written to be sung on the feast of Corpus Christi, during the part of the Mass when offerings of bread and wine are brought to the altar to be consecrated by the presiding priest. The text reads:

> The priests make an offering of incense and wine to God, and therefore they are holy to their God and will not defile his most holy name. Alleluia.

For a Roman Catholic this is a text that expresses the belief that priests have the power to offer the sacrifice of the Mass to the end that the faithful might be saved. It elicits one of Byrd's most joyful responses. This is achieved most obviously through syncopated rhythms. Where Palestrina's rhythms are smoothly flowing, Byrd's are exuberant. Byrd highlights the important first word of the text, *Sacerdotes* (the priests) by using root-position triads of C and G in pure homophony. This is immediately enlivened by the sopranos and tenors entering earlier than might be expected with *Domini* on the weak last beat of bar 2. Byrd emphasises this syncopation by setting it to the initial percussive 'd' sound of *Domini*.

The imitative entries at *incensum* begin on alternate weak and strong beats (a process that is rare in Palestrina). Similarly syncopated close imitation is evident in the setting of *et ideo* and *et non polluent*. In the soprano part *Deo* (God) is set to a jubilant melisma that is echoed by the weak-beat entry and melisma in the tenor part (bars 8–9). When God's name again appears (*Deo suo* in bars 13–15) it sparks off more melismas, the alto rising from its lowest pitch to the highest pitch it achieves in the first 19 bars. Notice too the off-beat syncopation in the tenor part of bar 24. Byrd's melodic contours also express the joyful text. Where Palestrina's melodies are predominantly conjunct Byrd's are, apart from the melismas, predominantly disjunct. For instance look at how the basses leap a 5th then an octave in bar 19, and then continue up to C in bar 20. Study the imitative entries of *Alleluia* and notice how flexibly Byrd varies the vocal textures. This final section kicks off with the outer parts singing in (compound) 3rds. They are answered four beats later by the two inner parts in 3rds. At the end of bar 21 a new vocal pairing (alto and bass) echoes the same idea. Byrd then quickly winds up the tension by introducing the next two imitative entries after only two beats (tenor, bar 22^2 then soprano, bar 22^4). The next entry (alto, bar 23) joyfully tumbles in only one beat after the soprano. Then the basses put the brakes on to herald the imminent ending by announcing the Alleluia motif in longer note values (a type of free augmentation of the rhythm).

Nominally this setting is in the mixolydian mode. The bass part has only one chromatic alteration, and there are short passages that entirely conform to the mode (eg bars 15–17). But for most of the motet sharps (never flats) add to the exultant mood by precipitating cadences in major keys (eg G major in bars 3–4, and D major in bars 8–9). The evolution from renaissance modality to baroque tonality is strikingly exemplified by these cadences in bright, sharp keys. The false relations between modal naturals and tonal sharps (eg C/C♯ in bar 5, and F♯/F♮ in bar 9) are also indicators of the transition

On the music printed opposite, draw circles round each of the syncopated notes in the soprano and alto parts of bars 12–18. Can you see why the alto part on *polluent* in bar 16 is syncopated, even though there are no tied notes in the setting of this word?

A false relation occurs when the normal and chromatically altered versions of the same note are sounded simultaneously or in close proximity *in two different parts*. The tenor F♯ in bar 9 forms a false relation with the alto F♮ in the same bar. But the alto F♮ in bar 23 is not a false relation.

Example 3   Byrd, Offertory motet for the feast of Corpus Christi

Sacerdotes Domini is sung by the choir of Winchester Cathedral on Hyperion CDA 66837. This CD includes other motets by Byrd (two from the collection mentioned below) and his Mass for Five Voices.

The *Second Chester Book of Motets* contains scores of 12 Latin motets from 16th-century England, including four by Byrd. It is part of a series (published by Music Sales) that encompasses a wide range of Latin church music from the renaissance, presented in cheap, reliable and informative editions.

between modality and tonality. Because of their dissonant effect false relations are sometimes used in slow, minor-mode music to express anguish, but in most cases they are simply a stylistic feature, particularly of 16th- and 17th-century English music. Here they add to the general exuberant effect, especially in bar 25 where a mixolydian F♮ descends stepwise to B in the alto while a tonal F♯ acts as a leading note and rises to G in the soprano. This type of perfect cadence, in which the tonic chord is approached by a false relation, is so characteristic of composers from Byrd to Purcell (see Example 31 on page 80) that it is often called an English cadence.

 Private study

1. (i) What features of renaissance church music were a cause of concern at the Council of Trent?
    (ii) To what extent do you feel that the recommendations of the Council addressed these concerns?

2. Which piece do you think most faithfully reflects the wishes of the Council of Trent, Example 2 or Example 3?

3. Explain the difference between the ordinary of the Mass and the proper, and give an example of a musical setting of each.

4. What is meant by (i) a false relation, and (ii) *musica ficta*?

5. Using Examples 2 and 3, or other music you have studied, show how modal styles of composition were modified to create an increasingly tonal style of writing in the late 16th century.

6. The illustration below shows the bass part of Example 3 as it appears in the original edition of 1605. Make sure you can identify the bass clef at the start of each stave and the **C** time signature. The diamond-headed notes are similar to the round-headed notes we use today. The square notes are breves (eight crotchets long) and the final note is a longa (16 crotchets long).

    Transcribe this bass part in notes of half their original length, adding barlines every four crotchet beats, as would be done by a modern editor. Start as shown *left* and compare your answer with Example 3. Notice how using barlines will require you to substitute tied notes for some of Byrd's original dotted notes.

The sign at the ends of staves 1–3 is called a 'direct' and gives advance warning of the next pitch – it is not a note in its own right.

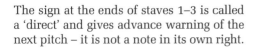

Sa - cer - do - tes   Do - mi - ni

Illustration from the *Bassus* part book of Byrd's *Gradualia* (1605) reproduced by kind permission of the Dean and Chapter of York.

Protestant church music

The creation of the Anglican Church was a typically English and therefore a particularly muddled affair. King Henry VIII had asked the pope to annul his marriage to Catherine of Aragón, the first of his six wives, largely because she had not produced a male heir to the English throne. The pope's continual delaying resulted in the king persuading parliament to pass a series of measures in the 1530s to deny the pope any jurisdiction over the church in England and to affirm a long-forgotten right of Christian monarchs to exercise supremacy over the affairs of the church within their domain.

The papacy was not popular in England and Rome seemed remote. The king received widespread support, not least because at first there were few changes to traditional catholic faith and practices. But religious reformers, led by Thomas Cranmer, Archbishop of Canterbury, soon gained the upper hand. The bible and some parts of the liturgy were translated into English, many church festivals were abolished and the king authorised the dissolution of the country's monasteries and nunneries.

When Henry died in 1547 he was succeeded by his only son, the sickly Edward VI. Since Edward was still a child, government was placed in the hands of his uncle, the protestant Duke of Somerset, who was given the title Lord Protector of England. Cranmer was now able to press ahead more rapidly with his reforms. The Latin liturgy was simplified and translated into famously elegant English under his direction. First issued in 1549, the use of this *Book of Common Prayer* was made compulsory in Anglican churches.

A year later a collection of simple music by John Merbecke for these new services was published under the title *The booke of Common praier noted* ('noted' meaning set to notes). The preface is shown *right*. If the four-line stave and the notes on it look like plainsong you are not mistaken, for Merbecke followed the cautious approach to reform that had been seen to work in England. He did this partly by adapting Latin plainsong melodies to Cranmer's incomparable English and partly by composing tunes of his own modelled on the ancient chants. But this is not music intended for trained choirs, it is church music for the whole congregation to sing. So instead of the flowing rhythms of real plainsong, Merbecke exactly quantifies the relative time values of the first three notes shown on the stave (a breve, semibreve, and minim) and adds that a *pryke* (dot) after the minim increases its length by a half. The word of God was of paramount importance for the reformers, so Merbecke completely rid plainsong of even the tiniest melisma. Instead there was a note to every syllable (see Example 4). This measured, syllabic chant was to have a profound effect on English polyphonic church music.

Merbecke was following in the footsteps of the Lutheran church, which had also adapted plainsong (and secular tunes) to provide music for chorales. These German hymns, sung to rhyming translations of the psalms and other religious texts, provided an important way of securing congregational participation in services. Harmonies (much simpler than Bach's elaborate harmonisations made 200 years later) were often added for choirs and once again this finds an English counterpart – in the metrical psalm.

In this booke is conteyned so muche of the Order of Commõ prayer as is to be song in Churches: wherin are vsed only these iiii. sortes of notes,

The first note is a strene note and is a breue. The second a square note, and is a semy breue. The iii. a pycke and is a mynymne. And when there is a prycke by the square note, that prycke is halfe as muche as the note that goeth before it. The iiii. is a close, and is only vsed at ý end of a verse.

Example 4 Merbecke, *Kyrie eleison*

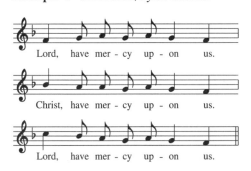

Lord, have mer - cy up - on us.

Christ, have mer - cy up - on us.

Lord, have mer - cy up - on us.

The metrical psalm

Below is the biblical text of Psalm 2 (from the translation in the Great Bible of 1539) on which Parker's version was based:

Why do the heathen rage, and the people imagine a vain thing?

The kings of the earth set themselves, and the rulers take counsel together, against the Lord, and against his anointed.

A problem faced by the reformers was how to enable church-goers to participate in services in an age when many people could not read. Following the example of the Lutherans with their chorales, a number of people in the Anglican church set about turning the psalms into metrical, rhyming verse that could be memorised – a process that led to the creation of the English hymn. Among them was Matthew Parker, Archbishop of Canterbury in the time of Queen Elizabeth I. Nine of his metrical psalms were set to music by Thomas Tallis (c1505–85) and printed in 1567. They include settings in each of the eight church modes and the eighth is the famous canonic setting known as Tallis' canon. Here is Tallis' setting of Archbishop Parker's paraphrase of Psalm 2 from the bible:

Example 5 Tallis, Psalm 2

This psalm tune is sung on track A37 of RDMS with the congregational melody in the soprano part.

The congregational melody is in the tenor. The psalm could be sung monophonically to this part, or with the homorhythmic soprano, alto and bass parts added. The setting is almost entirely syllabic, in keeping with its function as a congregational hymn.

Parker's verse is very regular in metre, with accents on alternate syllables: Why fum'th in fight the Gentiles spite, in fury raging stout. Notice how Tallis brings this to life with the irregular musical rhythm that is made clearer by the barlines we have added to Example 5 (the original edition did not have a time signature and barlines were used only to separate lines of the text).

The tonality of Tallis' setting is distinctly old fashioned. The tenor melody is in the phrygian mode throughout (E–F–G–A–B–C–D–E). Unlike the chromatic alterations in Example 3, the accidentals in the psalm do not suggest firmly established keys.

In one sense, the anthem is an English version of the Latin motet, but its function is different. Motets are settings of essential texts of the Mass. For instance the text of Example 3 would have been sung to plainsong in a church that did not possess a choir – the words are not an optional text that can be omitted. But the anthem, even though a characteristic part of much Anglican worship, is a non-liturgical addition tacked on to the end of morning or evening prayer. It is an adornment of the liturgy, not an essential part of it.

Like the motet, the words of an anthem are usually related to the specific theme of the service. Example 6, printed on page 44, shows the first half of an anthem by Tallis, possibly dating from 1575. Its opening text suggests that it was intended to be sung at Whitsun (Pentecost), a festival that celebrates the Holy Spirit. Notice that Tallis sets the word 'spirit' to a single note in bar 3, reflecting its pronunciation as a single syllable ('spreet') in the 16th century.

This anthem is a typical early-Elizabethan example of the genre. Unlike Byrd's motet (Example 3), the setting is largely syllabic, yet it is much more contrapuntal than Tallis' psalm tune (Example 5). Even in basically homophonic passages such as the first three bars Tallis adds interest by allowing one voice to sing out of step with the chords of the other three voices. Despite these more varied types of texture the words remain the primary focus, the textual repetition only adding to their audibility.

We noticed false relations in Byrd's motet and remarked that this was a stylistic feature that had little to do with word painting. The same is true of bar 5 in this anthem where the sharpened 7th of the mode (F♯) is immediately followed by a modal F♮ in another part. False relations of this sort are two-a-penny in 16th- and early 17th-century music. But the simultaneous false relation between alto and tenor in bar 11 is so exposed that its full bitterness is revealed. Given that it falls on the word 'fear' it is likely that Tallis intended word painting at this point. Contrast this passage with the serenity of bars 16–18 where Tallis uses pure B♭ major and a very modern-sounding cadential progression for his setting of 'all the days of our life'. The potential false relation in bar 20^3 is not observed in all performances but shows how dissonance may also have been used to highlight key words in the text. However, false relations remain a feature of the English style – Palestrinian purity would never allow such unprepared dissonance. Other features that distinguish the style of Tallis from that of Palestrina are:

✦ the melodic diminished 4th (B♮–E♭) in the alto part of bar 3

✦ the sounding of the note of resolution (A in the soprano) against the suspended B♭ (tenor) in bar 6

✦ the augmented triad on the first beat of bar 10: possibly another example of word painting since the unprepared dissonant note (B♭) again falls on the word 'fear'

✦ the leaping bass in bars 14–15 (covering a 9th in five beats).

Most of these English features derive from the opposing claims of modality and emergent tonality. The latter is most evident in the quasi-tonal cadences such as:

The anthem

The complete English anthems of Thomas Tallis are sung by the Tallis Scholars on Gimell CDG/M007.

Example 6 Tallis, anthem, *O Lord, give thy Holy Spirit* (bars 1–21)

- imperfect (phrygian) in G minor in bars 4–5
- perfect (with tierce de Picardie) in G minor in bars 12–13
- perfect in B♭ major in bars 17–18.

Anthems of this sort were intended for performance by a trained choir of boys and men – possibly the choir of Queen Elizabeth's own Chapel Royal, of which Tallis was a member. The choir of the Chapel Royal, which still exists, attracted many of the best church musicians of the day and acted as the focus for a great flowering of church music in Tudor England. Despite the dissolution of the monasteries and the loss of their musical tradition, trained choirs also continued to be employed in more than 40 cathedrals, churches and chapels in the late 16th century, and this choral tradition is still maintained by the Church of England today.

The type of anthem shown in Example 6 later became known as a full anthem, since it was intended to be performed by the full choir. Nowadays such anthems are usually sung *a cappella*, although contemporary evidence suggests that simple support by the organ may have sometimes been provided. Instrumental accompaniment was certainly essential in the verse anthems that became popular in the late 16th and early 17th centuries. In these composers set certain parts of the text ('verses') for solo voice(s), thus providing a vivid contrast in texture with sections for full choir. Verse anthems usually begin with an instrumental introduction played on organ or viols (or both). These instruments provided an accompaniment for the solo voices and doubled the choir in the choral sections.

Examples of verse anthems by Gibbons can be found in RDMS (A61) and HAM (172).

Private study

1. Outline some of the ways in which a performance of a choral work from the late 16th century might differ from the score.

2. Explain what is meant by word painting. To what extent is it important in the church music you have studied?

3. Suggest a reason why alto parts in church music of this period tend to use a rather low tessitura.

4. How did 16th-century composers differentiate congregational music from choir music?

5. State two ways in which an anthem differs from a motet.

6. What part did the singing of anthems play in Anglican worship at this time?

Secular vocal music

The madrigal originated in Italy, the first extant examples being published there in 1533. Unlike the sacred music we have studied so far, which was written for performance by choirs, madrigals were originally sung by solo voices, one per part.

The Italian madrigal

We noticed how the style of Tallis was more dissonant than that of Palestrina. But the desire to give forceful musical expression to Italian texts led to a much more revolutionary compositional style called *musica reservata* (probably because it was reserved for the

Example 7 Caimo, madrigal, *Piangete valli* (bars 1–23)

most accomplished singers). Example 7 dates from *c*1564 and is typical of this serious style of secular polyphony.

The dramatic text translates as 'Weep you valleys abandoned by the sun and you, earth, paint on your mantle [dark lilies and black violets]'. Such opportunity for word painting was too good to miss! Look at the imitative subject and identify precisely how Caimo chooses to depict the falling tears of the sunless valleys in the first 7 bars. Where and how does he first establish a tonal centre?

A new phrase (*E tu, terra, dipingi*) begins its long sequential descent to darkness – the sequence affects all parts, but is easiest to follow in the alto part of bars 9–20. The ruthless way in which Caimo pursues the pattern results in a simultaneous false relation of mind-boggling dissonance in bar 15. After the sequence has finished we are reminded how extravagantly the composer has responded to the doleful text when he tags on a modal cadence formula with normal chromatic alterations and a tierce de Picardie (bars 20–23). By now you should be able to recognise this type of cadential pattern as a feature of much renaissance music, be it sacred or secular.

The incredible range of the Italian madrigal may be judged by comparing Examples 7 and 8. The latter is also in the aeolian mode, but, apart from the sharpening of the seventh degree (the G♯ in bar 12) to form a cadence, there is not a single chromatic inflexion. Instead Marenzio focuses almost entirely on using word painting to illustrate the text, which refers to 'Charming birds among the green leafy branches [compete in practising their lusty notes]'. The songs of these charming birds are represented by virtuoso roulades starting in 3rds and ending with a perfect cadence in C major (despite the nominal modality most of the extract sounds as though it is in this major key). Like Caimo, Marenzio uses imitation and sequence as expressive resources (bars 6–12). The intertwining alto and tenor parts suggest the birds between the green leafy branches (*in fra le verde fronde*) while the scalic ascent (soprano, bars 7–12) and the rising sequence that accompanies it perhaps represents the eye of the poet as he follows the birds to the topmost branches.

Notice the curved line between words such as *valli abbandonate* indicating an elision (sung as 'vall yabbandonate').

Gioseppe Caimo's *Piangete valli* is sung by the Amarylis Consort on Carlton Classics 30367 0208, a CD that also contains an excellent selection of Italian madrigals by more famous composers such as Marenzio, Gastoldi and Monteverdi.

A good source of cheap and reliable scores of Italian madrigals is *The Oxford Book of Italian Madrigals*, edited by Alec Harman. *Oxford University Press.* ISBN: 0-19-343647-7.

Madrigals by Marenzio, including *Vezzosi augelli*, are sung by Concerto Italiano on OPS 30-117 from Opus 111.

Example 8 Marenzio, madrigal, *Vezzosi augelli* (bars 1–13)

The text of Example 9 translates as 'More than any other, Clori, you are beautiful and your looks please everyone'. A score of the complete balletto is given in HAM (158).

There were also simpler types of madrigal, the most common being the *canzonetta* (a short madrigal) and the *balletto* (a largely homophonic dance-like madrigal with *fa-la-la* refrains).

Example 9 is the first half of a *balletto* by Giovanni Gastoldi (c1556–1622). Here there is no word painting, instead everything is focused on the balletto's function as a dance (such pieces could be performed with any suitable combination of instruments and/or voices and could be used for professional or aristocratic dancing). Even the earliest examples were almost completely tonal. Notice that there is hardly any modality: F major is the tonic key (defined by the overwhelming number of primary triads of that key) with a touch of dominant harmony in bars 5–6. Although Examples 9 and 10 are the only five-part compositions discussed in this chapter, the sonorous effect that could be achieved with an extra voice was very popular and there are probably more madrigals for five voices than for any other grouping. Notice that we have not shown the word underlay for the whole of the *fa-la-la* refrain. This is in keeping with contemporary practice, the singers being left to their own devices when such nonsense syllables were used.

The English madrigal

Among the educated classes of late 16th-century England there was a craze for all things Italian, from furniture to the art and literature of humanism, a movement that took hold in Italy with greater tenacity than in any other European country. The English learned about life in Italian courts and wrote poetry in the style of the Italian sonnet. Fifteen of Shakespeare's plays have an Italian background.

'But supper being ended, and Musicke bookes, according to the custome being brought to the table: the mistresse of the house presented mee with a part, earnestly requesting mee to sing. But when after manie excuses, I protested unfainedly that I could not: everie one began to wonder. Yea, some whispered to others, demaunding how I was brought up ...'

Plaine and Easie Introduction to Practicall Musicke, in which the author and composer Thomas Morley explains how a pupil feels inadequate at his lack of musical skill.

The first anthologies of madrigals to be printed in England were translations of Italian madrigals, such as the appropriately named *Musica Transalpina* ('Music from across the Alps') published in 1588 and *Italian madrigals Englished* (1590). However English composers soon started to produce great quantities of their own music for the domestic vocal-music market, resulting in a brief but glorious age of English madrigals in the late 16th and early 17th centuries. During this period the madrigal became a naturalised English genre, the best examples of which compare favourably with earlier Italian models. Madrigal singing in the home became an important social accomplishment for educated Elizabethans, as suggested by the quotation *left* from a book published in 1597.

Example 9 Gastoldi, balletto, *L'Acceso* (c1591)

Example 10 is the first part of a ballett by Thomas Morley (1557–c1602). The similarity to Example 9 in title and use of a *fa-la-la* refrain will be immediately obvious. See how many other points of comparison you can make, considering the following elements:

+ number of voice parts
+ texture of the verses (bars 1–6 in Gastoldi, 1–4 in Morley)
+ keys and modulations
+ type of chords used (eg primary or secondary triads).

Now, equally importantly, examine the differences. Write in the chord names in the first four bars of each piece. Do you see how Gastoldi boringly changes chord on every beat of bars 1 and 3, almost like a hymn tune, while Morley gives his music much more pace by writing largely on chord I, craftily using chords IV and V at the ends of bars 1 and 3 respectively to give the text slight but unexpected off-beat accents?

Both examples begin with two-bar phrases, the second partially repeating the first. But Morley's repeat leads immediately to a modulation to D major and a perfect cadence in this bright dominant key, so producing a balanced pair of phrases – one of the things that makes his ballett sound surprisingly modern. Gastoldi only hints at the dominant before returning to the tonic key for the refrain and it is in the refrains that the greatest differences are apparent. Where Gastoldi continues in plodding crotchet chords, Morley breaks into dancing dotted rhythms (lower stave bar 5, imitated by soprano in bar 6), the dance-like effect being further enhanced by the syncopated middle part in bars 5–6. Morley's refrain is much longer than Gastoldi's, thus allowing the bright dominant harmony time to assert itself, and his final cadence (bars 9–13, including the approach chords) is also more extended to allow a convincing return to the tonic key of G major. There are just two modal touches in Example 10. At bar 7 Morley plunges straight from D major to a chord of C major (the chord on the flat 7th of D major) and the F♮s add modal colour in the next bar.

Having completed your comparison of these two short examples, what conclusions do you draw? Did English composers such as Morley slavishly follow the lead of the Italians or did they seek to improve on the style and, if so, how?

Ballett, the English equivalent of *balletto*, is pronounced like 'cassette', not like 'ballet' (*bal*-ay), even though both words are clearly related to dancing.

My bonny lass is directly based on another of Gastoldi's madrigals (*Questa dolce sirena*) but it is considerably reworked along the lines suggested by our comparison here. A score of the complete ballett is given in HAM (159). It is also appears in *The Oxford Book of English Madrigals* (*Oxford University Press*, ISBN: 0-19-343664-7). This collection includes 60 of the best-known madrigals from our period and will show much more of the variety of styles, light and serious, than we have room to include here.

My bonny lass, along with a representative selection of other English madrigals, is sung by the Amaryllis Consort (Carlton Classics, 30367 0175). This CD also illustrates the vivid word painting in Farmer's *Fair Phyllis I saw sitting all alone* – the same madrigal appears in *Aural Matters*, pages 101–2.

Example 10 Morley, ballett, *My bonny lass she smileth* (*c*1595)

The lute song

The lute is a plucked string instrument which has six courses (strings, or pairs of strings) and frets a semitone apart. In the 16th and early 17th centuries it was one of the most popular instruments for solo playing and accompanying songs.

The lute song or ayre (always spelled like this to distinguish it from the French *air*) was a genre that flowered and died in England in a period of little more than 25 years. The first published collection of lute songs was Dowland's *First Booke of Songes or Ayres* of 1597, the last a collection by John Attey published in 1622.

Lute songs were published in several different formats, but all include the solo melody set above a lute part printed in tablature. The latter shows the strings, with letters to indicate where they are to be stopped (a little like modern guitar 'tab'), and with note stems and tails to indicate the rhythm. Printed music was very expensive at this time and 'table scores' (like that shown below) allowed a group of friends sitting around a table to sing four-part harmony with lute accompaniment from a single copy. On the title page Dowland makes it clear that the bass part could be played on a viola da gamba (with or without a bass singer). It was also possible to play any or all of the vocal parts on viols, thus making the ayre one of the most versatile chamber-music genres ever invented.

Dowland achieved fame throughout Europe for his ayre *Flow my tears* (the first phrase of which is shown on page 52), but the range of his creative genius may be judged by comparing this sombre lament with the light-hearted strophic ayre shown in Example 11. In the poem the singer imagines himself as a poor beggar trying to sell trash to his beloved at a country fair. As so often in this period there is considerable word play (notice the two meanings of the word fair in the first verse) and the tone is ironic. There is no word painting, but the music echoes the playful poetry through lively and often syncopated rhythms. Notice particularly the rhythmic interplay between the syncopated tenor part at the start of bar 2 and the same rhythm beginning a beat later in the soprano part.

Dowland's *Fine knacks for ladies*, showing the four vocal parts as originally laid out in 'table score'. The lute part is printed below the Canto (soprano) part on the left page.

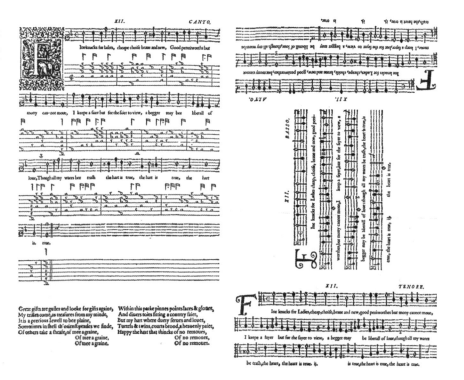

The same rhythm appears again at the start of bar 5 (alto and tenor), but this time against a lively dotted rhythm in the bass. The poetic irony is also mirrored in the music: Dowland reserves his loveliest arching phrase for the words 'Though all my wares be trash'!

Examples 9, 10 and 11 typify the tonal styles of late 16th-century secular music. Dowland's chord vocabulary is more extensive than Gastoldi's or Morley's, but like them he firmly establishes the tonic key before visiting the bright dominant key. This allows Dowland to reflect the structure of the poem in the two-bar phrases that are defined by tonal cadences (eg the perfect cadence in C major in bar 2, the perfect cadences in F major in bar 4, and the phrygian cadence in bar 6). The verbal repetition at the end of the verse elicits a wonderful six-bar phrase (bars 9–14) in which the cadences are disguised by contrapuntal overlapping as the soprano steps down from the upper to the lower tonic in ravishing melodic waves.

Dowland's ayres *Fine knacks for ladies* and *Flow my tears* are performed by Steven Rickards (countertenor) and Dorothy Linell (lute) on Naxos 8.553381. There are many other recordings of these two ayres for a variety of different vocal and instrumental ensembles.

Example 11   Dowland, ayre, *Fine knacks for ladies* (1600)

2. Great gifts are guiles and look for gifts again,
   My trifles come, as treasures from my mind,
   It is a precious jewel to be plain,
   Sometimes in shell th'orient's pearls we find,
   Of others take a sheaf, of me a grain,
       Of me a grain, of me a grain.

3. Within this pack, pins, points, laces and gloves,
   And diverse toys fitting a country fair,
   But in my heart, where duty serves and loves,
   Turtles and twins, courts brood, a heavenly pair:
   Happy the heart that thinks of no removes,
       Of no removes, of no removes.

Virginal music

The virginal was a small harpsichord for which English composers of this period wrote an extensive and highly influential repertoire of song arrangements, dances, variations, preludes and fantasias. Pieces with descriptive titles, such as *The King's Hunt* and *The Fall of the Leaf* were popular. A few works are actually programme music (they tell a story in music). For instance, Byrd's *Battel* is a keyboard suite of 15 movements with titles such as 'The march to the fight', 'The retreat' and 'The burying of the dead'.

Several English and continental composers arranged Dowland's *Flow my tears* for virginal or other instruments, and wrote variations upon it, all of them with the title *Pavana lachrimae* (Tearful pavan). These compositions bring together three genres, for they are simultaneously song arrangements, pavanes (dances in slow duple metre) and variations. At the same time they are ultimate examples of music inspired by words.

Example 12 First phrase of Dowland's ayre, *Flow my tears* (1600)

(Transposed up a perfect 4th)

Flow   my ___ tears,   fall _____   from   your   springs,

Any cultured listener of the period would have instantly recognised the first phrase of this ayre from its distinctive *fall* through a perfect 4th (D–A) and a diminished 4th (F–C♯). They would recall how these motifs relate to the text (*fall* from your springs), and would remember some of the baleful poetic images – such as 'night's black bird' – that characterise the original song.

Dowland's *Lachrimae Pavan* and variations on it by Byrd, Farnaby and Sweelinck are printed in volume 1 of the *Norton Anthology of Western Music*. Byrd's variations are recorded on Chandos CHAN 0574. This CD includes a representative selection of the virginal repertoire, played by Sophie Yates.

Example 13a shows how Byrd retains Dowland's melody with just one rhythmic change in his keyboard arrangement (some adaptation of the lute part is necessary, but Dowland's harmonies are also retained intact). In Byrd's variation of this phrase (Example 13b) Dowland's falling phrase is extended to encompass the interval of a 6th (D–F in bars 1–2) and to become the opening of a two-part canon (soprano and tenor, bars 1–3). This leads to further imitation (tenor and alto, bars 2–4) and another falling phrase at the cadence (soprano, bar 4). Thus, instead of Dowland's two falling motifs there are now six. And yet every note of Dowland's melody is contained in the uppermost part of the variation – see if you can trace them.

Example 13 Byrd, *Pavana lachrimae* (*c*1609)

(a) First phrase of the theme

(b) First phrase of variation 1

Private study

1. For what types of vocal ensemble did 16th-century composers write (a) anthems and (b) madrigals?

2. What is the difference between a madrigal and a ballett?

3. State what is meant by strophic and name a work in strophic form that you have studied from this period.

4. Why do you think the madrigal became so popular in Elizabethan England?

5. What evidence is there that lute songs were designed primarily for domestic entertainment rather than public concerts?

6. Name some of the ways in which composers of this period were inspired by words in their purely instrumental music.

The new style

From about 1573 to 1582 a group of humanist scholars, poets and musicians met at the home of Count Bardi in Florence to explore in great detail the relevance of classical literature, art and music to renaissance culture. They became convinced that ancient Greek drama was sung throughout and they sought ways of recreating the expressive power of Greek music as described by classical authors. Their deliberations related to changes that were already in progress, such as the evolution of a new style of music that could more powerfully express the moods of secular poetry, as in Example 7. More than this, they provided the philosophical foundations for a new type of monodic song – recitative – and a new type of drama – opera. A bitter dispute ensued between reactionary theorists such as Giovanni Maria Artusi (c1540–1613) and revolutionary composers such as Claudio Monteverdi (1567–1643). The former wished to perpetuate the conventions of 16th-century polyphony: the latter thought that music should be the handmaid of the words and that this could only be fully achieved by a single vocal melody that followed every rhythm and inflexion of speech. Soon the old style (*stile antico*) became known as the first practice (*prima prattica*) and this was opposed to the new style (*stile moderno*) of the second practice (*seconda prattica*).

Writers of music history often refer to this group as the 'Florentine Camerata'.

The earliest operas, dating from the very end of the 16th century, developed out of the spectacular musical entertainments laid on at Italian courts for events such as births, marriages and state visits. Like those entertainments, they brought together scenery, stage effects, dance and a variety of existing musical genres, including solo airs, duets and choruses. But unlike earlier spectacles, an opera was conceived as a single large-scale whole, and the new monodic recitative played a central role in welding the entire creation together as well as in providing a musical vehicle for conveying dialogue and narrative in the text.

Early opera

The first opera that is still regularly performed today is *Orfeo* by Monteverdi. Based on the classical legend of Orpheus who travels to the underworld and seeks to retrieve his dead bride by the power of his singing, it was written in Mantua (northern Italy) in 1607.

Example 14 Monteverdi, recitative from Act 3 of *Orfeo* (1607)

In bar 3 above the small notes show how a singer might embellish the single note B written by Monteverdi.

Examples 14, 15a and 15b can be heard on tracks A62, A65 and A66 of RDMS. An extended recitative from *Orfeo* can be heard on track A63. The entire opera is recorded on Naxos 8.554094–95. A vocal score and full score of the opera (edited by John Eliot Gardiner) are published by Chester Music.

Example 14 is taken from a recitative in *Orfeo* and, if you compare it with Example 2 (on page 36) you will immediately see the differences between the old style of Palestrina and the new style of Monteverdi. Instead of Palestrina's polyphony in which all four parts are melodic, Monteverdi writes a single vocal melody that follows the rhythm of spoken Italian, accompanied by a bass part for instruments. This bass is not melodic – it is there to define the chords and tonality, and is thus purely functional. Between these two parts a variety of keyboard and/or plucked string instruments were expected to improvise a harmonic filling on chords implied by the bass and melody. These instruments, along with those playing the bass, are known as the continuo.

As well as ensuring correct declamation of Italian texts composers of the *seconda prattica* also represented the *affetti* (moods) of the words through their vocal melodies. In this case Speranza (a personification of hope) quotes the famous words from Dante's *Inferno* – 'Abandon hope all you who enter here (the portal of hell)'. To express this dire warning Monteverdi resorts to a monotone that reminds us of a priestly intonation. The ensuing silence and rise to the highest pitch of the recitative throws a dramatic light on the word *voi* (you) so that, even without the stage action, we can almost see Speranza pointing a threatening finger at the unfortunate hero, Orpheus. Within a few seconds Monteverdi exemplifies the principles of what was known as the *stile rappresentativo* – a style of music in which the representation of the emotional significance of the text is of paramount importance.

Another important difference between the two practices is that, while ornamentation was possible in some types of renaissance music, embellishing sacred polyphony was difficult and frowned upon by The Council of Trent. But in the *seconda prattica* a display of solo vocal virtuosity was not only appropriate (provided it did not obscure the message of the text) but expected.

Improvised cadential ornamentation such as that in the last bar of Example 14 was commonplace, but it was in arias – in which the balance between text and music was tipped in favour of the latter – that singers were expected to display the full extent of their vocal virtuosity. What singers saw on paper was often as sparse as that in Example 15a, but what was expected of them was something like the hair-raisingly complex ornamentation shown in Example 15b (taken from Monteverdi's own embellished version of the aria). Often the only justification of such displays was the fact that Italians then (as now) regarded singing as something of a spectator sport. However in this case there is good reason for embellishment since this is Orfeo attempting (successfully) to charm the boatman of Hades to allow him passage across the river Styx.

Example 15 Monteverdi, excerpt from the aria 'Possente Spirito' from Act 3 of *Orfeo* (1607)

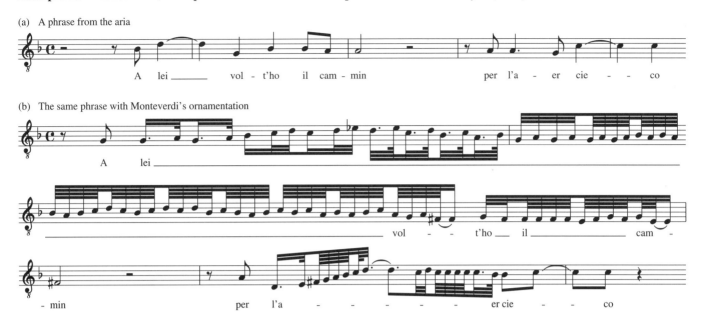

(a) A phrase from the aria

A lei _____ vol - t'ho il cam - min per l'a - er cie - - co

(b) The same phrase with Monteverdi's ornamentation

A lei _____

vol - - t'ho ___ il _____ cam -

- min per l'a - - - - - er cie - - co

It is essential to understand that the concepts of the two practices (*prima/seconda prattica*) or two styles (*stile antico/moderno*) were over-stated generalisations by early 17th-century composers. They were defending their stylistic experiments against the attacks of reactionary theorists such as Zarlino. A glance at Examples 7 and 8 instantly reveals that some of the most important principles of the *seconda prattica* were already observed in 16th-century secular vocal music. What was new, and what laid the foundations for newly emerging baroque style, was the emphasis on the solo voice, the free declamation of the text, and the subordination of the accompaniment to a functional bass with chordal filling.

Translation: To her [Euridice] I have made my way through blinding darkness.

The cold purity of Palestrina's style may have suited Rome, but the citizens of Venice preferred something altogether more spectacular. This tiny city, situated on a group of islands in a lagoon at the head of the Adriatic, accrued enormous wealth through trade with Asia. As a result Venetians were able to erect palaces and churches of the utmost splendour to line the banks of their city's canals. Most sumptuous of all was the palace of their elected leader (the Doge) and its chapel, now the cathedral, of St Mark.

To impress visitors and citizens alike, church music at St Mark's was organised on a magnificent scale. On major festivals 50 or more musicians were employed to perform polychoral church music – works written for multiple 'choirs' of voices and/or instruments. Spatial effects were created by placing the *cori spezzati* (divided choirs) in different galleries around the resonant building. Choirs could echo each other in antiphonal exchanges, voices could be combined with instruments on the opposite side of the building, or a solo voice could be contrasted with the full ensemble. Venetian church music was as theatrical as opera itself.

Giovanni Gabrieli was organist of St Mark's from 1585 until his death in 1612. His motet *In ecclesiis* was published in 1615 (by which time Monteverdi had become director of music at St Mark's). It is in the *stile concertato* (concerted style) of the early 17th century, in which voices and instruments are combined and contrasted.

Polychoral church music

Example 16   Giovanni Gabrieli, opening of *In ecclesiis*

The first section (Example 16) shows how the *seconda prattica* had been embraced in Venetian church music. Translated, the text of the extract reads: 'In the churches, bless the Lord. Alleluia'. The opening words are solemnly declaimed in mainly syllabic and priestly fashion by a solo voice. But this is monody, not plainsong, and so the music is metrical and the voice is supported by the continuo (which provides an unprepared diminished 5th between voice and bass on the second note). The *affetto* immediately changes and Gabrieli uses a lively, sequential phrase for 'bless the Lord'. The repetition in the vocal part sounds just like a written-out echo (perhaps it was performed that way), while the continuo adopts an ostinato-like figure. Metrical rhythm is all, and nothing could be further from the austere polyphony of Palestrina.

The first choral entry in bar 6 provides a *concertato* contrast with the solo voice. Triple-time *alleluias* were common enough in the renaissance style, but Gabrieli's sequential treatment, rising a tone from C-major to D, is altogether more modern. The third *alleluia* includes imitation between the soprano and tenor, but do you feel that Gabrieli's aim seems to be the creation of a dramatic climax rather than the construction of a truly polyphonic texture?

The complete score of *In ecclesiis* can be found in HAM (157). The CD *Music for San Rocco* by the Gabrieli Consort and Players includes this and other polychoral works by Gabrieli. For another motet by Giovanni Gabrieli, see *Aural Matters* pages 104–105.

Gabrieli uses the *alleluia* music as a refrain between sections for solo singers, duets and instrumentalists, creating a rondo structure that would have been unthinkable in the Palestrinian style of church music. Inevitably, the work reaches its climax when all the strands (four soloists, four-part choir, six instrumental parts and continuo) finally come together in luxuriant multi-voice counterpoint.

Such was the influence of the new style that a continuo part became a fashionable inclusion in almost every kind of music, however inappropriate. Thus Palestrina's *Missa Iste confessor* was published with figured bass for continuo in Rome in 1619.

The *seconda prattica* is the greatest change we have seen in this period and it laid the foundations of the new baroque style. Fired by opera, supported by the continuo (and often other instruments), and emphasising the polarity between melody and bass instead of polyphony, vocal music entered a new and highly dramatic phase in which declamation of the text became a principle focus.

Private study

1. (i) What do you understand is meant by the terms *prima prattica* and *seconda prattica*?
   (ii) What is the signficance of this distinction between styles?

2. What is the function of the continuo and what two main types of instruments would play from a continuo part in vocal music?

3. Explain the meaning of each of the following vocal-music terms: (i) monody, (ii) polychoral, (iii) *cori spezzati*, (iv) *stile concertato*, (v) *stile rappresentativo*.

4. The music below is from a motet for solo voice and continuo by Alessandro Grandi, Monteverdi's deputy at St Mark's. A translation is shown *right*. The words are from the Song of Solomon in the bible – an erotic text much more favoured in baroque Venice than renaissance Rome. Identify the musical features which indicate this is a work of the *seconda prattica*.

Oh, how beautiful you are. How beautiful you are my love, my dove, my shapely one, oh how [beautiful you are].

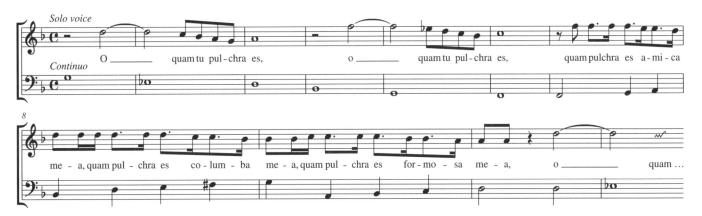

Sample questions

In the exam there will be three questions on your chosen topic, of which you must answer one. Always answer by referring to the composers and precise works you have studied.

Set A

1. Explain what is meant by the *seconda prattica* and outline the ways in which it established a new style in vocal music.

2. Did English madrigal composers slavishly follow the example of their Italian predecessors?

3. Discuss the similarities and differences between Latin church music of the counter-reformation and music written for the English liturgy of the reformed Anglican church.

Set B

4. Is it true to say that secular music in this period is often clearly tonal while sacred music remained largely modal?

5. To what extent was the Council of Trent's wish for restraint in the setting of sacred texts observed by composers in Venice?

6. What impact did the invention of opera have on the vocal music of the early 17th century?

Italian opera

You don't have to learn about the origins of opera for this topic, but you may wish to read the brief account in the section starting on page 53 of this book.

Opera as a sophisticated court entertainment was invented at the end of the 16th century in Florence, but opera as we know it now dates from the opening of the world's first public opera house in Venice in 1637. By the end of the century nine new opera houses were opened in the city to cater for the insatiable appetite of its citizens for this new form of entertainment. The public opera houses encouraged poets, composers, stage architects and scenic designers to change their focus from creating small-scale operas for the aristocracy to presenting large-scale works that would appeal to a broader range of educated society. To this end they abandoned their original aim of recreating the drama of ancient Greece and instead ransacked the literature of every period as sources for sensational stage representations of romantic love, heroic death, ghostly apparitions and the intervention of deities miraculously lowered to the stage by cunningly contrived machines.

Ground bass aria

Such diverse scenes demanded a wide a range of musical styles and genres. Example 17 is from an opera by the 17th-century Venetian composer Pietro Cavalli (1607–76), who was a pupil of Monteverdi. Although written before our period begins it is typical of many such arias throughout the rest of the century. It is built on a repeating bass melody that the Italians call a *basso ostinato* (known as a ground bass in England).

What do you notice about the texture of Example 17? This type of clear separation between melody and bass parts is sometimes called a polarised texture, and is characteristic of much baroque music – we shall see it time and again in the solo vocal music of this period. On paper it appears to be a thin, two-part texture but in practice the continuo part was played by more than one performer. A bass instrument (such as a cello) would play the music as written, but in addition keyboard instruments (such as the harpsichord) and/or plucked string instruments (such as the lute) were expected to improvise a light harmonic filling on the chords implied by the bass and melody. Composers sometimes added numbers and other symbols below the stave to clarify the chords required – a type of notation known as figured bass.

Example 17 Cavalli, closing bars of a lamento from *Egisto* (1643)

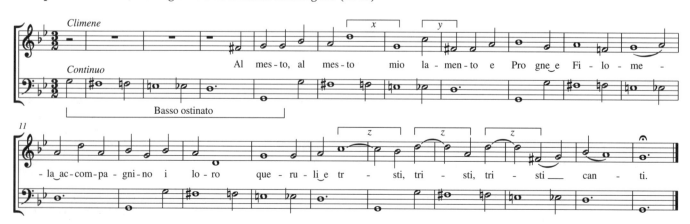

The key of G minor is clearly defined by perfect cadences and the sad chromatic descent of the bass from the tonic (G) to the dominant (D) is characteristic of many 17th-century operatic laments – this very word (*lamento*) occurs in the text. We do not need to know the details of the plot because the solemnly repeating bass and plaintive melody immediately tell us that Climene is in a state of utter despair. Notice the falling 5ths (*x*), and particularly the falling diminished 5th (*y*) that colours the crucial word *lamento*. Can you see how Cavalli draws attention to the key word *tristi* (sad)? It is twice repeated and all three occurences are syncopated. The first forms an unprepared 7th with the bass and is then held over the barline before falling a 2nd. In the second this falling interval is augmented from a 2nd to a 4th. The third most intensely represents Climene's grief. The note D is suspended over the barline to form a discord with the bass, but instead of resolving it falls by an even larger interval (a 6th) to form another discord with the bass that resolves upwards to a consonant G.

You will know from your own composing that regularly repeating four-bar phrases (such as that provided here by the *basso ostinato*) can produce a very predictable and regimented type of music. So next look at the way Cavalli skilfully disguises the repetitions of his *basso ostinato* by allowing Climene to begin her first phrase (*Al mesto mio lamento*) before the ostinato ends, and by allowing her next phrase (*e Progne e Filomela accompagnino*) to cover the join between two statements of the ostinato (bar 8). The whole aria is 71 bars long with 19 statements of the ostinato, yet, despite the fact that it never once leaves the tonic key of G minor, Cavalli ensures that this, one of the finest operatic laments of the century, never becomes monotonous.

At the beginning of the 17th century Italians such as Monteverdi had developed a type of music called recitative (see Example 14 on page 54). It was a vehicle for narrative texts and dialogue that not only allowed the singer to follow the natural rhythms of the words, but also permitted the music to reflect the changing moods of the text. But by the end of the 17th century, recitative had become little more than a link between one aria and the next.

This is also true of the secular cantata – an unstaged 'mini-opera' for one or two solo singers that was the most important type of vocal chamber music in 17th-century Italy. Example 18 on page 60 is taken from the cantata *Mitilde, mio tesor* by the Neapolitan composer, Alessandro Scarlatti (1659–1725). Like most cantatas of the time the text is about the pleasures and pains of love. Equally typical is the structure of the cantata, in which recitatives rapidly set the scene for the more contemplative arias that follow them.

Example 18 shows the recitative as Scarlatti wrote it. Example 19 shows how it might be interpreted in a modern performance. Here we touch on one of the most important aspects of baroque music – improvisation upon the bald skeleton provided by the composer. Although Example 19 is only one of many possible interpretations it is worth taking time to compare the two examples because it will help you to understand why what is printed and what is performed in baroque vocal music often seems so different.

Translation of Example 17:
To my sad lament let Progne and Filomela add their plaintive, sad songs.

Recitative

'Neapolitan' means from Naples, a city in the south of Italy that became an important centre for opera in the late 17th century.

Further extracts from *Mitilde, mio tesor* are printed in HAM (258). There is no recording currently available, but other cantatas by Scarlatti and Handel are included on the Virgin CD *Italian Cantatas* 5618032.

Example 18   Alessandro Scarlatti, recitative from the chamber cantata *Mitilde, mio tesor* (c1700)

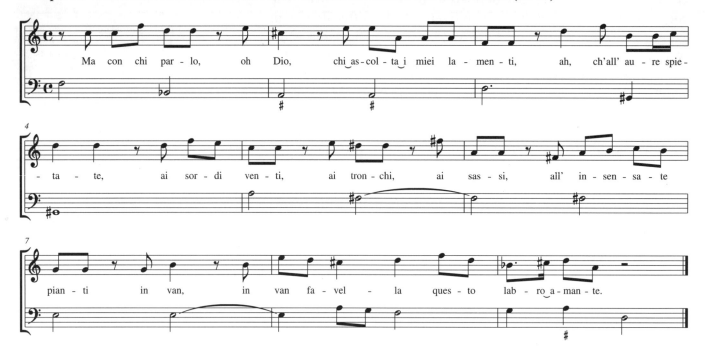

Ma con chi par - lo, oh Dio, chi as - col - ta i miei la - men - ti, ah, ch'all' au - re spie - ta - te, ai sor - di ven - ti, ai tron - chi, ai sas - si, all' in - sen - sa - te pian - ti in van, in van fa - vel - la ques - to lab - ro a - man - te.

Translation: But with whom do I speak, O God? Who listens to my laments? Ah, my loving lips speak in vain to these implacable breezes, these deaf winds, these trees, these stones, and these unfeeling plants.

Notice the following points:

✦ Scarlatti does not use a key signature, whereas Example 19 has a signature of one flat. Such incomplete signatures are found in most minor-key music of the baroque period, even though the music is obviously tonal. The rapid modulations (D minor, A minor, E minor and back to D minor) are typical of recitative.

✦ Scarlatti writes a continuous bass (*basso continuo*) in long notes, but we have notated the continuo part for the most part in short detached chords. This is the essence of *recitativo secco* (dry recitative) where the function of the continuo is, by and large, to provide basic harmonic support for the singer.

✦ Scarlatti's bass part is (apart from the last bar) consonant with the vocal part. In accordance with contemporary practice we have suggested appoggiaturas at the points marked * in Example 19. Precisely where these should be used is left to the soloist's interpretation and sense of style. In this connection you should be wary of attributing word painting to a composer when you hear such dissonances. Yes, we have introduced an appoggiatura on the emotive word *lamenti* (laments), but we have also included conventional appoggiaturas on non-emotive words such as *parlo* (speak) and *venti* (winds).

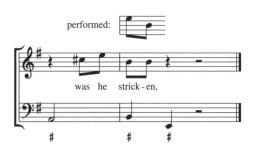

performed:

was he strick - en,

✦ At *(x)* Scarlatti wrote A but we have suggested F♯. It was a baroque convention that accented syllables should take a high note then fall to the unaccented syllable. In many scores of baroque music you will see two notes of the same pitch at a cadence, but will hear a high and a low note, as in the example *left* (the end of a recitative from Handel's oratorio *Messiah*).

✦ Scarlatti, like most composers of the time, included only sparse figuring in the bass part – just the sharps in bars 2 and 9. They indicate that the chord at these places should include a sharpened 3rd above the bass A, ie C♯ (implying a chord of A major). In bar 9 this would produce an horrendous discord (vocal D

Example 19   The recitative shown in Example 18 as it might be performed

against an A-major chord). In fact it was accepted practice to leave the singer to squeeze the last ounce of emotional juice from the written part, before the continuo played a delayed final perfect cadence, as shown at *(y)* above.

✦ It is impossible to show the final liberty that singers might take in their interpretation of *secco* recitative. In a good performance the vocalist will adapt the printed rhythms so that the text is delivered with the rhythm (and speed) of natural speech rather than the regular metre that is implied by the time signature.

Private study

1. (i)   What is a ground bass?
    (ii) Why do you think 17th-century composers were attracted to the ground bass for the setting of tragic texts?
    (iii) What is meant by the term polarised texture?

2. What is the function of the continuo and what main types of instruments would play the continuo part in vocal music?

3. What is a cantata?

4. What is the difference between an aria and a recitative?

5. (i)   How might continuo players have to adapt the rhythm of their part shown in the example at the foot of page 60?
    (ii) Explain some of the other ways in which the performance of a baroque recitative might differ from its notation.

The da capo aria

Example 20 comes from Pallavicino's opera *La Gerusalemme liberata* (Jerusalem delivered) of 1687. The text by Tasso (a late 16th-century Italian poet) also forms the basis of Handel's opera *Rinaldo*, mentioned later in this chapter. The text of this aria translates as follows:

A

Cruel lady, you laugh at me –
but I shall laugh at you.

B

I will offer prayers to the thunderer,
that with lightning in his right hand he may
one day burn the one who has offended me.

Example 20 is an aria by the Venetian composer, Carlo Pallavicino (died 1688). There could hardly be a greater contrast in style and form between this comic aria and Climene's anguished lament in Example 17. Look at (or preferably perform) the first 16 bars and then comment on the structure of the phrases. You almost certainly will have spotted that they are balanced in length, but did you notice that the first four bars rise to a high F♯ while the next four fall to end on a low F♯? This not only creates an elegant musical design but also reflects the antithesis in the text ('Cruel lady, you laugh at me – but I shall laugh at you'). The diatonic style and bouncy rhythms (eg bars 3–4) make the first eight bars instantly memorable, but in case the audience were not paying attention these bars are immediately repeated (Venetian audiences of the day were given to singing along with comic arias).

The final phrase of the first section (starting at bar 17) contains a jolly melisma that colours the crunch word *riderò* ('I will laugh'). At the end of the first section a modulation to A major is aborted by sequential repetition that clumsily returns to the tonic at the very last moment.

Example 20 Pallavicino, da capo aria from *La Gerusalemme liberata* (1687)

The second section (bars 26–44) strongly contrasts with the first because it is in the relative minor throughout. It also includes some vivid word painting, the thunder and lightning of the text being reflected in the vocal fireworks at *fulminante* ('lightning'). This sort of sequential melisma became a cliché of Italian vocal styles in the late baroque period. The performance direction *D.C. al fine* means that the aria should be repeated from the top (*da capo*) to the place marked *fine* (end). In other words, bars 1–25 should be repeated, so making a ternary-form structure (ABA). It is because of the use of this direction that this type of aria became known as a da capo aria. It became the most common type of aria in both secular and sacred music throughout the remainder of the baroque era.

The purpose of the fermata (⌒) in bar 25 is to show the precise beat on which to end the *da capo*. There should be no pause here when section A is performed for the first time.

French opera

It is ironic that the establishment of a truly French style of opera was largely the achievement of an Italian composer, Giovanni Battista Lulli (1632–87). In 1661 he was appointed superintendent of music to the French king Louis XIV. In the same year he became a naturalised French citizen and changed his name to Jean-Baptiste Lully. By the time our period begins he had turned his attention to the *tragédie lyrique* – a serious five-act operatic genre in which music and drama was combined with ballet and elegant verse. The inclusion of dance remained an important feature of French opera for centuries to come.

The primary aim of the *tragédie lyrique* was to glorify the king and provide refined entertainment for the court. So any show of extreme passion or ribald humour was avoided and the emphasis was on the correct declamation of the all-important text through lengthy *récits* (recitatives). Unlike Italian opera, these were often longer than the intervening arias – Example 21 (on page 64) is a complete air from Lully's opera *Armide*, although it is only 22 bars long.

Lully's *Armide* is brilliantly performed by the Collegium Vocale and Chapelle Royale, directed by Philippe Herreweghe, on Harmonia Mundi, HMC90 1456/7. A recitative and aria from *Armide* are printed in HAM (225).

The vocal melody in Example 21 is memorably tuneful, although notice that it is an entirely syllabic setting, and dancing triple-time rhythms are maintained throughout. Bars 0–7 are printed as Lully wrote them, but the remainder is edited to show the conventional dotted rhythms of French *notes inégales* – uneven rhythms that further enhance the dance-like style of the air.

Notes inégales refers to the performance of identical note-lengths as notes of unequal length, eg a run of quavers performed as quaver–semiquaver pairs. It is a feature of much baroque music in the French style. For an example of *Notes inégales* see RDMS A84.

Ballet was an important element in French opera and this *air* would almost certainly have been choreographed. Yet Lully also reflects the words in his music. Armide's urgent invocation of demons is represented by a leaping dotted figure on the words *Venez, venez* (Come, come). This is used again in a varied form for the equally urgent *Volez, volez* (Fly, fly).

Translation of Example 21:
Come, come you demons to strengthen my desires. Transform yourselves into pleasant breezes. I surrender to this conqueror, I am overcome by pity. Conceal my weakness and shame in the remotest of deserts. Fly, fly, lead us to the end of the universe.

Can you identify the form? It is, appropriately, in the same form as the majority of baroque dance music. Can you also work out the tonal scheme (ie the principal keys used)? Section A (bars 1–7) modulates from the tonic key of E minor to a perfect cadence in the dominant key, while Section B modulates through related keys back to a perfect cadence in E minor (bars 18–19). Finally the last phrase is repeated to underline the tonic key (bars 19–22, which form a little coda called, in this style, a *petite reprise*).

In the opera this air is preceded by an instrumental version of the same melody and bass (played on first violins and cellos) with inner parts for second violins and two sets of violas.

Example 21 Lully, air from *Armìde*, Act 2 (1686)

After Lully the next great composer of French opera was Jean-Philippe Rameau (1683–1764). He also wrote extensively about music, and his *Traité de l'harmonie* (Treatise on Harmony) of 1722 was important in codifying the principles of tonal harmony that had been developing throughout the baroque period – and some of his ideas still underpin our understanding of music theory today.

Rameau considered the chord to be the primary element in music, and he saw that a chord's function (eg as a dominant or tonic) was the same whether it was in root position or inversion. He recognised the 7th chord as a type of chord in its own right, albeit a more dissonant one than the triad. He identified chords I, IV and V as the main building-blocks of tonal harmony, and the progression V–I as fundamental in establishing a key. Furthermore, he showed how modulation might develop out of a change in the function of the chord. For instance, the chord of C minor at the start of bar 6 in Example 22 is chord IVb of G minor, the opening key. But in the context of the music that follows it is chord Ib of C minor. This dual function smooths the transition to the new key. In modern parlance we would call it a pivot chord.

Recognition that inversions do not affect the basic functions of chords led Rameau to emphasise the need to think about the roots of chords (which he called the *basse fondamentale*) as the key to understanding harmonic movement. In the next example we have added just such a 'fundamental bass' to Rameau's own music.

Example 22 Rameau, extract from the prologue to *Castor et Pollux* (1737)

Example 22 is taken from the first chorus of Rameau's opera *Castor et Pollux* (1737). Music for chorus appears in many early Italian operas, but choral writing was much more popular in France. Each of its four phrases establishes different (but related) keys according to the composer's own principles. First work out what these four keys are by looking at the cadences. Can you work out how they are related? Next note the chords that are used – the 'fundamental bass' (which is, of course, not part of Rameau's score) will help you.

If you play the choral parts alone you will find they make complete harmonic sense, and the same is true of the orchestral parts. Can you hear that, with the exception of the chord started in bar 15, all the harmonies are either tonic or dominant? But you might also have noticed that the choral parts use different inversions of these chords to those used in the orchestral parts. Listen to a recording (or, better still, play the score with a friend on two keyboards) and you will hear the same harmonic progression expressed through a sumptuous eight-part texture. Now add the fundamental bass and you will discover that this too fits perfectly with the combined harmonic progressions of the chorus and orchestra.

The most obvious feature of Example 22 is the alternation of texture between single bars of unison monotone and three-bar sections of full harmony. These balanced four-bar phrases form a majestic

Translation: He brings peace on earth when he rests under your law.

Notice that when French is sung vowels that are silent in normal speech are vocalised: eg *terre* (pronounced to rhyme with 'pear' in spoken French) is sung to two notes as *ter-re*.

A budget-price CD of highlights from *Castor et Pollux* is available from Harmonia Mundi (HMA 190 1501). This includes *Vénus ò Vénus* (the chorus from which Example 22 is taken). Three splendid recordings of the entire opera are also currently available, but they are expensive.

harmonic sequence that moves with a sense of total inevitability through part of a circle of 5ths (g–c–F–B♭). By the time Rameau wrote *Castor et Pollux* the use of tonality to define structure had become firmly established, but there are few passages of early 18th-century music in which you can *hear* the process with such immediacy. But Rameau is not just giving an object lesson in harmony and tonality, for he lengthens his final phrase (bars 13–17) by introducing a sustained and seductive discord (II^{7}b) decorated with a run of Lullian dotted rhythms played on treble instruments.

Another feature that helps express classical serenity is his use of dominant pedals (D in the first phrase, G in the second, and C in the third). When, in the last phrase, he abandons this technique the music is free to blossom in a way that is all the more effective for the harmonic restraint of the first three phrases. Rameau wrote *C'est l'harmonie qui nous guide, et non la mélodie* ('it is harmony, not melody, that guides us'). Of course he was capable of writing good tunes, but this extract admirably supports his deliberately contentious assertion.

Private study

1. What is a da capo aria? Refer to both form and tonality in your answer.

2. Mention some of the characteristic features of French baroque opera.

3. Why is Rameau's *Traité de l'harmonie* (Treatise on Harmony) important for an understanding of tonal harmony?

English opera

Opera took a long time to catch on in England. Theatres in England had been closed by Oliver Cromwell's dour puritan government in 1642 and were not reopened until the restoration of the monarchy under Charles II in 1660. The young Charles had lived in exile in France and with his return as king came a thirst for entertainment and a vogue for all things fashionable and Frenchified.

The word *libretto* (Italian for booklet) refers to the words of an opera or oratorio.

In 1685 John Dryden, (1631–1700), the famous English poet and dramatist, wrote the libretto of an English opera called *Albion and Albanius*, an allegorical tale which extolled the virtues of Charles II and his brother James II. The score, by the master of the king's music, a Frenchman called Louis Grabu, has been condemned to oblivion. But *Albion and Albanius* has a claim to be one of the first true English operas because, unlike the English masque (a courtly pot-pourri of poetry, songs, dances and spectacular sets), the libretto was set to music throughout. Even more important, from a historical point of view, is Dryden's definition of opera in his preface:

> An opera is a poetical tale, or fiction, represented by vocal and instrumental music, adorned with scenes, machines and dancing. The supposed persons of this musical drama are generally supernatural, as gods, and goddesses, and heroes, which at least are descended from them, and are in due time to be adopted into their number. The subject, therefore, being extended beyond the limits of human nature, admits of that sort of marvelous [sic] and surprising conduct, which is rejected in other plays.

This tells us a lot about opera in England in 1685. Firstly, the need to explain what is meant by opera reveals that the English were unfamiliar with 80 years of operatic development in Italy. Secondly, the adorning of the opera with 'scenes, machines [for lowering gods and goddesses to the stage] and dancing' is a sure indication that English opera was deeply indebted to the French *tragédie lyrique* of composers such as Lully. Thirdly, it suggests that Dryden regarded the 'marvelous and surprising conduct' of opera as a second-rate substitute for the spoken drama of Restoration plays.

Dryden reflected English public opinion of the late 17th century, and it was this no-nonsense attitude to the subject matter and paraphernalia of continental opera that helped ensure that serious opera in English never took root in Britain during our period (although, as we shall see later, opera in Italian was soon to take London by storm). Instead the masque continued to flourish, and many of Purcell's most famous songs come from semi-operas (ie operas with sections of spoken dialogue) such as *Dioclesian* (1690), *King Arthur* (1691) and *The Fairy Queen* (1692). The most famous song of all is 'Fairest Isle' from *King Arthur*. It is easily obtained, and you should study it as an example of pure diatonic melody in regular four-bar phrases.

But a few genuine, though short, English operas were composed in the late 17th century. One of the loveliest is *Venus and Adonis* by an unjustly neglected composer, John Blow (1649–1708). This, his only dramatic work, dates from the same year (1685) as the ill-fated *Albion and Albanius*. But where Grabu feebly imitates the style of Lully, Blow's music is a superb English re-creation of earlier continental styles such as the *lamento* shown in Example 17.

The best recording of *Venus and Adonis* is from L'Oiseau lyre (440 220) on which the part of Venus is ravishingly sung by Catherine Bott.

Example 23   John Blow, *Venus and Adonis*, Act 3 (1685)

Example 23 echoes several features of Cavalli's lament, particularly in its use of:

✦ expressive chromaticism (in the bass part of Example 17 and the vocal part of Example 23)

✦ tortured tritones (marked *y* in both music examples)

✦ a fragmentary melody with silences representing the sobbing of the heroine.

Blow's use of harmony and rhythm is more dramatic than that of Cavalli – notice how he increases the tension by frequently using dissonant intervals between singer and bass. And, while he uses 'French' dotted rhythms, many are in the order short–long rather than long–short. The origins of this pattern (the 'Scotch snap' or 'Lombardic rhythm', marked *x* in Example 23) are obscure, but its use is a fingerprint of the English restoration style, especially in the music of Blow's famous contemporary, Henry Purcell.

How many of the following dissonances between singer and bass can you identify in Example 23?
augmented 4th
augmented 2nd
diminished 7th
diminished 4th
major 2nd
minor 7th

Purcell

Henry Purcell (1659–1695), organist of Westminster Abbey and the Chapel Royal, was the leading English composer of the late 17th century, and is justly famous for the quality of his setting of the English language. His opera *Dido and Aeneas* was written for a girls' boarding school in Chelsea in 1689.

Of the many recordings of *Dido and Aeneas* currently available, the best value is Naxos 8.553108 with the Scholars Baroque Ensemble. Kym Amps sings both ground bass arias beautifully but with great restraint. Other well regarded recordings include Chandos CHAN8306, Harmonia Mundi HMC90 1683 and L'Oiseau-Lyre 436 992-2OHO.

Scores of *Dido and Aeneas* are available from several publishers including Novello/Music Sales and W. W. Norton.

In 'Ah! Belinda', Dido's first air in this opera, Scotch snaps and ordinary dotted rhythms are used, not just as conventional stylistic features, but with the obvious intent of expressing the text. This is evident in bar 7 of Example 24 where both types of dotted rhythm (made all the more jerky by Purcell's syncopated word underlay) uncannily suggest the physical twitching of a woman driven to distraction. Like Example 17 (on page 58) this air is based on a four-bar ostinato (called in English a ground), and, like Cavalli, Purcell carefully covers the join between the end of one statement of the ground and the beginning of the next (bars 4–5) by an overlapping melodic phrase. But Dido's air is made more expressive by weak-beat entries and silences that suggest uncontrollable sobbing.

Example 24   Purcell, bars 1–8 of the air 'Ah! Belinda' from *Dido and Aeneas* (1689)

In the last scene of the opera, Dido (queen of Carthage) has been deserted by her lover Aeneas. In total despair she prepares for death and fatally stabs herself at the end of this lament, after which the work concludes with a chorus during which cupids (who also appeared at the end of Blow's *Venus and Adonis*) scatter rosebuds on her tomb.

For example, the first vocal phrase ends on 'earth', halfway through the second playing of the ground.

Even more impressive is Dido's recitative and lament at the end of the opera (Example 25). Compared with the Olympian detachment of Lully's air (Example 21) Purcell's recitative contains word painting of the darkest hue. What vocal device does Purcell use to make the word 'darkness' particularly expressive? Notice how the sixth and seventh degrees of the scale of C minor are turned from light to dark (B♮ in bar 1 but B♭ in bar 2, and A♮ followed by A♭ in bar 2). Dissonances between Dido's melody and Purcell's bass proliferate. Finally the whole vocal melody falls in waves from the light of the first high C to the darkness of death an octave below.

The air which starts in bar 9 is often called 'Dido's lament' and is one of the most famous ground-bass arias in music history. The bass ostinato is similar to that used by Cavalli in Example 17 (a chromatic descent from I to V), but how does it differ in length? Purcell's assymetric pattern helps disguise the repetitions, as does his care in ensuring that the vocal phrases rarely coincide with the length of the bass pattern. Both composers also make use of prominent falling perfect and diminished 5ths (marked *x* and *y* in both examples). But Purcell's air is infinitely more expressive.

Where Cavalli's melody plods along syllabically in minims and semibreves Purcell introduces melismas to highlight key words. Where Climene is supported by a thin texture of continuo instruments, Dido is accompanied by the expressive timbres of a string orchestra. And it is here that the greatest difference is evident. The only real discords in Example 17 are the unprepared 7th in bar 15, the 4th in bar 16, and the 7th and 2nd in bar 18. Now listen to bars 15 and 16 of Dido's lament, and in just these two bars you will hear:

- ✦ a B♭ that is dissonant with three of the four string notes (*d1*)

- ✦ a B♮ heard over an accompanying D minor chord (*d2*)

- ✦ a C sounding against a suspended D in the accompaniment (*d3*)

- ✦ an A that clashes with the accompanying chord of C major (*d4*)

- ✦ an F♯ that is dissonant with all three notes of the accompanying C minor chord (*d5*).

Example 25 Purcell, recitative and lament from *Dido and Aeneas* (1689)

Of course such technical analysis cannot reveal the wellsprings of the genius that was at play in this, the greatest of all operatic laments, but it can identify some of the techniques through which Purcell transcended the conventions of his contemporaries. Try to listen to the entire aria, in which the ground is heard 11 times in all. As you do so, notice how Purcell shapes the vocal melody to give Dido a climactic top G on the words 'Remember me!' and how descending chromatic figures and yet more poignant dissonances permeate the instrumental *ritournelle* at the end of the air.

The complete aria from which Example 25 is taken can be found in HAM (255).

Private study

1. What is a semi-opera?

2. Explain what is meant by the term Scotch snap or Lombardic rhythm, and identify this rhythm in Example 25.

3. To what extent does Dido's lament reveal the influence of earlier composers such as Cavalli and Lully, and to what extent did Purcell improve upon such earlier examples?

A complete ground bass aria from Purcell's *Ode for the Duke of Gloucester's Birthday* can be found in *Aural Matters in Practice*, page 6. An extract from a ground bass aria that modulates (from Purcell's semi-opera *The Fairy Queen*) is given in *Aural Matters*, page 114. Also see RDMS A75.

Try to listen to the whole of Purcell's *Dido and Aeneas* – the entire opera lasts less than an hour but is astonishingly varied. It includes delightful duets and dances in the style of Lully, a jolly sailors' song and dance, a chorus with off-stage echoes – 'In our deep vaulted cell (-ed cell)' – music for cackling witches and a hunting scene – as well as the tragic lament that we have discussed here.

Opera buffa and opera seria

In 17th-century Venetian opera serious and comic characters and scenes could coexist in the same work, but by 1700 comic elements began to be excluded from opera. At first they were relegated to entertaining *intermezzi* (interludes) between the acts of what by now had come to be known as *opera seria* (serious opera). Later these *intermezzi* became completely independent comic operas (*opere buffe*). In fact the most famous early *opera buffa*, *La serva padrona* (1733) by the young Neapolitan Giovanni Battista Pergolesi (1710–1736) began life as a pair of intermezzi in his three-act *opera seria*, *Il prigionier superbo*. The serious opera was a flop, but the *intermezzi* were so famous that they were soon performed as an independent two-act *opera buffa* throughout Italy and then, in the presence of king and court, in Paris. This French performance set off the so-called *Guerre des bouffons*, a controversy between those who supported serious French opera and those who had been converted to the Italian *opera buffa*.

There is no need for us to quote from *La serva padrona* since the score (from Universal Edition) and several recordings are readily available. All we have said about Example 20 applies with equal force to Pergolesi's da capo arias except that they are much longer (listen to *Sempre in contrasti* and *Stizzoso mio stizzoso* in the first act, and *Son imbrogliato* in the second). The same is true of the purely functional, rapid-fire recitatives (compare *Questa è per me disgrazia!* from the first act with Example 18 on page 60).

The word 'school' in the context used here refers to music by various composers that shares common principles.

Shorn of comic elements, serious operas of the early 18th-century Neapolitan school soon developed into stylised music dramas in three acts, each containing a set number of arias linked by the sort of recitative we have already encountered in the work of the greatest Neapolitan composer, Alessandro Scarlatti (Example 18).

Much has been made of the reforms of the librettists Zeno and Metastasio, but in reality these men simply codified what was already beginning to happen in opera. From a purely musical point of view three principles were of paramount concern in early 18th-century *opera seria*. Firstly, the text for each aria expressed a *single* affection (ie a mood, such as sorrow, anger or love). The practical

Example 26 Handel, melody of a da capo aria from Act 2, Scene 4 of *Rinaldo* (1711)

consequence of this 'doctrine of the affections' was that composers tended to codify melody types that were supposed to reflect the emotional tenor of the text. Secondly, the composer's melody was specifically composed to be a suitable vehicle for the vocal talents of particular soloists. Thirdly, the musical form of the aria reflected the elegance of the librettist's verse. The practical consequence of these last two principles was the enthronement of the da capo aria, and the dominance of vocal display in the reprise of its first section.

These principles are evident in Example 26, which shows the melody of an aria from Handel's opera *Rinaldo*. The pervasive mood of the text is revealed in the first phrase 'Let me lament'. To represent this doleful affection Handel sets the text as a sarabande – a solemn dance in slow triple time that is characterised by accents on the second beat of the bar. In bars 1–4 Handel highlights the second beat by resting on the third. How is the second beat emphasised in bars 9 and 11? These and similar rhythms pervade the whole aria, so ensuring the desired unity of affection.

The ternary structure is tightly controlled. Section A consists of an eight-bar melody in F major and a six-bar melody in the related, but tonally contrasting, key of the dominant (C major). The opening melody is then repeated in the tonic, first by the singer (bar 15) and then by the orchestra (bar 23). This A section is thus a compact ternary form in its own right. The characteristic sarabande rhythm recurs in the minor-mode central episode (B) – can you work out how the keys here are related? The reprise of section A offers the singer an opportunity to display appropriate ornamentation and this, of course, will vary from one recording to another.

Translation of Example 26:
A: Let me lament my cruel fate and sigh for liberty.
B: Grief shatters these chains of torments only for pity.

Lascia ch'io pianga features on a CD from Carlton Classics, 'Let the Bright Seraphim' (30366 01182) which also contains relevant works by Purcell and Alessandro Scarlatti.

A ritornello means 'a little return': such instrumental reprises of the main musical material (often abbreviated) are a standard feature of da capo arias and many other musical forms of this period. Longer arias often begin with an instrumental ritornello designed to be played as the soloist enters.

Handel

George Frideric Handel (1685–1759) grew up in Germany but at the age of 21 he went to Italy for several years, spending time in those great operatic centres of Naples and Venice. He first came to England in 1710 and later made it his home for the last 42 years of his life. There was a buzz about London in the early 18th century. Much of the city had been grandly rebuilt after the great fire of 1666, it was the hub of a wealthy global trading empire and it was the seat of increasingly radical reform that had created a rich and powerful middle class. All of this undoubtedly appealed to the young and ambitious Handel. But the prime attraction must have been the new and insatiable demand for Italian opera that had suddenly arisen just before his arrival in 1710 – it was like the vogue for all things French 50 years earlier.

The first two sections of a da capo aria from Handel's opera *Orlando* (1733) are included in *Aural Matters*, page 118.

Handel soon got to work on the first of some 40 operas he wrote for the London stage – *Rinaldo*, from which Example 26 is one of the best-known arias. It was given the first of many performances on 24 February 1711 and was a triumph. Handel used a cast of seven Italian singers, including the great castrato Nicolini, who already had a popular following in London. Handel scored the work for a large orchestra (two flutes, two oboes, four trumpets, timpani, strings and continuo). Brass and drums were used to spectacular effect in the opera's battle scenes, while spectacle of a different kind was provided by a scene of fire-breathing monsters and another in which recorders imitated birdsong while a flock of live sparrows was let loose in the theatre! To further ensure success, Handel drew in the crowds by giving virtuoso improvisations on the harpsichord at the end of the second act.

Opera in 18th-century London

Going to the opera in the early 18th century was nothing like it is today. Some people treated the occasion as an opportunity to chat with friends during the least engaging parts of the music, others went to save the enormous cost of candle-powered light at home on dark winter evenings and perhaps to have a meal as they listened, while others went as fans to cheer their favourite singers and to boo the rival soloists. The immense vogue for castrati is difficult to understand today. These adult male singers had a soprano (or alto) voice, resulting from castration before puberty, that was reputedly of great power, virtuosity and beauty. Although the necessary surgical operation was cruel, castrati could earn vast sums of money and were star attractions in the operas of the time. Many of Handel's leading male roles were written for castrati and this creates a difficulty in modern productions. It is seldom possible for these parts to be sung an octave lower by a tenor, as the relationship between vocal line and accompaniment is then wrong. Sometimes castrato parts can be sung falsetto in the correct octave by a high male alto, but this type of voice is seldom able to achieve the brilliance and flexibility that the music demands. So it is often preferable musically (if not dramatically) for male heroic roles to be sung by suitably attired female sopranos. Other problems for modern producers of *opera seria* include the artificial plots, often based on obscure stories in classical literature, and the prevalence of reflective da capo arias that do not move the action forward. Nevertheless, Handel's operas include some of his finest music, especially in *Giulio Cesare* (1724) and *Rodelinda* (1725).

Ballad opera

The craze for Italian opera in London lasted barely 30 years, and in 1737 both the major opera companies, at Covent Garden and the Haymarket Theatre, collapsed. The end was undoubtedly hastened by the appearance of a new, comic and altogether more understandable type of dramatic entertainment, the ballad opera. This peculiarly English genre flourished in its original form between 1728 and 1735. Ballad operas were performed in English and had plots based on contemporary subjects. Instead of recitative they contained spoken dialogue, and the vocal numbers drew on popular tunes of the day and on traditional folk music.

The Beggar's Opera (1728) was the first and most famous ballad opera of the 18th century. John Gay (1685–1730) wrote doggerel verses that lampooned politicians, opera singers in general and Handel's Italian operas in particular. These were fitted to a motley collection of tunes derived from old folk melodies, contemporary broad-sheet ballads and music filched from contemporary Italian operas. *The Beggar's Opera* begins with an introduction in which a beggar (the supposed author of the libretto) says

> I hope I may be forgiven that I have not made my Opera throughout unnatural, like those in vogue; for I have no Recitative.

The ensuing French overture, composed along with 'basses for the airs' by the ineffable Dr Pepusch (1667–1752), lampoons the Prime Minister by using the defamatory ballad 'Walpole, or The Happy Clown' as a fugue subject. Further political satire is evident in the verses Gay fitted to the famous folk tune 'Lillibulero', to form a song that attacks financial corruption in high places ('twas ever thus in politics!):

Currently the only authentic recording of *The Beggar's Opera* is on Hyperion CDA 66591/2. Other recordings are based on re-arrangements of Pepusch's arrangements.

Further excerpts from *The Beggar's Opera* can be found in HAM (264).

Example 27 John Gay, melody of a popular song from *The Beggar's Opera* (1728)

Most of the airs are simple syllabic settings of this sort, but in Example 28 (page 74) Gay mocks highflown operatic coloratura by underlaying several notes of the original tune with just one monosyllabic word – 'dirt'! This air is a duet for two female characters who abuse each other with as much gusto as Francesca Cuzzoni and Faustina Bordoni, two of Handel's most notorious prima donnas whose disreputable off-stage behaviour caused as much concern in early 18th-century London as certain football stars do today.

Example 28 John Gay, melody of a duet from *The Beggar's Opera* (1728)

Reform opera

After the collapse of Italian opera in London, Handel turned his attention to oratorio (see page 78). *Opera seria* remained popular on the continent (where cultured people understood Italian) but there were constant attempts to remove some of its more stifling conventions – to make it more flexible and dramatic, to make it less of a vehicle for displaying the vocal prowess of the star singers, and to give the orchestra and chorus a more integrated role. By the 18th century the employment of a separate body of singers to form a chorus in Italian opera had fallen into disuse. Most of Handel's *opera seria* end with a vocal ensemble marked 'chorus', but this was just an opportunity for the assembled soloists to sing together (those who had been killed off in the third act being specially resurrected for the purpose of this generally happy finale).

The need for reform was obvious, and the most famous document about such reforms is the preface that Christoph Willibald von Gluck (1714–87) wrote for his opera *Alceste* (1767). The chief points of Gluck's manifesto are:

✦ Simplicity, truth and nature are the great principles of beauty in any art

✦ Music should therefore serve poetry by simple expressiveness and by closely following the dramatic developments of the libretto

✦ To this end superfluous ornamentation, cadenzas, meaningless roulades and unessential orchestral ritornelli are to be avoided

✦ If da capo arias are to be included, the central section, upon which the poet has laboured so hard, should not be passed over quickly in order to hurry on to the vocal display of the embellished reprise (see Example 26 on page 71, in which section B is only 12 bars long)

✦ Recitative and aria should not be so independent or contrasted in style that they 'wantonly disturb the force and heat of the action'

✦ Instruments should be used 'in proportion to the interest and intensity of the words'.

It is surprising that Gluck fails to mention the role of the chorus since they play such an important part in his first two reform operas (*Orfeo* and *Alceste*). In these operas it is Gluck's clear intention to break the Metastasian recitative-aria mould and instead to integrate all types of music in service of the drama. This he magnificently achieves at the start of Act I of *Alceste* (Example 29).

Example 29 Gluck, music at the raising of the curtain on Act 1 of *Alceste* (1767)

As the curtain rises the tumultuous, doom-laden overture (a) leads without break (but with a dramatic interrupted cadence) into a short chorus (b). Its homophonic texture and slow tempo allow the words to be heard and the chromatic D minor harmony makes it plain that a tragedy is about to unfold. The first solo instrument is a trumpet (c) – what could be more 'in proportion to the … intensity of the words' than this dramatic fanfare announcing the arrival of the herald? His recitative (d) follows and chromatic harmony returns as he unfolds his bad news (see how many diminished-7th and augmented-6th chords you can spot in the extract). In bars 23–24 the herald sings a conventional operatic cadence formula, but the equally conventional perfect cadence is immediately followed by two chords that with utmost urgency effect a modulation to B♭ major. It is by such means that Gluck achieves his objective of returning to the original aims of the founding fathers of opera.

Translation of Example 29:
Chorus: O gods, save our king, our father.
Herald: People, listen and double your tears. You will be tested by a terrible misfortune.

Philips produce an excellent recording of *Alceste* (470 293-2PH2). It uses the revised version of the opera that Gluck produced for Paris in 1776 – and this is the version from which the example above is taken. Note that Gluck's original version of 1767 was in Italian and differs from the Paris version in numerous details.

Private study

1. An *opera seria* generally begins with an overture and ends with a vocal ensemble for the soloists. What two vocal genres predominate in the rest of the work?

2. (i)   What is a ritornello?
    (ii) What does the fermata (⌢) signify in a da capo aria?
    (iii) How might a baroque composer differentiate the middle section of a da capo aria from the outer sections?

3. Explain what is meant by 'the doctrine of affections'.

4. (i)   What is the difference between *opera buffa* and *opera seria*?
    (ii) How does ballad opera differ from both of these?
    (ii) For which type of opera is Handel famous?

5. Why was *opera seria* in need of reform?

Sacred Music

Passion settings

In 1724, more than 40 years before the first performance of *Alceste*, J S Bach (1685–1750) used recitatives and choruses with equally dramatic force in his St John Passion. The following discussion is based on the extract from this work shown in B4 in RDMS, but scores and recordings of the complete work are easy to come by.

The reformed Lutheran church in Germany perpetuated an ancient tradition of solemnly recounting the story of Christ's last days on earth as a human (commonly known as the passion story) during Holy Week, the week leading up to Easter. Many earlier composers had written passion settings, sung in German so they would be clearly understood by the congregation. But Bach's two settings of the gospel story (one a reflection on the account by St John and the other on the account by St Matthew) far surpass all others in scale and depth of expression. In common with his other church music, Bach (who never wrote an actual opera) drew on almost all the operatic genres we have discussed, and integrated them with the Lutheran tradition of hymn (chorale) singing with which the Leipzig congregations would have been familiar.

Near the start of part two of Bach's St John Passion, Jesus is interrogated by Pilate who, unable to find any fault with him, asks the crowd whether he should release Jesus. The crowd (*turba* in Latin) cry out 'Not this man, but Barabbas'. The interrogation is conducted in rapid recitativo secco (explained on page 60) as is the response by the Evangelist (narrator): *Da schrieen sie wieder allesamt und sprachen* ('Then cried they all again saying …'). The *turba* that follows (*Nicht diesen, sondern Barrabam*) is sung almost as fast as the recitative and with strong, brutal accents on *Barrabam*. Without pause the Evangelist begins the next recitative on his highest note with 'Barabbas was a murderer' (*Barrabas aber war ein Mörder*). Bach then reveals the full expressive potential of recitative when the Evangelist tells how Pilate had Jesus flogged (*Da nahm Pilatus Jesum und geisselte ihn*). The melisma on the first syllable of *geisselte* must rank as one of the most graphic examples of word painting in the history of music: the jagged rhythms of the chromatic vocal line being intensified by the flailing leaps of the bass.

This dreadful scene is followed by an arioso (*Betrachte, meine Seel*) with enticingly beautiful accompaniment for lute, viola d'amore (literally 'viola of love' – a tenor string instrument with multiple sympathetic strings that help produce the most tender tone) and continuo. Arioso is another operatic genre that can take the form of a melodic flowering within a recitative or, as here, can be an independent short aria without a da capo repeat. In his Passions Bach used both full-blown da capo arias and shorter ariosos as meditative interludes between passages of recitative.

In listening to this arioso, note how key words are underlined by melodic contours and how the latter relate to the basso continuo. Notice, for instance, how the rising minor 7th at the start is replicated a fourth higher in bar 3, reaching the flat (therefore mournful) 7th of the scale on the adjective *ängstlichem* ('anxious'), at the same time forming a diminished 7th with the bass.

We encountered the secular cantata on page 59. Its counterpart in sacred music, the church cantata, was performed in large Lutheran churches as part of the main service on Sundays and festivals, as a way of dramatising the biblical readings appointed for the day. Although there is considerable diversity in the precise format, a typical church cantata in Bach's time was written for one or more solo voices, choir and small orchestra and would be about 20 minutes in length. There were usually between four and eight movements, including recitatives, arias and duets for the soloists. Many of Bach's cantatas begin with an elaborate movement for choir and orchestra, and end with a simple four-part harmonisation of a German hymn tune (known as a chorale). The chorale melodies, many of which date back to the 16th century, would have been very familiar to the congregation and Bach often incorporated them into other movements of the cantata. This is so in his Cantata No. 140 (*Wachet auf*), excerpts from which are shown in Example 30. The melody appears in the first movement as a treble cantus firmus:

Church cantatas

Translation of Example 30:

(a) Chorale, verse 1:
Wake, arise, the [voices call us] …

(b) Chorale, verse 2:
Zion hears the watchmen singing, …

(c) Chorale, verse 3:
'Gloria' now be sung to thee, …

Example 30 Bach, excerpts from Cantata No. 140, *Wachet auf!* (1731)

Beneath the cantus firmus, the lower voices weave a contrapuntal texture of fugal entries, and the entire edifice is supported by an independent orchestral accompaniment that is extended to create a large-scale ritornello form for the movement as a whole.

After an Italianate recitative and duet the chorale melody recurs as a cantus firmus for tenor voices against an obbligato string part with continuo harmony – part of this trio-sonata-like texture is shown in Example 30 (b). Following another recitative and duet, the cantata ends with a *Schlusschoral* (final chorale) in which the melody is harmonised in syllabic style (Example 30 (c)). If you are studying chorales for your techniques option you will be familiar with simple settings of this type, most of which come from Bach's cantatas.

Oratorios

Handel's oratorios are not strictly church music – they were written for secular venues such as the opera house and a few are not even on religious subjects, although most are based on biblical stories, mainly from the Old Testament. Handel first started writing oratorios for performance in Lent, when it was the custom not to mount staged productions. In many respects these works were like *opera seria* without the costumes or stage-play. But there were two important differences: they were in English and they included dramatic choruses as well as solo singing. Both innovations greatly appealed to audiences and, after the collapse of Italian opera in London in 1737, Handel spent much of the next 20 years writing a succession of oratorios, of which the most famous is *Messiah* (1742).

Most schools and libraries will have scores of *Messiah*, so we have not included printed music examples here. If you do not already have access to a good recording of the work, an excellent authentic performance by the Scholars Baroque Ensemble is available at a bargain price on Naxos 8.550667/8.

In *Messiah* Handel's setting of St Luke's account of events associated with the birth of Christ consists of six short movements that exemplify several typical operatic genres. Together they form what, in contemporary opera, would have been called a *scena* (scene). This *scena* begins with an instrumental interlude which Handel called *pifa*. This is either an abbreviated form of the Italian *piffaro* (shawm) or *piva* (bagpipe). Both words are related to performances given by Italian shepherds who, in the weeks running up to Christmas, used to come down from the mountains to play shawms and bagpipes in Rome in honour of the Christ Child. In baroque operas such instrumental interludes were called *sinfonie*, so the title most often used today – 'Pastoral Symphony' – exactly describes the nature of this illustrative music in which violins represent shawms and lower strings the drone of a bagpipe.

The second movement of Handel's *scena* is a secco recitative ('There were shepherds abiding in the field') accompanied by continuo instruments – with the bass instruments continuing the bagpipe drone of the *piva*. The third movement ('And lo, the angel of the Lord came upon them') is *recitativo accompagnato* – accompanied recitative, in which the singer is supported by more than just the continuo group. Here, Handel writes parts for high strings, giving a brilliantly luminous picture of the arrival of the angel.

The additional instruments in accompanied recitative are often used to throw a particular light on what is sung. For instance in Bach's *St Matthew Passion* the words of Jesus are accompanied by a halo of upper strings (as well as continuo) whereas the recitations of all other characters are accompanied by continuo instruments only.

The fourth movement ('And the angel said to them') is another secco recitative. Notice how its rapid modulations not only increase the excitement but also provide a transition from F major of the third movement to D major in the fifth ('And suddenly'). The latter is another accompanied recitative and here, to escalate the drama, Handel confines the vocal part to a high tessitura and adds to this obvious word painting by imitating the quivering of angels' wings with a flashing semiquaver figure.

The last movement of the *scena* is a setting of the angel's hymn of praise. The musical metaphors of the preceding recitative are maintained in the first four bars where bass voices are omitted. Semiquaver string figuration continues and distant trumpets (their first appearance in the oratorio) add a further touch of baroque drama. In bars 5–7 the semiquavers stop and unison low voices illustrate 'and peace on earth' in another obvious example of word painting. Finally the fugal texture starting at bar 18 suggests a multitude of angels, the close imitation giving the impression of countless overlapping shouts of praise.

Listening to *Messiah* will introduce you to a wide range of late-baroque vocal forms and styles. The choruses include:

✦ simple homophony ('Since by man came death')
✦ homophony with elaborate accompaniment ('Hallelujah')
✦ antiphony ('Lift up your heads')
✦ fugue ('And with his stripes')
✦ fugue with independent accompaniment ('And he shall purify')
✦ ritornello form ('And the glory of the Lord')

Many choruses combine two or more of these techniques, such as the ever-famous 'Hallelujah' chorus. The solo vocal writing in *Messiah* includes:

✦ secco recitative ('There were shepherds')
✦ accompanied recitative ('All they that see him')
✦ arioso ('Behold, and see')
✦ ritornello-form aria ('Ev'ry valley shall be exalted')
✦ aria with obbligato trumpet solo ('The trumpet shall sound')
✦ da capo aria ('He was despised')
✦ duet ('O death, where is thy sting?)
✦ an operatic 'pastoral' style aria ('He shall feed his flock')
✦ an *aria di bravura* full of operatic coloratura ('Rejoice greatly')
✦ an operatic 'rage' aria ('Why do the nations so furiously rage')
✦ an *aria all' unisono* ('The people that walked in darkness')

Again, there are many composite forms, including 'O thou that tellest good tidings to Zion' which is essentially a da capo aria in which the final section is written for chorus. Finally, the two purely instrumental movements are a French overture (the type Handel used in most of his operas) and the 'Pastoral symphony' mentioned earlier. Such diversity within such unity is just one of the reasons why *Messiah* remains the most famous choral work ever written.

A French overture consists of a slow first section, featuring dotted rhythms, followed by a fast fugal section.

Private study

1. (i) Explain the difference between secco and accompanied recitative.
   (ii) What is (a) an arioso, and (b) a cantus firmus?

2. Briefly describe some of the variety of ways in which Bach incorporated chorale melodies into his cantatas.

3. Outline the main similarities and differences between Handel's operas and oratorios.

English anthems

The English anthem is not part of the liturgy of the Church of England, but provision was made in the Prayer Book for an anthem to be sung as an optional extra in churches with competent choirs. During the Commonwealth (1649–1660) church choirs had been disbanded, but with the restoration of the monarchy in 1660 they were re-established and new anthems were written, often in the fashionable French style of the day. Spearheading the musical restoration was the Chapel Royal where, in 1662, a band of 24 strings was established in imitation of the French *vingt-quatre Violons du Roi* (the King's 24 string instruments). Here composers such as Blow and Purcell wrote church music with accompaniment for strings (and organ continuo) that reflected the style of composers such as Lully. The most popular genre was the verse anthem, in which parts of the text ('verses') were set for soloists, contrasting with sections for the full ensemble. Sometimes these included orchestral ritornelli, which composers of the time called 'symphonies'. The entire anthem, with its contrasting sections, was thus similar to a short cantata in structure.

The famous diarist Samuel Pepys went to a Chapel Royal service in September 1662 and noted that there was a 'most excellent anthem with symphonies between'. But his fellow diarist, John Evelyn, was more disapproving, complaining of the '24 violins between every pause, after the French fantastical light way, better suiting a tavern or playhouse than a church'.

String orchestras were seldom feasible in churches other than the Chapel Royal, and in most cathedrals verse anthems were performed with just organ accompaniment.

Example 31 comes from the end of a verse anthem of this type, although the verses here are unusually short – typically such solo sections were several dozen bars in length. Its dancing triple metre, with dotted and double-dotted rhythms (some of which are editorial) are clearly in the French style – compare the music with Example 21. These, and the joyful second-beat syncopations reflect the key word 'rejoice', while the simple homophonic texture and largely syllabic underlay ensure that the text will be clearly heard. The frequent repetition of words is justified by the text ('and again'), but Purcell skilfully avoids monotony by a varied tonal scheme.

Example 31 Purcell, last 22 bars of verse anthem, *Rejoice in the Lord alway* (c1685)

The first phrase begins in C major and ends in A minor. The A-major chord at the end of bar 6 is treated as a dominant, which propels the second phrase through D minor before the modulation back to C major in bars 9–10. The last word ('again' – again!) is wittily echoed by the three verse parts who steer the music towards G major (a key confirmed by the perfect cadence in bars 13–14). This time the echoing verse parts return the music to C major, the key of the last phrase. When this phrase is repeated the tenor introduces a cheeky flattened 7th in bar 20 (B♭) which causes a false relation with the treble B♮ in the same bar. Such colouring of a cadence with a false relation is not only characteristic of Purcell but also of much other 16th- and 17th-century English music (see page 40).

Look closely at the part-writing in the last three bars and you will see a multitude of dissonances as Purcell simultaneously uses a variety of different types of melodic decoration (passing notes, échappée, suspension and notes of anticipation as well as the false relation). Thus the tenor's B♭ forms a 9th with the treble, and the soprano and alto proceed in parallel 7ths at the start of bar 20. All is resolved by the final perfect cadence, of course. There are no words in the text to suggest such discords – English composers of the middle baroque simply relished their piquant effect and they are thus a characteristic fingerprint of the style.

Even such strictly liturgical music as the Mass was influenced by opera in the baroque period. Increasingly elaborate instrumental accompaniment was used and the longer texts (*Gloria* and *Credo*) were often subdivided into shorter movements in which aria-like sections for solo voice, sometimes incorporating operatic coloratura display, were contrasted with dramatic choral writing. Old style (*stile antico*) polyphony still sometimes had a role to play in fugal choruses, but the music was little like that of the renaissance – baroque composers preferred a thoroughly tonal approach, often with independent orchestral accompaniment.

In 1733 Bach wrote a setting of the *Kyrie* and *Gloria* (the only movements of the Mass that were commonly sung in Lutheran liturgies) for a visit to Leipzig of a new ruler, Friedrich August II, Elector of Saxony. Towards the end of his life, perhaps around 1748, Bach decided to add three further movements to these two, thus creating a setting of the complete ordinary of the Mass. Quite why is a mystery – Bach was not a Catholic, and the entire work, with its 25 substantial sections, is on too large a scale for liturgical performance (it is more likely to be heard in a concert hall today, and if presented in a church it will normally be as a concert work, not as part of a service). Bach skilfully adapted much of the new material from his earlier church music, and it is possible that he conceived the complete Mass as a work for posterity, as was the case in several of his last works, in which he summed-up the art of late baroque sacred music and his lifetime as a church musician. If so, it was an extraordinary act of faith because very little of Bach's music continued to be performed after his death in 1750. The new classical style increasingly became the rage and many scores of Bach's 'unfashionable' baroque music were lost or destroyed. It was not until 1859, more than a century after Bach died, that his Mass in B minor received its first complete performance.

Rejoice in the Lord alway is often known by its nickname 'The Bell Anthem' because of bell-like scales in the opening symphony. A score is published by OUP, ISBN: 0-19-395312-9. Better value is *A Purcell Anthology* (OUP, ISBN: 0-19-353351-0) – a collection of 12 anthems including this one. Of the many recordings, the best is in volume 5 of 'The Complete Anthems and Services of Henry Purcell' by the choir of New College Oxford with The King's Consort on CDA 66656 (Hyperion).

Try to listen to *The Coronation of King George II* by the King's Consort. This is a bargain-price double CD, produced in 2001 by Hyperion (CDA 67286) and consists of a vivid recreation of the 1727 coronation service, including anthems by Purcell, Blow and Handel.

The Mass

One of the best modern recordings of Bach's Mass in B minor is by Robert King and the King's Consort on Hyperion CDA 67201/2. A bargain-price recording is available on Naxos 8.550585/6.

Example 32 Bach, final bars of the *Crucifixus* from the Mass in B minor (*c*1748)

However it came to be written, Bach's Mass in B minor remains one of the mightiest monuments of western music. Example 32 shows the last 17 bars of the *Crucifixus*, part of the text of the creed. The Latin words can be translated as follows: *Crucifixus etiam pro nobis* – For our sake he was crucified; *sub Pontio Pilatus* – under Pontius Pilate; *passus* – he died; *et sepultus est* – and was buried.

The vocal parts conform to the principles of the *stile antico,* but they are accompanied by antiphonal wind and string chords, and the continuo, thus combining elements of the old style with the new *stile concertato.* But the most striking elements are the agonised chromaticism and extreme dissonance. At bar 2, beat 1, the soprano part is a diminished 7th above the bass. On beat 2 it falls a diminished 3rd to A♯, an augmented 5th above the bass. On beat 3 it rises to B, an augmented 4th above the alto part – and then forms intervals of an augmented 2nd and diminished 5th with the alto on the first two beats of bar 3. These tortured intervals are clearly intended to reflect the dreadful pain of crucifixion.

What holds such expressive chromaticism and dissonance just within the tonality of E minor is the *basso ostinato.* This ground, which is heard 13 times in all, comes from Bach's Cantata No. 12, *Weinen, Klagen, Sorgen, Zagen* (Weeping, wailing, lamenting, fearing) written in 1714. By now, you will recognise it as the same weeping bass formula – a chromatic descent from tonic to dominant – as that used by Cavalli (Example 17) and Purcell (Example 25).

So, have we returned full circle to the beginning of our period? Well, no – not quite. At the end of Example 32, as all the parts descend to their lowest tessitura and the flutes and upper strings fall silent, the basso ostinato doubles back on itself. Thus, by means of a chromatic chord known as an augmented 6th (labelled **A6** in bar 15), the *Crucifixus* ends, not in the tonic key of E minor, but in the relative major key of G. This unexpected ending provides a wonderful point of repose – the agony is ended – and it also offers a smooth transition to the next movement of the Mass (*Et resurrexit* – he was raised on the third day) where the full ensemble, with trumpets and drums, blaze out in glorious D major. Furthermore, the final five bars enabled Bach to extend his ground bass from the 12 appearances that occur in Cantata No. 12 to the 13 used here, so echoing in his music for the *Crucifixus* the tragic symbolism of that ill-fated number.

Programme music

We tend to think of programme music as an invention of the romantic period, used in character pieces and tone poems. In fact there are thousands of examples of illustrative music ranging from 16th-century *battaglias* (works depicting the sights and sounds of battle) to 18th-century harpsichord pieces illustrating, for instance, the clicking of knitting needles (Couperin's *Les Tricoteuses*).

We have already seen how Handel's *Pifa* (Example 33a) evokes the pastoral scene of shepherds watching their flocks by night. In fact Handel was drawing on the style of the siciliana – a lilting dance in slow compound time that was also the foundation of many arias with a pastoral text. The Concerto Grosso Op. 6, No. 8 by Corelli (1653–1713) ends with a siciliano entitled *Pastorale* (Example 33b) which he added for occasions when the work was performed at Christmas. In his set of four violin concertos called *The Seasons* Vivaldi (1678–1741) added specific programmatic texts to the score. The first concerto is called 'Spring' and Vivaldi labelled its last movement *Danza Pastorale* – its opening is shown in Example 33c.

Example 33 Siciliana movements

(a) Handel (1742)

(b) Corelli (1712)

(c) Vivaldi (1725)

A recommended recording of Corelli's Op. 6 concertos is available on Naxos 8.550403. There are more than 100 recordings of *The Seasons* in the catalogues, although some are rather old and others are arrangements (eg for flute) which don't accurately reflect the composer's intentions. The best bargain basement recording is on ASV Quicksilver CDQS 6148.

A recording of part of Bach's chorale prelude on *Wachet Auf!*, related to Example 30(b), is included in *Aural Matters*: CD2, track 24. Bach's chorale prelude, *Nun freut euch, lieben Christen*, arranged for piano by Busoni, can be found on page 48 of *Aural Matters in Practice*.

Above this opening music, Vivaldi's text refers to the 'festive sound of pastoral bagpipes', which he imitates by the tonic-dominant drone (the tied notes in Example 33c). Apart from similar lilting compound rhythms the three extracts from programmatic compositions shown in Example 33 all have melodies doubled in thirds above tonic and/or dominant pedals, and all have simple and slowly changing diatonic harmonies that evoke the peaceful emotions always associated with programmatic music of this type. Many more examples of programme music can be found in *The Seasons*.

The chorale prelude, played on the organ before the congregation intoned the chorale in Lutheran services, is another type of baroque instrumental music written in response to words. Bach transcribed Example 30(b) on page 77 as a chorale prelude, assigning the violin melody to the right hand, the chorale cantus firmus to the left, and the bass to the organ pedals (which are played with the feet).

 ## Private study

1. (i) What is a verse anthem?
   (ii) Which French composer influenced the style of Anglican church music in the late 17th century?
   (iii) Why is the Chapel Royal important in the development of restoration church music in England?

2. (i) In what ways did opera influence late-baroque church music?
   (ii) Why is Bach's Mass in B minor unsuited to liturgical performance?

3. We have studied vocal music from Italy, France, Germany and England in this chapter. Name one characteristic of each of these four national styles.

 ## Sample questions

In the exam there will be three questions on your chosen topic, of which you must answer one. Always answer by referring to the composers and precise works you have studied.

Set A

1. To what extent is it true to say that church music of the period 1685–1765 was operatic in nature?

2. Describe the conventions of *opera seria* and explain why Gluck felt that this type of opera needed reform.

3. Why did ballad opera have such popular appeal?

Set B

4. Why have most of Handel's oratorios remained so popular and yet his operas are now only rarely staged?

5. Show how Bach combined elements from several different traditions of music in his vocal works.

6. Explain what is meant by recitative, and outline some of the performing conventions of baroque recitative.

Topic 3: 1815–1885

Aspects of romanticism

If romanticism means the vivid expression of an artist's own emotional and spiritual experiences then it can be found in the works of poets and composers ranging from the renaissance to the present day. For instance what could be more subjectively expressive than Shakespeare's Sonnet 97 (published in 1609)?

1   How like a winter hath my absence been
From thee, the pleasure of the fleeting year!
What freezings have I felt, what dark days seen!
What old December's bareness every where!

5   And yet this time removed was summers time,
The teeming autumn big with rich increase,
Bearing the wanton burthen of the prime,
Like widowed wombs after their lord's decease:

9   Yet this abundant issue seem'd to me
But hope of orphans, and unfathered fruit,
For summer and his pleasures wait on thee,
And thou away, the very birds are mute;

13   Or if they sing, 'tis with so dull a cheer
That leaves look pale, dreading the winter's near.

The poem bears several of the hallmarks of romanticism. The subject is love: not the antique love of Anthony for Cleopatra, but the poet's own vibrant and immediate experience of love for a living being. The subject is specific: every line is imbued with a sense of longing for a time when the poet can once more embrace the distant beloved. Finally love and longing are expressed through images of the natural world which, in the poet's eyes, reflect his suffering. The last of these attributes is an example of the 'pathetic fallacy' that is such a common feature of 19th-century poetry (the birds do not really fall silent or sing sadly because the poet is separated from his beloved, nor do leaves dread the onset of winter).

When you read the texts of 19th-century vocal music, particularly German texts, you will constantly encounter the same subjects of love (*Liebe*), and longing (*Sehnsucht*), often for a distant beloved (*ferne Geliebte*), as well as an almost pagan worship of nature (*Natur*). It is because Shakespeare dealt so vividly with such subjects that he became for romantics throughout Europe the greatest and most influential poet of all time. But notice that the expression of emotions in Sonnet 97 is contained by poetic form. The first quatrain (lines 1–4) clearly establishes the simile between absence and winter, and all of its images (freezings, dark days, December's bareness) derive from the simile. Each line of the first quatrain also establishes the metre of the whole sonnet (every line is a pentameter containing five stressed syllables) and the ABAB rhyme scheme of the other two quatrains. The second and third of these qualify the subject matter of the first: we learn that the period of separation was in fact summer and autumn (lines 5–8), but that without the beloved the rich harvest of these seasons seemed barren (lines 9–12). Finally the rhyme of the couplet ('cheer' and 'near' in lines 13–14) chimes with the rhyme scheme of the first quatrain ('year' and 'where') as the sonnet returns full circle to the initial image of

Much of the discussion in the first part of this chapter is about *Lieder* (German songs). A useful resource for this topic is a CD-ROM from Deutsche Grammophon called *Erlkönig: The Art of the Lied* (455-188-2GH). It consists of a representative selection of songs (including several that we discuss here) by Schubert, Schumann and Brahms, in highly respected performances from the past. It is part of a 'CD-pluscore' series that includes automatically scrolling scores of the music, and a MIDI facility to enable you to listen to the accompaniment separately from the vocal part.

winter. So Shakespeare's romantic expressiveness is balanced by a satisfying structure that contains what could otherwise have been a formless outpouring of emotion.

Similarly, in music written before the 19th century we can find romantic emotional intensity reined in by purely musical structures. For example, between about 1765 and 1775 Haydn wrote a series of minor-mode symphonies in a tempestuous style that prefigures the *Sturm und Drang* ('Storm and Stress') movement of authors such as Goethe. In the last movement of his Symphony No. 44 (the *Trauersinfonie* or Mourning Symphony) Haydn wrote demonic, wildly leaping melodic lines that give rise to complex contrapuntal textures which reinforce the stormy, stressful mood – yet simultaneously the emotional intensity is balanced by canonic writing that provides purely musical satisfaction. And just as the sonnet structure of Shakespeare's poem disciplines his romantic rhetoric, so the sonata form of Haydn's Presto disciplines his tempestuous melodic style.

The romantic era

The period from 1815 to 1885 coincides with, or is at least contained within, what most historians would define as the romantic era. But why, since we have noticed that romanticism is not confined to the 19th century, should this period be singled out as peculiarly romantic? The answers are many, but one of the most important is that literature and music of the romantic era often lacked the strong formal restraints that we have noticed in Shakespeare and Haydn. It was an age of extremes in which poetic and musical fantasy – expressed in anything from tiny miniatures to vast epics – was prized above formal beauty.

On the one hand, the poet William Blake (1757–1827) assembled a set of fragments known as *Auguries of Innocence* (1803?) that are so lacking in order and punctuation that no one is sure how they ought to be compiled. The first quatrain, for instance, is not even a sentence:

> To see a World in a Grain of Sand
> And a Heaven in a Wild Flower
> Hold Infinity in the palm of your hand
> And Eternity in an hour

But it is pregnant with romantic imagery (nature in the form of a grain of sand and a wild flower, and eternity – which was another romantic preoccupation).

On the other hand, *Childe Harold's Pilgrimage* is an epic account of the wanderings of the knightly hero of the title by that arch-romantic Lord Byron (1788–1824). In the first three cantos Childe Harold visits romantic locations such as the Alps, the Rhinelands, the Balkans, and the islands of the Aegean. In the last canto Byron writes in the first person about his lonely pilgrimage through Italy – wanderings that were to be the literary stimulus for *Harold in Italy* (1834), an epic programmatic symphony by another arch-romantic, Hector Berlioz (1803–69). Among the many romantic themes of the poem is Byron's use of the medieval word 'childe' for a noble youth awaiting knighthood. Where writers of the 18th-

Haydn is well before our period, but you can hear an excerpt from the finale of his symphony No. 44 in RDMS, B21.

BBC Radio Classics/Carlton Classics (15656 91532) contains excellent live recordings of Berlioz's *Harold in Italy* and *Les Nuits d'été* (the latter discussed later in this chapter). Other fine performances of *Harold in Italy* include Philips 446 676 (on period instruments) and Naxos 553034.

century Enlightenment regarded all things gothic as barbarous, artists of the 19th century were attracted to the romance of the middle ages and tried to recapture it in words (eg Walter Scott's novel *Ivanhoe* of 1820) and music (eg Wagner's opera *Tannhäuser* of 1845). A theme that runs throughout *Childe Harold* is the pilgrimage itself, in this case not a journey to a particular shrine, but a journey undertaken in answer to a restless need to seek out the strange and exotic – a quest that the Germans call *Wanderlust*. This is a central theme in some of the greatest vocal music of the romantic era, notably Schubert's song cycle *Die schöne Müllerin* (1823). In 20 songs it tells of a youth setting off to follow a stream from source to sea, his encounter with a beautiful miller's daughter, her rejection of him, and (yet another romantic theme) his eventual desire for death in the embrace of the fateful brook.

The best recent CD of *Die schöne Müllerin* is by Ian Bostridge and Graham Johnson on Hyperion's prize-winning CDJ33025.

Schirmer's *First Vocal Album* contains scores of *Die schöne Müllerin* and all the other Schubert songs mentioned in this chapter. Many of these songs are also in volume 1 of the collected edition of Schubert's songs published by Peters Edition. Good translations of Schubert's songs are given in *The Schubert Song Companion* by John Reed (Mandolin, ISBN: 1-901341-0013). English translations can also be found on the web at http://www.recmusic.org/lieder/

Romantic Lieder and character pieces

Many romantic composers sought to capture evanescent emotion in fragmentary works that begin like a half-remembered dream and melt away at the end as a dream fades with the morning. They found the ideal media through which to express themselves in the *Lied* and the character piece (a single-movement work designed to express a mood, image or scene). Example 34 on page 88 comes from the first song in *Dichterliebe* (A poet's love), a cycle of 16 *Lieder* set to music by Robert Schumann (1810–56). It was composed in 1840, often known as Schumann's 'year of song' for it was the year in which he married and in which he wrote some 124 songs. The words are by Heinrich Heine (1797–1856):

The German noun *Lied* (plural *Lieder*) can mean a short, simple, lyrical poem, or a musical setting of such a poem.

Schumann selected the texts of *Dichterliebe* from Heine's *Lyriches Intermezzo*. This set of 66 lyrics is prefaced by a prologue which sets the scene – a knight, who is also a dreamy poet, is suddenly catapulted back from the fantasy of his illusions about life and love into a lonely poet's cell. Such is the very essence of romanticism!

Im wunderschönen Monat Mai,	In the beautiful month of May,
Als alle Knospen sprangen,	When all the buds opened,
Da ist in meinem Herzen	It was then in my heart
Die Liebe aufgegangen.	That love sprang up.
Im wunderschönen Monat Mai,	In the beautiful month of May,
Als alle Vögel sangen,	When all the birds sang,
Da hab ich ihr gestanden	It was then I confessed to her
Mein Sehnen und Verlangen.	My longing and desire.

Schumann's setting is strophic and Example 34 shows the second verse (the music of the first verse is the same). It begins with a suspended C♯ that seems as though it were a part of music that had already been sounding before our ears caught its first strain, and ends without resolution on a dominant 7th.

Example 34 also shows another characteristic of much romantic music – a deliberate blurring of tonality. Is the song in F♯ minor? The piano introduction suggests this key, but the first vocal phrase immediately veers towards the warmth of A major (as shown by chord symbols below the staves). The same A-major phrase is repeated for the second line of the verse. And if the song really is in F♯ minor, then why does the vocal part end with a G *natural* and F♯ (bar 23), and why are these notes supported by piano harmony in D major? The answer is that tonal ambiguity is an important element in Schumann's romantic armoury. Its vagueness helps express the poet's intoxication with the beauty of nature (*Im wunderschönen Monat Mai*) as well as his longing (*mein Sehnen*) and his unfulfilled desire (*Verlangen*) for the beloved.

Dichterliebe is performed by Ian Bostridge and Julius Drake on EMI Classics 7243 5 56575 (although there are also many excellent earlier recordings, including a famous one by Dietrich Fischer-Diskau).

Scores of *Dichterliebe* are available from several publishers. Volume 1 of the complete edition of Schumann songs (Peters Edition) includes this and several other song cycles, together with a good selection of other songs by the composer.

Example 34 Schumann, 'Im wunderschönen Monat Mai' (second stanza) from *Dichterliebe* (1840)

Similar moods to those in his *Lieder* prevail when Schumann writes characteristic pieces for piano alone, even when the title is as vague (but as significant) as *Romanze* (romance being the noun from which the adjective romantic derives).

Schumann's *Faschingsschwank aus Wien* and *Carnaval*, played by Daniel Barenboim, are available on a bargain-price CD from Deutsche Grammophon Classikon, 449 855.

Example 35 shows the opening of the *Romanze* from Schumann's set of five 'fantasy pictures' called *Faschingsschwank aus Wien* ('carnival jest from Vienna'), a collection of character pieces that were completed in the same *annus mirabilis* (1840) as *Dichterliebe*.

Example 35 Schumann, *Romanze*, opening bars (1840)

Like Example 34 the music drifts in with a poetic suspension (9–8) followed by another dissonance (7–6) which plainly tell us of the pain of love without need of words, while the complex rhythm of the melody suggests dreamy improvisation.

Example 36 Schumann, *Romanze*, bars 22–25 (1840)

G minor: IV   V⁷   VI   ♭II   V   I

Example 36 shows the last four bars of the *Romanze* (which is only 25 bars in length). This ending begins with a reminiscence of the opening bars, but now with an interrupted cadence (V⁷–VI). This leads to quite unexpected Neapolitan harmony (♭II – an A♭-major triad on the flat supertonic of G minor), enriched by a double suspension (D♭ and F). After this foray into such a flat tonal area the ensuing perfect cadence in the tonic major sounds strange, ambiguous and as unnerving as the pangs of love.

Many of Schumann's basic chord progressions (such as IIb–V⁷–I in Example 34) would have been familiar to classical composers of earlier generations. But his use of patterns in which the length and impact of dissonance becomes a prime objective, and resolution of the dissonance a secondary matter, became a driving force in German romanticism for decades to come. Look, for example, at the entry of the singer in Example 34. Three quarters of the first beat of bar 16 lingers on the tension between the C♯ in the vocal part and the D in the bass. In comparison, the singer's resolution to B vanishes in a single semiquaver.

Schumann was fascinated by words. His father was a bookseller and the young Schumann was widely read in both classic and modern literature and poetry. He founded and edited the magazine *Neue Zeitschrift für Musik* (New Musical Journal) to champion the high poetic nature of new music and to deride the shallow musical taste of those who wrote showy but empty virtuoso-style music. In the magazine Schumann created an imaginery *Davidsbund* (band of David) to fight these philistines, peopled with characters that reflected different sides of his own personality. Thus he would sign articles of an impulsive, extrovert nature with the name Florestan, while thoughtful, contemplative articles were signed Eusebius.

These literary figures also appeared in Schumann's compositions. The *Davidsbündlertänze* (Dances of the band of David) of 1837 consists of 18 character pieces. Using his favourite image of a masked ball at carnival time, each one suggests a fleeting portrait of an elusive figure, and each is signed E or F (or sometimes both) to reflect the composer's mood. Instead of Italian tempo directions, Schumann uses German words to spark the imagination of the performer – *Innig* (Intimately – obviously 'by' Eusebius) or *Etwas hahnbüchen* (Impetuously – a Florestan piece). But sometimes he

The *Davidsbündlertänze* are performed by Benjamin Frith on a fine bargain-price CD from Naxos (8 550493).

takes literary images much further than this. At the head of the ninth piece Schumann wrote:

> *Hierauf schloss Florestan und es zuchte ihm schmerzlich um die Lippen.* (Here Florestan stopped and his lips trembled painfully).

And above the final piece he again hints at a hidden programme:

> *Ganz zum Überfluss meinte Eusebius noch Folgendes; dabei sprach aber viel Seligkeit aus seinen Augen.* (Entirely redundantly Eusebius added the following, with great ecstasy in his eyes.)

Schumann's music is full of literary allusions, word games and hidden meanings. After meeting the Countess von Abegg in 1830 he chose the letters of her name to make the theme (A–B–E–G–G) for his 'Abegg variations'. Five years later Schumann wrote the piano cycle *Carnaval*, the ninth movement of which he named 'Sphinxes'. Example 37 shows the entire, inscrutable piece – just 11 breves. Below the stave are shown the German letter names of the notes: E♭ in German is *Es* (= 'S'), A♭ is *As* and B♮ is known as *H*. The bars marked No. 2 and No. 3 are a musical play on Asch, the home town of Schumann's girlfriend at that time. And these are the pitches on which the other 20 movements are based. The first bar of Example 37 is an anagram of Asch, in which Schumann rearranges the letters to match the musical pitches that can be derived from his own name (SCHumAnn). Thus, instead of starting with a theme and varying it, Schumann waits until the ninth movement and then introduces a riddle. This is music to intrigue the cultivated amateur playing the piano at home, not music for the concert platform.

Schumann rarely made public the literary allusions and hidden references in his music. For instance he never revealed that the movements in his piano cycle *Papillons* (Butterflies, 1831) are each related to specific paragraphs in his favourite novel, Jean-Paul's *Flegeljahre*. Furthermore, 20th-century musical research has uncovered the probability that in a number of his works Schumann used a cipher-code to encrypt the complete alphabet as musical pitches, enabling this most introverted of composers to embed private thoughts and memories in his thematic material.

Example 37 Schumann, 'Sphinxes' from *Carnaval* (1835)

One of the many recordings of *Carnaval* is mentioned in the margin note on page 88.

For example, according to this theory, the theme of the last movement of the *Davidsbündlertänze* decrypts as 'There was utter stillness…' while its countermelody spells out the name of Schumann's wife, Clara.

Private study

1. (i) What is meant by the terms *Lieder* and strophic song?
    (ii) Justify the statement that the singer's accompaniment in Example 34 is 'nothing more than a cobweb of support'.

2. (i) What is a character piece?
    (ii) Which of the following titles do you think might most likely suggest a character piece? – Prelude, Whims, Minuet, Fugue, Clowns, Daydreams, Sonata, Nocturne.

4. Look again at Example 34 and:
    (i) explain how Schumann gives special impact to the wonder of the keyword *wunderschönen* (beautiful)
    (ii) suggest a reason why the only part of the song that is not entirely syllabic in style is the setting of the word *Vögel*.
    (iii) identify the technical means by which Schumann conveys a romantic sense of 'longing' in the vocal part on the words *gestanden* (confessed) and *Verlangen* (desire).

Goethe and 19th-century vocal music

Goethe (1749–1832) is as dominant a figure in German literature as Shakespeare is in English literature. While an undergraduate he wrote short lyric poems in his *Leipziger Liederbuch* (Leipzig Song Book, 1770) – we should not be surprised by the title for we have already seen that *Lied* applies to lyric poetry as well musical settings, and one of Goethe's aims was to integrate poetry and music (an idea that became important in the romantic era). A severe illness in 1768 marked the beginning of his *Sturm und Drang* period when he asserted many of the ideals of romanticism. His greatest achievement in this period was *Die Leiden des jungen Werthers* (The Sufferings of Young Werther, 1774), a semi-autobiographical novel that tells of the hero's unrequited love and his eventual suicide. It was a seminal work in the development of romantic sensibility and was source for *Werther*, an opera by Massenet (1842–1912) written at the end of our period and still in the repertoire of many opera companies. Both the novel and opera focus on another romantic pre-occupation – death (remember that Schubert's *Die schöne Müllerin* ends with the young wanderer's death-wish).

Less familiar, but perhaps more important as a source for romantic composers, was *Wilhelm Meisters Theatralische Sendung* (Wilhelm Meister's Theatrical Mission), a novel that contains four enigmatic songs supposedly sung by a female character called Mignon. Two of them (*Kennst du das Land* and *Nur wer die Sehnsucht kennt*) were set by composers ranging from Beethoven to Hugo Wolf (1860–1903). We will return to them later when we shall see that one of Mignon's songs deals with another characteristically romantic theme – the longing of northern European poets and musicians for the literal and metaphoric warmth of southern Europe (Goethe himself visited Italy in 1786–88 and 1790).

It was during his *Sturm und Drang* period that Goethe began work on his masterpiece, Faust, a monumental version of a legend about the man who sold his soul to the devil. The first part of the tragedy (published in 1808) deals with Faust's pact with the devil, his seduction of Gretchen, his moral degradation and inevitable doom. Thus it introduces two more typically romantic themes – guilt and damnation – and, being based on an ancient legend, it illustrates a final strand of romanticism – a fascination with gothic art and architecture. The second part (published in 1832) concerns Faust's eventual redemption. Faust became one of the most influential texts in the development of romantic literature and music. It directly inspired Berlioz's dramatic legend *La Damnation de Faust* (1846), Schumann's late choral work *Szenen aus Goethes Faust* (1853), Gounod's five-act opera *Faust* (1859) and many other compositions.

We have chosen to concentrate on Goethe's role in German romanticism not only because he was, with the exception of Shakespeare, the most influential author in this period, but because all the themes we have identified as being characteristically romantic can be found in his works. Love (unrequited and consummated), loneliness, suffering, guilt, damnation and death, pantheism, *Wanderlust* and a restless longing for the strange and exotic – all expressed through literature that ranges from fragmentary lyrics to vast epics.

A useful source of scores for many songs by Schubert and other 19th-century composers is http://www.schubertline.co.uk/

Schubert and Goethe

See page 87 for details of scores and English translations of Schubert's *Lieder*. Recordings of all three of the songs discussed in this section can be found in the resources mentioned in the margin notes on pages 85 and 95.

We have already seen that the essence of *Lieder* is the use of poetry in which the audience is addressed directly and expressively, wedded to music which reflects the emotional tenor of the lyrics. This intimate art form was, like the character piece for piano, designed for private performance in the home, not for presentation in concert halls. Schumann, whom we discussed earlier, followed in the footsteps of Franz Schubert (1797–1828), three of whose settings of Goethe we will explore next.

Gretchen am Spinnrade

'Gretchen at the Spinning Wheel' was the first poem by Goethe that Schubert set to music – it was composed in 1814 when he was 17.

There are many fine recordings of this song: Audivis E7783 includes a performance of this song sung by Elizabeth Söderström in a Schubert recital that includes *Nur wer die Sehnsucht kennt* D877/4 (discussed below).

Gretchen is a familiar name for Margareta, the innocent girl whom Faust seduced. In the play she is alone at her spinning wheel lamenting her lost peace of mind. The poem falls into ten four-line stanzas which, in Schubert's setting, begin in bars 2, 13, 21, 31, 42, 50, 58, 73, 84 and 92. The first (*Meine ruh ist hin … und nimmermehr*) is repeated as a refrain in stanzas four (bar 31) and eight (bar 73). Here are the opening bars:

Example 38   Schubert, *Gretchen am Spinnrade*, bars 1–6 (1814)

At the end of the song Schubert repeats Goethe's first two lines ('My peace is gone, my heart is heavy') as a dramatic closing refrain (bars 114–118). In addition he repeats crucial lines of the text in order to achieve a musical climax that intensifies the poetic expressiveness to an almost unbearable degree (bars 100–112).

As in many of his *Lieder*, Schubert's accompaniment is based on a musical figure suggested by the text, which he uses to unify the entire song. Here, spinning is represented by an almost continuous semiquaver figure in the piano part. This retains its basic outline throughout, but it is sufficiently elastic for Schubert to be able to vary it to fit his wide-ranging harmonic progressions. But this is not just naive pictorialism – the continuously whirring figures also express Gretchen's endless distress. After 65 bars the spinning stops – Gretchen is overcome with the memory of Faust's kiss.

When, at first haltingly, the spinning resumes it heralds the return of the hopeless refrain. The tonal structure has a purely musical logic, but it also reflects every inflexion of the poem. Static harmony and pedals in D minor accompany the refrain (Example 38), but when Gretchen dreams of Faust's noble figure (bars 51–54) the music moves into F major and the nagging left-hand quaver figure disappears from the accompaniment. As her daydream becomes more impassioned (bars 55–62) an ascending harmonic sequence rises through G minor and A♭ major to B♭ major. Then, as Gretchen recalls the touch of Faust's hand and his kiss (bars 63–68) a G♯ is added to the B♭-major triad, creating an augmented-6th chord, which allows an ecstatic chromatic rise to the dominant of D minor (bar 68). This dominant discord also permits an immediate return to the tonic key of D minor, a resumption of the spinning music and, of course, a return to hopelessness.

Another harmonic sequence begins at bar 85 where the music rises through E♭ major, F major and G minor before getting stuck on the dominant of A minor (bars 93–96) followed by the dominant of the home key, D minor (bars 97–99). It is as though Schubert is trying to break free from the doom-laden tonic key just as Gretchen tries to break free from her forebodings. This sensation becomes even more acute as the bass circles around the dominant of D minor (notice the obsessive *sforzandi* in bars 101–107) while the repetitive vocal part twice escapes to a top A. But the return to D minor is as inevitable as Gretchen's fate.

We can better understand the revolution Schubert wrought in *Lieder* if we compare a setting of Goethe's *Erlkönig* by Reichardt (1752–1814) with Schubert's setting of 1815. The song comes at the start of a *Singspiel* (an opera with spoken dialogue), and it was written, as Goethe says, 'to be sung to a strictly regular and easily memorable tune'. Reichardt's setting of 1794 (Example 39) exactly fits the bill. Each line of the poem contains four stressed syllables (eg *Wer reitet so spät durch Nacht und Wind?)* so each of Reichardt's four phrases is precisely four bars long (as shown by slurs). Textual clarity is ensured by syllabic underlay and a homorhythmic piano part that doubles the vocal melody. The entirely diatonic melody is easily memorable because there are no modulations, only two leaps, and it describes a simple arch shape, rising in the first two phrases from the lower to the upper dominant and falling in the last two phrases back to the tonic:

Erlkönig

Reichardt was a personal friend of Goethe and one of the most versatile composers of *Lieder* before Schubert. Fourteen of his settings of texts by Goethe are sung by Dietrich Fischer-Dieskau in a recital of Reichardt songs on Orfeo C245921A.

Translation of Example 39:

Who rides so late through the night and the wind? It is a father with his child; He has the boy safe in his arms and keeps him warm.

Example 39 Reichardt, *Erlkönig*, bars 0–16 (1794)

Goethe's poem is a ballad in which three characters (the father, his sick son and death, personified as the Erl King) appear in direct speech. But Reichardt's setting is strophic. So when, in the second stanza, the father asks his son why he is so scared and the son asks his father why he cannot see the Erl King, the music of the first verse has to suffice for this dramatic dialogue. In the third stanza the Erl King tries to entice the boy to come with him by promises of lovely games, flowers and golden clothes. Yet the same piano music is repeated, while the Erl King sings mainly on a D monotone.

Schubert's setting of Goethe's poem is totally different. It is not strophic but through-composed (ie there are differences in the music for each verse) and it begins with a substantial introduction in which the piano sets the mood of a wild ride through the night, represented by continuous triplets and threatening bass figures. And Schubert's setting does not merely reflect the general mood of the poem but also its finer nuances. So a modulation to the relative major (bars 22–24) suggests the warmth of the fatherly embrace, and in bars 36–54 Schubert sets the father's words in a much lower tessitura than those of the son. Greater contrast comes at bar 57 when the Erl King entices the boy with a flowing melody in B♭ major, while the frenetic repeated notes and menacing bass figures of the piano part give way to a much simpler chordal accompaniment, a tonic pedal and slow-moving, consonant harmony. As the song reaches its climax Schubert sets the child's terrified screams of 'Father, my father' at a higher pitch in each stanza, producing searing dissonances against the piano's unstoppable triplets:

Example 40 Schubert, *Erlkönig*, bars 73, 98 and 124 (1815)

But finally the triplets do stop, and Schubert ends the song with a three-bar recitative of the utmost drama – for when the desperate father at last reaches home, 'the child in his arms was dead'.

Heidenröslein

In complete contrast, Schubert responded to the sophisticated naïvety of Goethe's *Heidenröslein* (Meadow rose) with a strophic setting that is almost as simple and folk-like as the style that Reichardt used far less appropriately in Example 39.

The words of *Heidenröslein* are based on a traditional folksong about a boy picking a rose, but its sexual subtext, in which the picking of the flower becomes a metaphor for its rape, is attributable to Goethe. Schubert captures the simplicity of the poem with diatonic two-bar phrases supported by a piano accompaniment in a very basic 'oom-cha' pattern (Example 41) and a conventional modulation to the dominant in the middle of each verse. But he also reflects the poem's sophistication in the knowing stepwise rise of a 7th to a pause on the tonic (bars 12, 28 and 44) in a phrase enticingly marked *nachgebend* ('giving way' or 'indulging').

Example 41 Schubert, *Heidenröslein*, bars 1–2 (1815)

In tiny miniatures such *Heidenröslein* and extended dramas such as *Gretchen am Spinnrade* and *Erlkönig* Schubert had proved his mastery of the *Lied* by the age of 18.

Mignon's songs from *Wilhelm Meister*

In Goethe's *Wilhelm Meisters Theatralische Sendung* Mignon is the naive child of an incestuous relationship who leaves her foster parents to wander in the mountains. She is kidnapped by a troupe of acrobats but is ransomed by Wilhelm Meister to whom she becomes submissively attached as a father figure (though secretly she loves him as a man). The full extent of her sufferings is only revealed when, at the end of the novel, she dies.

Nur wer die Sehnsucht kennt, expresses her longing (*Sehnsucht*), suffering (*leide*) and loneliness (*Allein und abgetrennt von aller Freude*). Beethoven wrote four simple strophic settings of the poem, but none compares with the six settings Schubert composed, the first in 1815, the last in 1826. The finest is D877/4 (1826). Like Beethoven's third setting it is in the minor, in compound time, and features a broken-chord accompaniment. It is through-composed with a chromatic, agitated triplet accompaniment that fully expresses the words *Es schwindelt mir, es brennt mein Eigeweide* ('My head swims, my bowels burn within me'). Goethe, however, would not have approved of the textual repetitions that can be justified only on purely musical grounds (the unnerving, shifting tonality in bars 27–33 could not be achieved without repeating this line of the poem). Notice too how the piano solos that frame the song set the emotional tone of the whole song. As early as bars 2–3 the A-minor tonality is upset by a sequence in which a highly dissonant and chromatic chord (the dominant minor 9th of IV over a tonic pedal in bar 3) that at a stroke reaches to the depths of Mignon's grief.

Beethoven composed five songs entitled *Sehnsucht*. The four catalogued as WoO 134 are four settings of Goethe's *Nur wer die Sehnsucht kennt*. The fifth (WoO 146) is a setting of a completely different poem. All five are included in a recital of Beethoven's songs on CPO999 436, which also includes his song cycle *An die ferne Geliebte* and his setting of *Kennst du das Land* (see below). Schubert's setting of *Nur wer das Sehnsucht kennt* (D877/4) is recorded on a CD from Auvidis/Astrée (AUE 7783) with the three Schubert *Lieder* discussed earlier. There are many alternatives, of which the best value for our purposes is the Schubert recital by Barbara Bonney and Geoffrey Parsons (Teldec/Warner 4509 90873) which includes *Gretchen*, *Heidenröslein*, and *Kennst du das Land* as well as D877/4.

Tchaikovsky wrote a setting of the same poem in 1869 which shows just how long and far Goethe's shadow fell. With an English translation ('None but the lonely heart') that was sufficiently ambiguous for bourgeois sensibilities, it proved to be a popular parlour song in late-Victorian England and even became a hit for Frank Sinatra in the 1940s. What distinguishes Tchaikovsky's setting from those of Beethoven and Schubert is the role of the accompaniment, its consistent syncopation ensuring the coherence of the entire song:

In order to help clarify Tchaikovsky's use of tonality in this song, Examples 42 and 43 show the song transposed for a low voice to the key of C major.

Hyperion CD VCA66617 (by Joan Rodgers and Roger Vignoles) includes 'None but the Lonely Heart' and four other songs from Tchaikovsky's Opus 6.

Example 42 Tchaikovsky, *None but the lonely heart*, bars 9–14 (1869)

Tchaikovsky achieves a satisfying ternary structure by returning to the opening melody and text at bar 30, but the climax comes in bars 38–42 with a second repetition of the words *allein und abgetrennt von aller Freude* ('alone and cut off from every joy'). Clearly the composer saw Mignon's loneliness, her alienation from normal society, as a mirror of his own sexual isolation and as the kernel of Goethe's poem – the bit about fiery bowels (just plain 'burning fire' in some English versions) is relegated to the dying close of the song.

In an extended preparation for the central climax the pianist begins a long *cantabile* melody at bar 17, incorporating inversions of the falling 7th and 6th from the first two bars of the opening melody. With the vocal part it forms a love duet of mounting passion that reaches its climax when the rising motif from the third and fourth bars of the opening melody is used sequentially in contrary motion to the voice, leading to *fortissimo* chords of D minor:

Example 43   Tchaikovsky, *None but the lonely heart*, bars 38–43 (1869)

There are a number of cadences in D minor during the course of the song, but the open key signature suggests C major, confirmed by the perfect cadences at the end of the introduction and in the final bars. This less clear-cut approach to tonality arises from a combination of Russian modality (the melody begins on A and is harmonised with mainly secondary triads and 7ths) and romantic chromaticism. It ensures that the musical messages are as ambiguous as the secret desires of Mignon and Tchaikovsky.

CD CPO999 436 (mentioned on page 95) contains Beethoven's *Kennst du das Land*. Teldec/Warner 4509 90873 (also mentioned earlier) includes Schubert's setting and four other songs by Schubert mentioned in this chapter. Liszt's setting is on Decca (IMS) 430 512 and there is a stunning performance of Wolf's setting on Chandos 8726.

If you wish to trace developments in *Lieder* composition through another of Mignon's songs you should look at some of the numerous settings of *Kennst du das Land* in which Mignon tries to persuade Wilhelm Meister to lead her through dreadful mountains to the lemon-scented lands of the south. You will find the journey most rewarding in the company of Beethoven (1809), Schubert (1815), Liszt (1841), Schumann (1849) and Wolf (1888). The journey begins with classical pictorialism and ends with the vocal equivalent of a tone poem.

Translation of Example 44: Do you know the land where the lemons blossom? Where golden oranges glow among the dark leaves.

Example 44 is from Wolf's setting of this poem and shows that his piano writing is almost as dense as an orchestral accompaniment by Wagner – indeed, Wolf orchestrated the song a few years later. The treble melody is above the vocal solo in the first five bars, thus ensuring that it is heard as a vital countermelody. In the third bar the counterpoint expands to three parts with the addition of the rising chromatic scale in the alto register of the piano, an ascent that culminates in its assumption of the role of principal melodic line at the end of the extract. These contrapuntal textures are supported by the richest possible chromatic harmony, shifting tonal centres and prominent discords that fully express Mignon's aching longing in this ripe fruit of late romanticism.

Example 44 Wolf, *Mignon*, bars 5–13 (1888)

Programme music

In his overture *A Midsummer Night's Dream* (1826) Mendelssohn combined a traditional sonata-form structure with musical ideas that vividly evoke the main groups of characters in Shakespeare's play of the same name. Orchestral works designed to portray explicit visual, literary or philosophical ideas without recourse to a sung text, became increasingly popular at this time. Berlioz's *Symphonie fantastique* (1830) illustrates an 'episode in the life of an artist' (the artist being the composer himself) while his next symphony, *Harold en Italie*, is based on an epic poem by Byron. Liszt (1811–86) developed the symphonic poem (or tone poem) as an important type of programme music – and found inspiration in Shakespeare for his symphonic poem *Hamlet* (1858).

One of the most famous orchestral works to be based on a play by Shakespeare is Tchaikovsky's 'fantasy-overture' *Romeo and Juliet* (1869). Like Mendelssohn, he does not attempt to 'tell a story' in musical terms (few programmatic works can hope to do this). Instead he portrays three main strands from Shakespeare's drama (Example 45). The introductory theme (a), modal and chorale-like in style, portrays Friar Lawrence, but its fateful quality also anticipates the dreadful end to the drama. The first subject (b), with its rapid contrasts, syncopation and off-beat cymbal clashes, is a clear picture of the cut-and-thrust street fighting between the families of Romeo and Juliet. The famous second subject represents the young lovers – a tenor-range melody (c) for cor anglais and violas (Romeo) followed by delicate violin palpitations that blossom into Juliet's version of the same tune on soaring violins.

Recommended recordings of Mendelssohn's *A Midsummer Night's Dream* overture and Berlioz's *Symphonie fantastique* are listed in our OCR AS Guide. Some CDs of Berlioz's *Harold in Italy* are mentioned on page 86 of this book. There are many fine recordings of Tchaikovsky's *Romeo and Juliet* overture, and most schools will already have at least one version and probably a score as well.

Example 45 Tchaikovsky, themes from *Romeo and Juliet* (1815)

1. Explain the difference between a through-composed song and a strophic song, and give an example of each.

2. To what extent is it true to say that in his ballades, Schubert set poetry with the intensity of a miniature opera for home performance? Refer to specific songs in your answer.

3. Find a copy of Schubert's song *Die Forelle* (The Trout) and explain how the figuration in the piano part (a) relates to the poetry and (b) unifies the song, even in the minor-key section.

4. Look again at Example 44 and identify the harmonic device that underpins the harmonic complexity.

5. Show how literature played a part in 19th-century programme music by briefly discussing a symphonic poem of your choice.

French music

You probably know that the French for song is *chanson*. But this term applies to any type of song, from the medieval *chanson de geste* to the latest pop song. *Mélodie* is a word that specifically identifies French art songs of the 19th and 20th centuries.

The French counterpart of the 19th-century German *Lied* was the *mélodie*. Like the *Lied* it can be traced back to simple strophic songs of the 18th century with regular musical phrases and subordinate keyboard accompaniments. The initial impetus for the development of the *mélodie* came when Schubert's songs were published in Paris with French translations. A second stimulus was the independent development of French romantic literature, including the composition of short lyrical poems suitable for musical settings.

Les Nuits d'été is coupled with *Harold in Italie* (see earlier) in an excellent performance on Carlton Classics 15656 91532. Also at bargain basement price is a performance by Janet Baker on a Virgin Classics Double CD VBD5 61469, although the other works on this recording are not particularly relevant to Topic 3.

The only French author of the period who can compare with Goethe was Victor Hugo (1802–85). Like his German counterpart he was master of both the poetic fragment and of epic novels such as *Les Misérables*. Hugo wrote an extravagant epitaph on the death of his protégé, Théophile Gautier (1811–72), and it was this younger man who wrote six poems in his *La Comédie de la mort* (1838) that were set as the first French song cycle by Hector Berlioz, under the title *Les Nuits d'été* (The Summer Nights, 1841).

Example 46 Berlioz, *Villanelle* from *Les Nuits d'été*, bars 47–62 (1841)

The song cycle was originally written for voice and piano, but later Berlioz produced the sumptuous orchestral accompaniments that are so frequently heard today. The subject matter (the poet's reactions to the death of his beloved) and some of the titles ('The spectre of the rose' and 'At the cemetery') might seem as romantically death-obsessed as much contemporary German verse. But the sensuous beauty of Gautier's diction and imagery counterbalance morbid introspection, so the prevailing mood is nostalgic rather than melodramatic. Berlioz responded to Gautier's typically Gallic sense of proportion and sensuous beauty with an entirely new style of music, the chief characteristics of which are melodic subtlety allied with sumptuous and often elusive harmony.

Example 46 is an extract from the first *mélodie* of *Les Nuits d'été*, a villanelle (pastoral poem) about spring and young lovers. The complete stanza from which the example is taken reads:

Le printemps est venu, ma belle;	Spring has come, my lovely one;
C'est le mois des amants béni;	This is the blessed month for lovers;
Et l'oiseau, satinant son aile,	And the bird, smoothing its wing,
Dit ses vers au rebord du nid.	Recites his verses on the edge of the nest.

Beauty of sound becomes apparent when the poem is read aloud – for instance, notice the sensuous sibilants in the third line. Berlioz responds with sensuously shifting tonality. Sing the vocal melody and you will be surprised and delighted by the way an exact sequence (shown in Example 47) is avoided by a last-minute plunge into C♯ minor (Example 46, bars 59–60).

Elliptical tonality is more pronounced in the accompaniment of Example 46. B♭ major has only one note in common with B minor (B♭ – which, when enharmonically notated as A♯, becomes the leading note of B minor). When Berlioz modulates to C♯ minor he introduces an exquisite dissonance, caused by the canonic bass on the first beat of bar 59. It may seem strange that an arch-romantic like Berlioz should write a canon at the 9th below (starting in the vocal part at bar 53 and the bass at bar 54). But this is not an academic exercise, rather it is a simple enrichment of the texture (there is no canon in the same position during the first verse of this strophic setting). The canon is not strict (the rising 4th in bar 55 is answered by a rising 3rd in the next bar), but, as Example 47 shows, it could have been. Berlioz would have been well aware of this possibility, but he obviously rejected it because the result would have forced him into the conventional modulation between related keys shown in the following reworking (which is about as tasty as a glass of distilled water):

Example 47   A reworking of bars 53–60 from Example 46

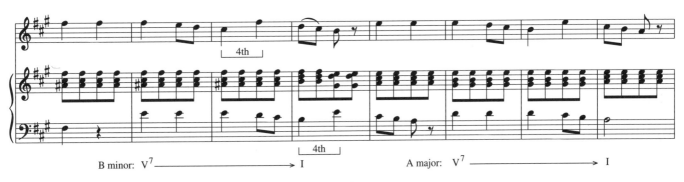

Volume 1 of REM Edition's recordings of all of Fauré's *mélodies* (REM311175) contains both *Lydia* (Op. 4, No. 2) and the whole of *La Bonne Chanson* (Op. 61).

It was this sort of wayward approach to harmony, tonality and counterpoint that caused so much antipathy between Berlioz and his teachers at the Paris Conservatoire, but these are precisely the elements that so delight us today. The same is true of the style of Gabriel Fauré (1845–1924). Example 48 is from *Lydia* (*c*1870), a *mélodie* set to words by Leconte de Lisle:

Example 48 Fauré, *Lydia*, opening bars of verse 1 (*c*1870).

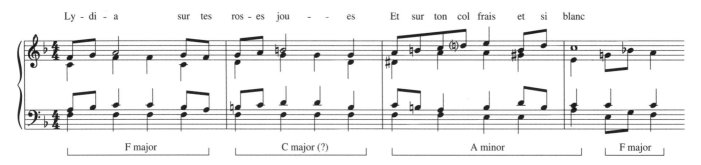

Inspired by the poem's title, Fauré wrote this four-bar vocal melody in the Lydian mode (F–G–A–B–C–D–E–F). The accompaniment is in F major in the first bar, but when the top three parts move up a step in bar 2 the bass remains on a tonic pedal, thus forming the dominant 7th of C major. The pedal note remains unresolved in the first two beats of bar 3 as the sequence rises another step. The chromatic chord that is formed above this obstinate bass is the augmented 6th of A minor and it is the dominant of this key to which the pedal resolves to form the bass of chord V^7 (with 4–3 suspension). The perfect cadence (bars 4–5) seems to confirm this key, but with a deft move Fauré returns to the tonic key of F major in the space of just two beats. This tiny fragment from an early song (*c*.1870) exemplifies the way Fauré combines modality (the melody) with simple diatonic harmony (bars 1 and 4), ambiguous tonality (bar 2) and chromatic harmony (bar 3).

Both *Lydia* and *Après un rêve* will be found in the first volume of *20 Mélodies* by Fauré published by *Hamelle* and distributed by *Leduc*. Both songs are also in *Fauré: 30 Songs for voice and piano* (published by *IMP*) in an edition which also includes line-by-line translations. The discussion here of *Après un rêve* is based on the first nine bars of the song in its original key of D minor.

In his most famous song, *Après un rêve* (*c*1878), the same stylistic features are even more subtly combined. The melody of bars 2–4 and 6–8 is in the aeolian mode (the scale A–B–C–D–E–F–G–A, here transposed to D), but the E♭s and C♯ in bar 5 add sensuous chromatic colour to otherwise pure modality. Meanwhile the piano part, beginning on a simple D-minor triad, slides through the dominant 9ths of C, F and B♭ (bars 3–5), then moves through an augmented triad on B♭ and a half-diminished 7th on E before reaching the proper dominant 7th of D minor in bar 7. This in turn resolves to the tonic triad at the start of the next vocal phrase. The glue that holds this wonderfully sensuous passage together is the bass part which describes a complete diatonic circle of 5ths (D–G–C–F–B♭–E–A–D) in bars 1–9.

The finest of Fauré's *mélodies* are to be found in his terrific song cycle *La Bonne Chanson* (1894) and you could have endless pleasure comparing this cycle with Berlioz's *Les Nuits d'été*. But if you want to dig beneath the sensuous surface you really need to come to grips with Verlaine's difficult French (impossible to translate adequately) and Fauré's equally difficult harmony. The songs are a challenge to perform, but well worth the effort – and there is no better way of getting to know the music.

Music in England

In the 19th century Germans used to call England *Das Land ohne Musik* ('the land without music'). A cruel jibe, and not entirely accurate. In reality England was a land without any native world-class composers. Instead a stream of continental musicians crossed the channel hoping to make their fortune in what was then the richest country in Europe. Chief among them was Mendelssohn, who soon became one of Queen Victoria's most welcome guests (she and Prince Albert sang some of his early songs when he visited Buckingham Palace in 1841).

Oratorio

An aspect of the romantic period that runs clean counter to most of the trends we have so far noticed was a new scholarly interest in ancient music that led to the publication of the complete works of composers such as Bach and Handel. Mendelssohn, who edited and conducted several of Handel's vocal works, was one of the leading figures of this movement and it was under the influence of Handel that Mendessohn composed his oratorio *Elijah*. He set a German text, but it was the English version that was used for the world premier in Birmingham in 1846. The words derive from the dramatic story of the life of the Old Testament prophet, found in the Book of Kings, chapters 17–19.

Like Handel before him, Mendelssohn gave the chorus a central role, and this is evident in Nos. 35–38 (which together illustrate most of the forms and styles to be found in the oratorio). The alto solo at the start of No. 35 ('Above him stood the Seraphim') is a recitative that could have been written by Handel, except that a single orchestral chord replaces the baroque continuo group. The ensuing chorus includes antiphonal exchanges which find their counterpart in oratorios by Handel, but the choral recitative flowing seamlessly into Elijah's arioso and accompanied recitative (No. 36) is entirely original.

The recording of *Elijah* by Paul Daniel and the Orchestra of the Age of Enlightenment is electrifying but expensive (Decca 455 688-2DH2). A good older recording at a bargain price is available on EMI/Double Forte CZS5 68601-2.

Elijah's air (No. 37) takes the form of a duet between the vocal part and the equally important orchestral melody. Here the baroque obbligato aria is the obvious model. No. 38 finds its counterpart in Handel's raging choruses such as 'With thunder armed' (*Samson*), but the frenetic syncopations of the accompaniment and Mendelssohn's dramatic use of tonality are entirely modern.

Elijah soon joined Haydn's *Creation* and Handel' *Messiah* as part of the staple fare of British amateur choral societies. Works by native composers were not entirely unknown, but it has to be admitted that in 'the land without music' the sentimental choral music of Victorian composers such as Maunder, Stainer and Sullivan pale into insignificance in the light of music such as this.

Parlour songs

With the advent of the piano as a 'must-have' adornment for the front parlour of every English middle-class home there came a demand for songs that were simple enough for amateur performance. But the finest examples of the genre were imported from the continent – often with tacky English translations (as we saw earlier with Tchaikovsky's *None but the lonely heart*). But the finest examples, such as Mendelssohn's 'On wings of song' (*Auf Flügeln des Gesanges*), are still sung in both home and concert hall.

As with oratorio so with the parlour song, native composers seemed constitutionally incapable of avoiding banality and sentimentality. Perhaps the most infamous example is 'The Lost Chord' by Arthur Sullivan (1840–1900). Adalaide Proctor's dire verse …

> Seated one day at the organ, I was weary and ill at ease,
> And my fingers wandered idly over the noisy keys

with its tawdry rhymes (ease/keys) is matched by a boring *parlando* vocal part (hardly worthy to be called a tune) and predictable harmony. Sullivan never did manage to find what he lost, and the whole effect is so dreadful that the publishers were obliged to add the following to the usual copyright notice: *The Public Performance of any parodied version of this composition is strictly prohibited.*

Operetta

Yet Sullivan did achieve lasting fame as a composer of operettas (small-scale comic operas). He could write pretty tunes and dress them up in skilful orchestrations, and he had a gift for pastiche. But the success of his operettas was in no small measure due to the witty librettos written by W S Gilbert, a master of satirical verse. Soon Gilbert and Sullivan became a national institution, and in 1885 'G & S' reversed the trend of musical importation when *The Mikado* achieved world-wide renown.

A vast amount of information about *Trial by Jury*, including lists of recordings and videos, can be found on the web at http://diamond.boisestate.edu/gas/trial/html/trial_home.html

Unlike their other operettas, the one-act *Trial by Jury* (1875) is sung throughout. Every trifling detail of what is said in court is rendered in solemn recitative or melodramatic song. In No. 12 the Judge sings an operatic roulade on the word 'wit' (fair enough), but he is cheekily outdone by learned counsel whose answering phrase ends with a much more elaborate flourish on the words 'settle it':

Example 49   Sullivan, *Trial by Jury*, No. 12, bars 4–8 (1875)

And at this stage, ____ it don't ap - pear   That we can set - - - - tle it.

The incongruity of using another roulade simply because 'wit' rhymes with 'settle it' could not be more obvious. In fact this elaborate sestet and chorus is a direct parody of the finale to Act 1 from Bellini's two-act opera *La sonnabula* (1831). The fun comes from the many repetitions of the mundane words 'A nice dilemma we have here that calls for all our wit' as a tragic ensemble for six soloists, four-part chorus and full orchestra.

? **Private study**

1. What name is given to the French equivalent of a German *Lied*?

2. Many romantic composers coloured tonality with the frequent use of chromaticism. What else did Fauré use to enrich the simpler tonal styles of earlier composers?

3. Why were continental composers so dominant in Victorian England?

4. Outline some of the vocal music that would have been heard in England during the period 1815–85.

5. What is (a) an operetta, and (b) a roulade?

Italian opera

At the beginning of our period Rossini (one of the composers whose style Sullivan parodied) was working on his most famous comic opera, *Il barbiere de Seviglia* (The Barber of Seville, 1816) which Sullivan edited with English words for Boosey & Co. The plot is based on the early life of Figaro, the eponymous hero of Mozart's opera *Le nozze di Figaro* (The Marriage of Figaro, 1786). The source of both librettos was a pair of subversive comedies by the French playwright, Beaumarchais (1732–99) which satirise the social and sexual mores of late 18th-century aristocrats and their servants.

Rossini's debt to Mozart and his lack of interest in German romanticism are everywhere apparent. Of course Rossini did not simply copy Mozart's style, in fact he was responsible for introducing genres, forms and styles in his comic and serious operas that became standard modes of dramatic expression in Italy right up to the end of our period. One of these was the *cavatina*, a genre, which, by the early 19th century, simply meant an aria sung by one of the principal soloists at his or her first entry.

Perhaps the most famous *cavatina* ever written is that sung by Figaro when he takes centre stage (metaphorically as well as literally) in the first act of *The Barber*. He boasts that, as well as being a barber, he is the general factotum of Seville who can arrange anything for paying customers. His bombast could not be more brilliantly expressed than in Rossini's setting of *Largo al factotum* ('make way for the factotum'). The terrific speed, very high tessitura and huge leaps of the virtuoso vocal part are wedded to a brilliantly orchestrated accompaniment featuring a cunning utilisation of sudden, unexpected modulations. Yet the repetition of tiny melodic motifs ensures that the audience will be able to whistle or sing snatches of the aria long after the opera is over. The patter singing at *Pronto a far tutto, La notte e il giorno*, is built on an easily-remembered descending triad of G major, but this is immediately followed by a three-note figure that climbs a chromatic scale to the distant key of E♭ major. There is no modulation – just tonal shock tactics. Starting a bar and a half before *Tutti mi chiedono* the song builds to a climax 25 bars later. This is achieved through the agency of the famous 'Rossini crescendo'. Repeated motifs (rising 4ths and 5ths in the vocal part) are moved closer together, the rate of harmonic change speeds up from one chord for four bars to two chords per bar, more and more instruments are added, the orchestral melody moves up an octave, and, of course the dynamic level increases.

At the climax Figaro silences the orchestra and repeats his own name, unaccompanied, to a 'Three blind mice' figure in C major. Then, without warning (but with a fortissimo orchestral tutti), he launches into the unexpected key of A♭ major. The *cavatina* ends with another 'Rossini crescendo'. It is designed to milk thunderous applause from the audience and it always succeeds.

Although Rossini wrote more than 20 serious operas he is chiefly known for his comic operas, and in many ways he was a fish out of water in the burgeoning romantic era. The reverse was true of Verdi, the dominant figure in Italian opera from 1841 (when his first opera was launched at La Scala in Milan) to 1893 (when his

Rossini

Figaro's *cavatina* is available on hundreds of compilation discs of operatic favourites. The complete opera is available on CD at a bargain price from Naxos (8.660027/29).

Patter singing involves the enunciation of tongue-twisting words at high speed. Patter songs were a feature of many 19th-century comic operas and operettas, especially those of Gilbert and Sullivan. One of their most famous examples is 'I am the very model of a modern major general' from *The Pirates of Penzance* (1879).

Verdi

last opera was premiered at the same opera house). Of his 28 operas only two are comic (though one of them, *Falstaff*, is a masterpiece). His serious operas deal with most of the romantic pre-occupations we have already encountered, not least love and death in medieval settings, especially as recounted by Shakespeare (*Macbeth* and *Otello*). But in the 1840s Verdi immersed himself in contemporary literature, including the works of Victor Hugo (whom we have already encountered in another context). The result was a bending of the conventions of the Rossinian number opera to accommodate greater dramatic continuity and deeper musical characterisation.

Bargain-price CDs of the complete opera are available on Naxos 8.660013/14 and Opera Double Decca 443 853-2DF2. A very good mid-price recording (with Plácido Domingo as the Duke) is Deutsche Grammophon 415 288-2GH2. There is no shortage of full-price recordings if you prefer Pavarotti. *Rigoletto* is also available on video and DVD.

Rigoletto (1851) is one of the finest of Verdi's operas. It is based on Hugo's dramatic tragedy, *Le Roi s'amuse* (1832), a play that was so revolutionary it was banned after its first performance in Paris. It was the grotesque and macabre elements of the play (elements that are as typical of romanticism as Goethe's theme of moral degradation in *Faust*) that stuck in the gullets of the French censors, and in their turn Italian censors insisted on major revisions to the libretto of the opera. Nevertheless, in the finally approved version, the libertine 16th-century Duke of Mantua still proclaims his determination to enjoy his carnal pleasures wherever and whenever he chooses, and Rigoletto (the hunch-backed court jester) still cruelly mocks Monterone, the father whose daughter the Duke has ravished. Monterone solemnly curses both the Duke and Jester. But Rigoletto himself has a daughter, Gilda, and she is to be the Duke's next victim. Courtiers trick Rigoletto into allowing himself to be blindfolded while they carry off Gilda. Only when he hears her cries does Rigoletto realise the potency of the curse.

In Act 2 Rigoletto discovers that the Duke's seduction has been successful as he listens in tears to his daughter's shameful story. When he sees Monterone being escorted to prison he assures him that he will be avenged. In the last act Rigoletto engages the services of an assassin whose sister, Maddalena, has lured the Duke to a ruined tavern. Gilda and her father secretly observe the Duke's overtures to Maddalena, his intended third victim. Rigoletto plans his revenge while his daughter despairs.

It is at this point that Verdi wrote for the Duke, Maddalena, Gilda and Rigoletto one of his finest operatic ensembles (*Bella figlia dell' amore*). Each role is assigned its own characteristic melodic line, which is maintained even when all four voices sing together.

The Duke's sexual overtures ('Come, beautiful daughter of love – with one word you can assuage my suffering') are represented by a *cantilena* with seductive grace notes (*amore*), oily chromaticism (*puoi, Le mie pene*) and impassioned discords (eg the appoggiatura at *palpitar*) that exactly reflect his duplicitous character.

Maddalena's sardonic response ('My laughter mocks you, random words are cheap') contrasts strongly. Rapid, staccato semiquavers suggest her flirtatious character while her teasing appoggiatura at *core* mocks the Duke's impassioned appoggiatura.

Gilda's melody begins in semiquaver figures with appoggiaturas, but they are broken by rests, and the appoggiaturas (B♮, G♮ and E♮) are chromatic. The climax of her melody (*infelice*) mirrors the

Duke's ascent at *palpitar*, but now, instead of an appoggiatura, Gilda's ascent precipitates a stunning modulation to the remote key of E major (enharmonically notated as F♭ major).

Finally Rigoletto's melody literally mirrors that of his daughter in the sequence at *Chei mentiva or sei secura*. The miracle of this passage is that each voice retains its individual characteristics throughout 32 long bars of counterpoint.

In the rapid action of the rest of the opera, the heart-broken Gilda offers herself as the victim in the plot to assassinate the Duke. Just when Rigoletto is about to dispose of the body, wrapped in a sack, he hears the Duke singing in the distance. He rips open the sack and, in the type of dramatic ending typical of Italian grand opera, discovers that his desire for revenge has resulted in the murder of his own beloved daughter. As the curtain falls, Rigoletto cries out that Monterone's curse has been fulfilled.

German opera

Weber's *Der Freischütz* (1821) is the earliest German romantic opera to retain an enduring place in the standard operatic repertoire. It is set in a vast Bohemian forest where the hero of the plot, Max, having lost a shooting competition, is now in danger of losing the hand of the heroine, Agathe. His rival, Caspar has made a pact with Samiel, the diabolic Black Huntsman (shades of *Faust*!) in which he has traded his life for magic bullets that unerringly hit their targets. Caspar, by demonstrating the effectiveness of one of the bullets, lures Max to the Wolf's Glen at midnight, supposedly to obtain more magic bullets, but in reality to offer Max to Samiel as a substitute victim. The meeting in the Wolf's Glen (Act 2, scene 4) is a *locus classicus* of romanticism: the stage sets depict a romantically wild ravine; the plot involves rivalry in love; death and damnation are threatened; and we are introduced to a romantic theme we have not yet touched on – magic.

Weber treats the libretto as a melodrama in which the text is spoken with minatory orchestral interjections and accompaniments. After the midnight hour has been announced by a tolling bell, *fortissimo* strings play a tritone (an interval that has represented diabolic powers from the early middle ages onward). Caspar summons the Black Huntsman (*Samiel! Samiel! erschein'*). The orchestra plays a darkly-scored, soft diminished 7th (another sonority associated with evil). Caspar swears by the skull of the magician (*Bei des Zaub'rers Hirngebein*). Then, to the accompaniment of chromatic chords played by tremolo strings swelling to *fortissimo*, Samiel himself appears.

The harmony and scoring of this melodrama appear periodically throughout the opera and they are always associated with Samiel. As such it is a *Leitmotif* – a clearly defined musical idea that represents a person, object, idea or mood, and that appears several times in an opera or programmatic composition. Wagner (1813–83) is famous for his use of the device, but he went much further than Weber by integrating *Leitmotifs* within lengthy melodic lines that often form strands in rich symphonic textures. By his integrated use of *Leitmotifs* in overlapping contrapuntal lines, by avoiding

An extract from the Wolf's Glen scene can be found in RDMS, B60. Compare it with bars 25–30 of the opera's overture, shown in RDMS 59.

perfect cadences, by resolving one discord to another, and by intense, tonality-defying chromaticism Wagner was able to build immense unbroken musical paragraphs in his music dramas (as he called his operas). All of these techniques are used to devastating effect in the famous *Liebestod* (Love-death) at the end of *Tristan und Isolde* (1859) – nine minutes of continuous symphonic argument beginning 79 bars from the end of the opera.

An extract from the *Liebestod* is given in Aural Matters: CD2 track 42, page 134.

Indeed, so symphonic is this music that it makes complete sense without Isolda's vocal part and is sometimes performed as an orchestral piece. Through the texture the most important melodic line (which Germans call a *Hauptstimme*) weaves its way, changing from instrument to instrument, but nevertheless completely continuous. This is Wagner's 'unending melody'. Above the symphonic swell Isolde declaims the text in phrases that sometimes coincide with the *Hauptstimme* (eg *Mild und leise* – a *Leitmotif* from the love duet at the end of Act 2, scene 2). Sometimes they are unrelated melodic fragments (eg *säh't ihr's nicht?*) and at other times they form a more extended countermelody (such as the vocal melody at *sternumstrahlet hoch sich hebt?* and the cello *Hauptstimme* with which it is paired). Often Wagner writes an impassioned dialogue between voice and orchestra. For instance at *Wonne klagend* the vocal melody with its characteristic semiquaver figure (another leitmotif from the love duet in Act 2, scene 2) is imitated in diminution by treble instruments.

A comparison of the *Liebestod* with the ensemble in *Rigoletto* will reveal how different were the aims and techniques of the two composers. Verdi focuses on vocal melodies leaving the orchestra to provide a largely homophonic accompaniment. Wagner focuses on a symphonic argument that is, at the very least, an equal partner of the vocal melody and the unfolding dramatic argument.

But in *Tristan* and his other late operas Wagner sought even greater integration in what he called the *Gesamtkunstwerk* ('total artwork'). By this he meant a fusion of literature (his own libretti), music (radically integrated with the text as we have seen), art (his scores contain exact instructions for stage artists), architecture (he designed his own opera house in Bayreuth) and philosophy (which he comprehensively expounded in his books *The Artwork of the Future* and *Opera and Drama*).

There are numerous recordings of the Prize Song but many are ancient recordings of long-dead heroic tenors. Avoid these like the plague. The best bet is Belart 450 121 in which Plácido Domingo not only sings the *Prize Song*, but also sings extracts from several other operas we have mentioned in this chapter, including Massenet's *Werther*, Verdi's *Macbeth* and *Rigoletto*, and Berlioz's *La Damnation de Faust*.

The fusion of many aspects of romanticism is nowhere more evident than in the Prize Song in the last act of Wagner's music drama *Die Meistersinger von Nürnberg* ('The Mastersingers of Nuremberg', 1868). The theme is love – like Max and Caspar in *Der Freischütz*, Beckmesser and Walther have to compete for the hand of the lady they both love – the setting is 16th-century Germany, the sub-text is nationalistic (Hans Sachs extravagantly praises 'Holy German Art' in Act 3, scene 4). The magnificent melody of the prize song itself is in medieval bar form (AAB), but the cadence at the end of the first section is interrupted by the acclamation of the mastersingers and ordinary folk. The same happens at the end of the second A section, but the crowds are silenced by the beauty of Walther's final section (B). However, this time the folk, unable to restrain their admiration for Walther's prize song, enter before the end, and when the song is finished they take up phrases from it in a mighty choral apotheosis. Total integration is further assured by an orchestral *Hauptstimme* (derived from bars 7–10 of the first section of the song) that runs through the polyphony of the two choral interruptions.

This chapter began with an examination of a tiny fragmentary song by Schumann (Example 34). The other extreme of romanticism is represented by *Tristan*, *The Mastersingers* and by the unsurpassed epic that is Wagner's *Der Ring des Nibelungen* (1876). Commonly known as 'The Ring', it is a cycle of four totally integrated operas that inspired Tolkien, but it completely overshadows *The Lord of the Rings*.

Private study

1. State what is meant by each of the following: (a) patter song, (b) cavatina and (c) leitmotif.

2. How did Rossini achieve such enormous success as an opera composer?

3. What are the principal differences between Italian and German opera in this period?

4. Make a list of concepts that appealed to romantic composers, (such as nature, dreams etc) and try to identify a piece that you know from the period that reflects each item on your list.

Sample questions

In the exam there will be three questions on your chosen topic, of which you must answer one. Always answer by referring to the composers and precise works you have studied.

Set A

1. Describe some of the techniques used by **either** Schubert **or** Schumann in setting words to music.

2. Show how ideas from literature were important in the purely instrumental music of this period. Refer in detail to at least one specific work.

3. Explain why one of the following groups of vocal works was so popular in Victorian England: **either** the operettas of Gilbert and Sullivan **or** the oratorios of Mendelssohn.

Set B

4. Discuss the influence of **either** Goethe **or** Shakespeare on romantic composers.

5. Show how romantic composers used tonality as a dramatic and expressive element in their music.

6. What contribution can music make to the dramatic effectiveness of action on stage in opera? Refer to specific examples from two contrasting works that you know well.

Topic 4: 1945 onwards (music and drama)

Introduction: the age of technology

Until shortly before 1900 the only way to hear music was to hear it live – either by performing it yourself or by listening to other musicians around you. The invention of a way to record music (the gramophone) and to play music to a huge and widely-dispersed audience (the radio) had a profound effect on the development of music in the 20th century. New music could be disseminated at an unprecedented speed, and the technology fed on its own success. For example, gramophone records only became truly popular in 1917 with the advent of jazz. People wanted to hear jazz so they purchased a gramophone, and once the public had the equipment more jazz was recorded and sold – leading to the 'jazz age' of the 1920s that we explored in the AS Guide.

The effects of this new market for music were not limited to jazz. Before 1900 popular music was primarily a music for people to perform, but it soon became a music for people to consume – to listen to or dance to. In the totally different field of opera, singers such as Enrico Caruso who could master the technical requirements of early recording, achieved enormous sales of records to people who would never have dreamt of setting foot inside an opera house.

Other new technologies quickly followed and each made its own impact on music. The invention of the microphone and amplifier led to a new style of singing in jazz and pop music. Because a microphone could pick up the softest vocal nuances there was no longer a need to project the voice over a great distance and new techniques, such as humming or using a light head-voice, could be used effectively and expressively. The first successful sound film (*The Jazz Singer*, 1927) was entirely structured around the moment when the lead character cries 'Say, Ma, listen to this' and breaks into the song 'Mammy' – which not only became an immediate popular hit but which also paved the way for a new genre – the film musical – of later decades. The principle of amplification was also applied to the guitar (the first commercial electric guitar appeared in 1937). Not only did this allow the instrument to be heard against the large brass and reed sections of contemporary big bands but it also led to new playing styles and techniques.

The invention of the long-playing record in 1948 increased the continuous playing time of records from three minutes to more than 20 minutes. This not only allowed substantial classical works such as symphonies to be heard with few or no interruptions but also enabled jazz performers to record the long improvisations that were becoming increasingly popular. Stereo recordings, which gave a new realism to home listening, first appeared in 1958.

The ease with which music could be disseminated had far-reaching consequences. Composers such as Debussy, Stravinsky, Milhaud, Satie and Walton heard the new popular music from America and drew on elements of ragtime and jazz in their own works. Greater awareness of non-western music encouraged the American composer Henry Cowell to run classes in world music which were attended by John Cage in 1934. Cage was profoundly influenced by these and by the potential of the technology of the age. In 1942 he wrote *Credo In Us*, a work that includes a part for radio (tuned to whatever happens to be on) or gramophone (set to play an arbitrary recording of classical music), thus introducing the idea of random sound-sources to interact with his own music.

The development of the tape recorder in the 1940s made it possible to record multiple 'takes' of a piece of music, the best parts of which could be spliced together when the musicians had gone home – thus giving control over the final product to the editor or producer. This same technology also enabled composers to find new ways of processing sound after it had been recorded, by editing the tape in unusual ways, creating loops of sound, or by applying various types of distortion for artistic effect. In 1951 the French broadcasting authority RTF established a studio for the development of *musique concrète* – music created by manipulating recordings of natural sounds. This attracted some of the major composers of the day, including Messiaen and his pupils Boulez and Stockhausen. The latter went on to run his own Studio für Elektronische Musik in Cologne, Germany, where he also explored the use of electronically-generated sounds. In 1958 the BBC established a Radiophonic Workshop for similar work in this emerging technology.

At first such work was highly experimental and attracted tiny audiences, but in 1963 the BBC Radiophonic Workshop produced Ron Grainer's theme music for a new television sci-fi series called *Dr Who*, and its success brought this new type of studio music to national attention. The equipment used – wave generators, filters and ring modulators – was bulky and cumbersome, but this was all to change. The commercial development of the transistor made it possible to produce complex electronic devices on a small scale. During the 1960s multitrack recording started to be used widely in pop music and the first practical synthesisers, designed by Bob Moog, became available. Again it was one particular recording that excited the public and illustrated the potential of this new instrument – *Switched-On Bach*, a recording of well-known movements by Bach recorded on a Moog synthesiser in 1968 by Walter Carlos.

Synthesisers rapidly became more sophisticated and in 1983 the introduction of MIDI (the Musical Instrument Digital Interface) provided a standard way to link them with other electronic instruments and with another important new technology – the computer.

Digital recording, in which the waveforms of sound are stored as a series of numbers, has been the most significant invention in more recent years. It led to the introduction of the CD (compact disc, 1982), DAT (digital audio tape, 1987) and DVD (digital versatile disc, 1995). It also led to the development of the sampler and the resulting dance-music phenomenon. Digital technology has facilitated the creation of sophisticated, but small and affordable, studios based around the personal computer. The result has been a reversal of the trend we discussed at the start of this chapter. The age of technology has produced a return to the creation of music in the home and a new facility to exchange the results between enthusiasts via the Internet.

The synthesiser was by no means the first electronic instrument. A number of experimental instruments were pioneered in the first half of the 20th century and at least one, the Hammond organ, became widely used for light-entertainment music.

See http://www.obsolete.com/120_years/ for pictures and audio samples of a huge range of electronic musical instruments.

The American musical is sometimes called the Broadway musical – a reference to the street (Broadway) in New York where many theatres hosting these elaborate spectacles are located.

West Side Story: Resources

A vocal score, full score and libretto of West Side Story are published by Chappell. The full score is expensive but the vocal score is fine for study purposes and will make it easier for you to perform some of the songs – always the best way to get to know music. The libretto shows details of the stage action and includes the full spoken dialogue (very little of which appears in the vocal score).

The 1961 film version of West Side Story is available on video and DVD. Like many film versions of musicals there are various differences between this and the original stage version.

There are a number of CD recordings available. One of the best is that made by the original Broadway cast in 1957, now digitally remastered on Sony SK 60724 – note that Sony SK 48211 is a CD of the film version. Bernstein's own 1985 recording (the only time he ever conducted the work) surprisingly uses opera singers for the parts that he originally insisted were for actors. It is on Deutsche Grammophon DG 457199-2. A 1993 recording based on the Leicester Haymarket production of the musical comes on a two-CD set from Ter (TER 1197). It is expensive but it is the most complete recording and has been well reviewed.

Avoid scores or CDs that are limited to 'highlights' since these often omit some of the most dramatic parts of the whole work. Far better is to look out for an opportunity to attend a live production which will probably prove to be irresistibly memorable.

Try to see a production of Romeo and Juliet. Franco Zeffirelli's film version of 1968 is available on video and DVD, and is broadcast on television from time to time. It uses teenage actors in the title roles and was shot on location in Italy. The scenes of street fighting between rival clans are particularly vivid and make a striking comparison with West Side Story.

The integration of music and drama

The principal focus for our topic is the integration of music and drama and we shall take as our starting point Bernstein's musical West Side Story (1957). As we noted on page 26, the term 'musical' originated in the USA as an abbreviation of musical comedy – a popular and tuneful theatrical work that developed out of 19th-century operettas such as those by Gilbert and Sullivan. Like those operettas it consisted of a number of different musical genres (solo songs, duets, vocal ensembles and choruses), separated by passages of spoken dialogue. Many musicals also draw on much older operatic traditions by including dance and elaborate spectacle, but the music is always popular in style (in the widest sense).

Jerome Kern's Show Boat (1927) established the musical as a new and essentially American art form. It is a musical play, not just an entertainment, with a credible plot, three-dimensional characters, pathos, high drama and a succession of hit songs. The book and lyrics were written by Oscar Hammerstein II, who went on to work with the composer Richard Rodgers in a team that was to dominate the musical in the 1940s and 1950s. Their works include Oklahoma! (1943), Carousel (1945), South Pacific (1949), The King and I (1951) and The Sound of Music (1959). All were filmed and all achieved remarkable success. But the raw energy of Oklahoma! (with its use of exciting dance sequences and songs that emerge naturally from the drama) and the beautiful subtlety of Carousel were not always equalled in their later works, despite some exotic settings. The Sound of Music made it all too apparent, in an age of increasing cynicism, that Rodgers and Hammerstein were depending on a nostaglic romantic style, with its traditional accompaniment of a large symphony orchestra. By the late 1950s there was clearly a need for a new approach if the musical was not to become a quaint museum piece.

West Side Story

Leonard Bernstein (1918–90) was a many-talented American musician who established a reputation as a pianist, conductor, broadcaster and composer. In the last of these areas he followed in Gershwin's footsteps, often working at the frontier between popular and art music. But Bernstein's music reflects the styles of his own, later age – especially bebop jazz, with its hard-edged dissonance and driving rhythms, and the urban blues. He had written the musicals On the Town (1944), Wonderful Town (1952) and Candide (1956) as well as the score for the film On the Waterfront (1954). The last of these is a direct predecessor of West Side Story, both musically and dramatically – for it, too, deals with harsh inner-city tensions, human conflict and social realism.

The idea of a musical based on Shakespeare's play Romeo and Juliet was suggested to Bernstein by the choreographer Jerome Robbins. The setting was changed from renaissance Italy to modern-day New York. Romeo and Juliet, the young lovers who defy a running feud between their families, become Tony and Maria from rival teenage gangs, the Jets and the Sharks. And Shakespeare's famous balcony scene is mirrored by the meeting of Tony and Maria on the fire escape of a bleak New York tenement.

Some early sketches were made in 1949, but it was not until 1956 that Bernstein began work in earnest on the project. The screenwriter Arthur Laurents was engaged to write the book and Stephen Sondheim was asked to provide the lyrics – Sondheim was a close friend of Oscar Hammerstein II and later became a composer of musicals in his own right. Robbins had envisaged the conflict of loyalties that is so central to the drama to be interpreted as a conflict between Catholic and Jewish communities. Bernstein seized on the idea that current racial tensions in New York caused by a large influx of immigrants from Puerto Rico would provide a more powerful scenario – and he undoubtedly saw that this would also offer him the opportunity to use a range of Latin-American dance rhythms, for he later said: 'Suddenly it all sprang to life. I heard rhythms and pulses, and – most of all – I could sort of feel the form.'

Much about *West Side Story* was revolutionary. Instead of the nostalgic romanticism of earlier musicals, this is a story of bleak despair. In place of the rousing finale, it ends in murder. Extended dance sequences convey the drama, and Bernstein stressed that he wanted the principal parts to be played by actors who could sing, not singers who might happen to be able to act. The impact of *West Side Story* was enormous. It was a new type of musical with a plot rooted in violence and tragedy, that explored social tension, that made extensive use of contemporary dance and that had music which integrated ideas from opera, jazz, music hall, popular song and Latin-American traditions – a combination that far exceeded the ambitions of any earlier work in this genre.

Although Shakespeare's text is not used, his characters are clearly identifiable:

Romeo and Juliet	*West Side Story*
The Montague family	The Jets (Americans)
Mercutio (Montague's nephew)	Riff (their leader)
Romeo (Montague's son)	Tony (a member of the Jets)
The Capulet family	The Sharks (Puerto Ricans)
Tybalt (Capulet's nephew)	Bernardo (their leader)
Juliet (Capulet's daughter)	Maria (a member of the Sharks)
Friar Laurence	Doc
Nurse	Anita

Bernstein originally envisaged starting the work in a conventional way with an overture and opening chorus. But instead he found a much more dramatic solution. The curtain rises immediately on a long sequence in which action and tension are conveyed in dance, mime and music without words.

The opening bars, shown in Example 50, illustrate Bernstein's jazz-based approach to harmony. A strong chordal sequence (a) is brought to life with the blues-like added notes shown in (b) and by syncopation – the anticipation of the beat (known as a push) shown in (c). At the start the Jets are in control of the city streets and they are cool. Arrogant finger-snaps (notated in the score) introduce a slinky saxophone melody at the end of bar 11, and we hear for the first time the motif that permeates the entire musical, the tritone.

Throughout the following pages we refer to Bernstein's ability to capture and interpret styles of Latin-American music. As a jazz pianist he played the Afro-Cuban jazz that was popular in the 1940s and 1950s. His marriage to the Chilean Felicia Monteleagre resulted in personal contact with the music of South America on their visits to the region. He was also greatly influenced by the composer Aaron Copland, who had started to explore a new and simpler style based on Latin-American music in *El Salón Mexico* (1936).

Example 50 Bernstein, opening bars of *West Side Story* (1957)

The tonal instability of this interval, known for centuries as the *diabolus in musica* ('devil in music'), has long been associated with evil and here it sets the scene for the ruthless violence of the Jets and the Sharks – see Example 52(a). When the texture thickens at bar 22, notice how the accompaniment uses a three-beat riff (shown by brackets below) which cuts across the duple pulse of the $\frac{6}{8}$ metre. The pitches of this part sway between a suggestion of F♯ minor (C♯–F♯) and a dominant 7th of G. This tonal ambiguity supports neither the sustained saxophone part (which hints at D minor) nor the countermelody in 3rds, which is clearly in A minor.

Example 51   Bernstein, *West Side Story*, No. 1, Prologue

Riffs, cross-rhythms, bitonality and layered textures of independent parts are all fingerprints of Bernstein's style and are here used to build dramatic tension for the entry of Bernardo, leader of the Sharks. This is signalled by the motif of evil – the tritone, played on muted trombone – Example 52(b). It is now inverted and therefore notated as an augmented 4th rather than a diminished 5th. Bernardo is taunted by two of the Jets, to another characteristic Bernstein sound – a solo break for drums of different pitches.

The tritone doesn't merely provide musical glue, it also has a clear dramatic purpose. For instance, in bars 108–109 we hear Example 52(b) in shorter note values – see Example 52(c). This *pp* version in bare octaves underlines the baiting going on between the rival gangs. And when a Shark deliberately trips up a Jet at bar 140, and thereby sets in motion the train of events that will lead to the final tragedy, we hear a curiously tripping figure in which our motif appears twice in succession, splitting the octave into two tritones, followed by a figure from bar 49 – see Example 52(d).

Bernstein builds the tension of this confrontational opening scene over a long period – notice how he frequently drops back from intermediate climaxes by thinning the texture and reducing the dynamic, in order to give space for yet another build-up. But the underlying quickening of intensity eventually leads to a searing semitonal dissonance at bar 241, where Bernardo attacks one of the Jets, and then to chaotic *fff* cross-rhythms as free-for-all fighting breaks out. A police whistle (notated in the score) is heard and there is time for only six more bars of fighting. When the police appear they are greeted by a sudden pretence of dreary normality – what's up? nothing's wrong, the music seems to say, as the prologue ends with a nonchalant repeat of its first main melody (Example 52(a)).

We have spent some time discussing this Prologue because it is important to realise how faithfully Bernstein's music reflects the drama even in the absence of words. The gradual transition to vocal music is equally skilful. The second number ('Jet Song') begins with motifs from the Prologue played under spoken dialogue. When Riff breaks into song the accompaniment is based on the syncopated $\frac{6}{8}$ pattern from the start of the musical (Example 50(c) on page 111) that we have already associated with the Jets. But above this Bernstein writes a vocal part in crotchets, effectively in $\frac{3}{4}$ time. The forceful cross-rhythms, angular melody and entirely syllabic setting give enormous weight to Riff's authoritarian statement as gang leader: 'When you're a Jet, You're a Jet all the way'. The middle section of the verse develops the saxophone melody from the prologue (Example 52a)). Its disjunct motion and prominent tritone, along with the chord clusters in the accompaniment, leave no doubt that Riff is a hard man – see Example 52(f).

Riff's best friend, Tony, is growing disillusioned with the Jets. His first song ('Something's Coming') anticipates the excitement of the dance to be held that night at the gym and also reveals his desire for a different and better future. The urgency is conveyed in the driving tempo, the constant push on the third beat of the bar and the short riffs that permeate the accompaniment. You should have no difficulty in spotting the ever-present tritone, which is used not only melodically but also harmonically (look at the very first chord).

A short scene of spoken dialogue after this song introduces Maria and Anita, who work in a bridal shop. As it ends Maria imagines the dance to be held that night and whirls across the stage in the dress she has made for the occasion. As she does so the music of No. 4 starts and, in a spectacular stage transformation, the bridal shop flies out of sight, streamers fall from above and we are in 'The Dance at the Gym'. This long dance sequence reveals Bernstein's superb ability to recreate different styles of music in his own unique terms. The initial heavy blues begins with simultaneous descending and ascending tritones and from bar 16 it makes clear reference to the added-note harmony and syncopated rhythms first heard at the very start of the musical. The rhythm becomes greatly fragmented at bar 34 as the Jets and the Sharks withdraw to opposite sides of the dance floor. Glad Hand, a well-meaning adult, tries to break the ice by getting the boys to form a circle around an inner circle of girls. The two circles promenade in opposite directions until a whistle blows – couples facing each other at this point are then expected to dance together. Bernstein writes this 'Promenade' in a deliberately old-fashioned, ragtime-like style using essentially just tonic and dominant harmonies. But notice the rasping Gb in the bass of bars 6, 7, 10 and 11 – Bernstein makes it clear what the teenagers think of this kind of dancing!

The whistle blows, the music stops – and each Jet boy is left facing a Shark girl, and vice-versa. The groups separate in disgust and begin a Mambo, a Latin-American dance from Cuba with driving rhythms. The dance itself begins at the rhythmic shout of 'Mambo! Mambo! Go!' and, as it turns into a challenge dance between the leading couples from each rival gang, the malevolent tritone makes its presence known – see Examples 52(g) and (h) and notice how the three-beat motifs in the latter (shown by the pecked brackets) once again create cross-rhythms with the prevailing duple metre.

Example 52 Bernstein, *West Side Story*
Tritone motifs (i)

Example 53 Bernstein, *West Side Story*
Tritone motifs (ii)

(a) Cha Cha

(b) Meeting Scene

(c) Maria

(d) Maria

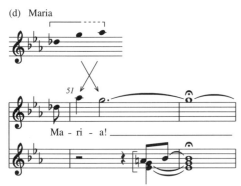

Towards the end of the Mambo Tony and Maria see each other for the first time. The lights dim, the dance floor clears, and they begin another popular Latin-American dance of the 1950s, the Cha Cha – its name comes from the prominent use of the 'cha-cha-cha' rhythm at the ends of phrases, here heard in bars 10 and 18. The tritone appears in a new and very unthreatening guise – Example 53(a). The dissonant C♯ is treated as a chromatic appoggiatura above G-major harmony, and its momentary tension is immediately dissipated by a resolution to D. The melody is, of course, a stylised version of the song 'Maria' that we shall hear in a few minutes.

In the 'Meeting Scene' the anticipation of 'Maria' becomes more obvious as this extended motif adopts a slower speed and more legato style (Example 53(b)). But before we hear the song itself the gangs return to a reprise of the Promenade. This is followed by 'Jump' – a dance from the swing era that looks forward to rhythm-and-blues with its strong backbeat and use of blue (ie flat) 3rds and 7ths from the natural minor scale – by now you will need no help in spotting the tritones, harmonic or melodic! 'Jump' is played very quietly because over the music Bernardo pulls Maria from Tony's arms and plans with Riff a big showdown between their rival gangs.

Tony is left alone and begins the *parlando* introduction to 'Maria'. Sondheim's lyrics deserve special mention – he clearly realised that a love song about a girl Tony had met only five minutes ago would be implausible. And so the song is not about the girl herself, but the magic of her name. The accompaniment to the song is based on the rhythm of the habanera (another Cuban dance) that can be heard in every bar of the bass from bar 9 until the pause in bar 46. But the vocal part is much freer in rhythm, the crotchet triplets in particular giving the sense of expressive rubato.

This song also sees a beautiful transformation of the tritone motif – Example 53(c). Adapted to fit perfectly the rhythm of Maria's name, it is rising and aspirational. The slower speed means that the tension of the chromatic appoggiatura (now A♮) is more obvious, but it finds immediate release by resolving to the dominant (B♭). Bernstein leaves little doubt that Tony has found a resolution to conflict, musical and dramatic, in Maria.

'Maria' was one of the first songs Bernstein wrote for the musical, drafted during the preliminary sketches of 1949. It is thus possible that Example 53(c) is the original source of the interval that came to pervade *West Side Story*. Bernstein himself acknowledged that it forms the kernel of the musical '… in that the three notes pervade the whole piece, inverted, done backwards. I didn't do all this on purpose.' This last comment is fascinating. It suggests that what to us seems a brilliantly planned compositional device was actually generated at a subconscious level – the result of a skilled composer working with enormous intensity and clear unity of purpose.

Notice how Bernstein reflects every nuance of the text. The circling triplets around B♭ ('I've just met a girl named Maria') echo Tony's whirling emotions. Triplets suddenly give way to firm quavers for 'suddenly that name'. The phrase is repeated but it is not actually the same when he sings 'will never be the same'. The third phrase rises higher, to D, as he thinks of the kiss, but it is the sound of her name that is inspirational, taking the following phrases ever upward to E♭ and then F (and much higher later).

Bernstein is not afraid of more obvious word-painting, such as the sudden *pp* at 'Say it soft' and the repetitions of Maria suggested by the phrase 'I'll never stop saying Maria' – but notice how he builds into the music the very way that a star-struck lover might repeat her name over and over with different nuances. Thus the final syllable is accented in bar 28, then Tony tries different ways of stressing the second syllable in bars 30–32, leading to tumbling triplets on her name in bar 33.

As we approach the central climax the tessitura becomes increasingly higher and the vocal demands become operatic in nature. The top G in bar 34 is marked *p* *crescendo* and is immediately followed by a sustained top B♭ which must increase still more in dynamic as it leads without a break into the high triplet minims of bar 39.

In fact, the entire song resembles a showpiece tenor aria from a romantic opera (perhaps justifying Bernstein's use of opera stars in his 1985 recording). The melody lines are mainly conjunct in motion and when leaps occur they are often used to heighten the expression (as in bars 34–36). Contrast this with No. 7 ('America') where almost entirely disjunct melodic motion captures the very different style of the Puerto Ricans. Also rooted in romantic opera is the way Bernstein uses the orchestra to play the principal melody in counterpoint to the vocal gymnastics throughout bars 28–39. But beneath all this, with its lush, western instrumentation, Bernstein's pervasive habañera rhythm reminds us of how totally Maria's Puerto-Rican world has now started to infiltrate Tony's thoughts.

In bars 47–48 the vocal melody of bars 28–29 is repeated with a new accompaniment which in bar 48 echoes bar 10. Bars 49–50 return to the *parlando* style of the introduction by repeating the vocal part of bars 1–2 an octave higher (the enharmonic notation doesn't make this immediately apparent) but with a very static accompaniment. Finally and most magically, Bernstein reverses the last two notes of the 'Maria motif', so making the rising interval a perfect 5th (D♭–A♭) which then allows the previously rising semitone to fall to G – Example 53(d). Below this the accompaniment poignantly condenses the version of the motif heard in bar 9 into a *ppp* cadential figure in which the tritone is heard harmonically.

The focus of the 'Balcony Scene' (No. 6) is the duet 'Tonight'. Here the interaction between the two soloists is very simple – they sing mainly in alternation or together in octaves. The choice is probably deliberate, probably to indicate that they are already of 'one heart' (to quote a later duet). But Bernstein turns an old trick of tonality on its head. To create an illusion of excitement, many composers of popular music used to transpose successive verses of songs up by semitones. Here Bernstein does the reverse. As the lovers become more intimate the tonality first nestles down from B♭ to A major and then snugly sinks a semitone further to A♭ major. As the tempo gets slower and the tessitura gets lower, much of the last part of the duet dissolves into spoken dialogue above music. In the last four bars notice how the accompaniment looks both forward to Act 2 ('There's a place for us') and backward to 'Maria'.

'America' (No. 7) combines two Latin-American musical traditions. The initial speed direction refers to *seis*, a type of vocal music from Puerto Rico – *seis* ('six') most probably refers to the six-string guitar used to accompany these songs. The mood is established from the outset with cross-rhythms between claves and guiro, instruments frequently used in Latin-American dance music. From bar 5 the clave pattern is developed into a bass ostinato – you may recognise the habanera rhythm since we have encountered it before – and the guiro's crotchet triplets develop into a melodic accompaniment-figure played in thirds. Further cross-rhythms occur as Rosalia introduces minim triplet figures. Once again, we can see how Bernstein builds up a complex texture in separate layers.

The *seis de bomba* featured a verbal blow (*bomba*) aimed at one of the singers. We can see this in bar 21, where Anita mockingly interrupts Rosalia's reminiscences of Puerto Rico with a well-aimed blast about the 'island of tropical diseases'. The ten-line structure of a *seis* lyric would conventionally end at bar 34 ('Always the population growing,') but Anita gets so carried away with her own reportage of life in Puerto Rico that she cannot stop herself adding further sour comments. Bernstein marks the change musically by first reducing the complex accompaniment to fragmented quavers, marked 'rhythmically'. And when Anita reveals that she is totally won over by America ('I like the island Manhattan – smoke on your pipe and put that in') he supports the lazy triplets of the vocal line with sustained and voluptuous 7th chords.

The second Latin-American tradition on which Bernstein based this number is the *Huapango*, mentioned in the tempo direction at bar 46. This Mexican dance is characterised by a fast tempo, alternate bars of $\frac{3}{4}$ and $\frac{6}{8}$, and frequent use of tonic pedals. Bernstein draws on all these features, cleverly using the hemiola rhythms to emphasise the word 'America' (see Example 54). He interprets the pedal as the I–V ostinato pattern also shown in this example. Above the ostinato simple triadic harmony provides a series of sparkling clashes – diatonic in bars 50–53 (chords I, IV, I and V) but chromatic in bars 54–56, where the triads are formed on the blue (flat) 3rd, 7th and 6th of the scale (E♭, B♭ and A♭ respectively).

In the verses, notice how Bernstein takes great care to prevent the *Huapango* rhythm from becoming too predictable. He syncopates the expected $\frac{3}{4}$ vocal rhythms in bars 63 and 65, adds an extra bar at bar 66 (which combines a $\frac{3}{4}$ pattern in the bass with a $\frac{6}{8}$ pattern in the higher instruments) and entirely stops the accompaniment at bar 69 to allow Anita's low chest-register notes to be heard.

The dance interlude starting at bar 82 contrasts the distantly related keys of A♭ major and C major, maintaining the *Huapango* rhythm and providing an instrumental version of the chorus at bar 104. After a third verse and chorus (bars 112–137) a repeat of the dance interlude leads to the fourth verse. But in place of the usual sung chorus there is an orchestral coda in which the music of the chorus is first played delicately and very high in C major, and then rumbustiously and loudly to finish in the key of E major. Notice that the principal key of 'America' is C major and that Bernstein arranges his two subsidiary key centres symmetrically a major 3rd below C (A♭ major) and a major 3rd above C (E major).

Example 54   Bernstein, *West Side Story* 'America'

I like to be in A - mer - i - ca!

'America' fulfills several functions in the musical. Firstly it offers light relief in a drama preoccupied with tension and despair ('Gee, Officer Krupke' serves a similar purpose in the second act). The sudden change in the audience's emotional response generated by these amusing interludes serves to intensify the high drama that follows. Secondly 'America' provides another dance number – a fine choreographic opportunity for colourful skirt-swirling. Thirdly it is the only musical number for the Sharks independent of the Jets (but only for the Sharks' girls). In an otherwise superbly-crafted drama, 'America' has been criticised for limiting the voice of the immigrant Puerto Ricans to a glorification of the American way of life, at the expense of making fun of their own homeland. But we must remember that the purpose of *West Side Story* is not social engineering and that it reflects the understanding of its own age.

In the 1950s the expression 'cool' referred to a calculated display of controlled energy. As Riff explains in the dialogue immediately before No. 8 ('Cool'):

> No matter who or what is eating at you, you show it, buddy boys, and you are dead … You wanna live? You play it cool.

Bernstein starts the display of pent-up energy in 'Cool' with a *pp* ostinato – we should call it a riff in this style of music, but at the risk of confusion with the character Riff (whose name can hardly be a coincidence). This is shown in Example 55 and the continued use of augmented 4ths is obvious. But this example also shows how tightly Bernstein's almost symphonic integration of *West Side Story* is developing. Within the riff the rising perfect 4th followed by an augmented 4th (shown by a bracket) is none other than the three-note motif from the prologue that we heard when we first became aware of the tension between the rival gangs – compare it with Example 52 (b) and (c) on page 113. And fatefully combined with this motif is another augmented 4th variant – the 'Maria' motif.

Example 55 Bernstein, *West Side Story* 'Cool'

Bernstein portrays the nervous energy in stark bare octaves that contrast with passages of highly dissonant harmony. Riff delivers his terse, clipped phrases to a fragmentary melody (based on the ostinato) which Bernstein marks 'almost whispered'. Although the harmony is enriched by the use of complex jazz subsitution chords the underlying C-major tonality should be clear. For instance look at how the bass in bars 17–24 uses only the notes C, F and G.

But the most innovative aspect of 'Cool' is the use of fugue for the first dance episode, starting at bar 45. To employ this most learned of contrapuntal textures, often associated with church music, in a musical was bold indeed. But Bernstein already had experience in writing jazz fugues, most notably in his *Prelude, Fugue and Riffs*, which is a clear antecedent to 'Cool'. And he perceived how vividly the independent musical strands of a fugue could portray the way each individual Jet lets off steam and could allow the whole exciting edifice to be built up with increasing contrapuntal complexity.

Bernstein's *Prelude, Fugue and Riffs* for solo clarinet and jazz ensemble was composed in 1949 and first performed in 1955. It is thus very much a work of the *West Side Story* years.

The fugal subject is first announced on muted trumpet at bar 45, embellished by references to the bracketed figure in Example 55. This figure is developed as a separate contrapuntal strand through-out much of the fugue (eg on the small upper stave from bar 72). Notice how Bernstein uses long notes for the subject to ensure that

it will stand out against the jazz quavers of the countersubject (first heard in the upper part at bar 60). The starting pitches (and bar numbers) of the first four entries of the fugal subject are shown in Example 56. You will see that they outline the tonally ambiguous chord of a diminished 7th, with alternate pairs of entries (shown by the brackets) a tritone apart. This tonal instability, reinforced by the dissonant chromatic writing, adds to the increasing tension as the dance builds to a climax.

At bar 106 fugal texture gives way to bare octaves as the individual Jets come together to work out their frustrations in a ritualistic communal dance. After a loud restatement of the opening ostinato (bar 121) and a yell (bar 126), we hear Riff's melody from bar 9 which then alternates with phrases from the fugal countersubject in a very loud and highly dissonant big-band style. Riff calms the gang down with a final verse, but only just – notice the *ff* outbursts. The number ends with finger-snaps, disintegrating fragments of the countersubject and an inversion of the 4ths motif (Example 57) from the opening riff. All is under control again. All is cool.

We do not have space to study every number in *West Side Story* and neither is it necessary for you to know the entire work (although the experience is very rewarding). The integrity of the drama is Bernstein's prime concern right until the end. Thus there is no rousing finale of the type found in many musicals. Look at the closing bars and you will see, as Tony's lifeless body is carried off, an ethereal *ppp* chord of C major decorated with the resolution of 'Maria'. But several octaves lower, the tritone below C (F♯) is still tolling its awesome warning. Bernstein has so totally integrated his 'tragic musical comedy' that music and drama become as one, two sides of the same coin, working in an indissoluable partnership.

Private study

1. Explain the difference between conjunct and disjunct melodic motion and give an example of each from *West Side Story*.

2. What are the main characteristics of Bernstein's musical style, as exemplified in *West Side Story*?

3. How does Bernstein convey a sense of time (1957) and place (the back streets of New York) in both the musical style and the instrumentation of this musical?

4. Outline some of the ways in which Bernstein uses purely dance music for dramatic purposes.

5. Show how Bernstein uses the tritone not only as a unifying device but also as a way to transform one musical idea into another in *West Side Story*.

6. Discuss Bernstein's use of Latin-American musical genres and styles in *West Side Story*.

7. Choose a number that we have *not* discussed in this chapter and write your own account of the ways in which it shows an integration of music and dance or drama. (Any one of Nos. 9A, 10, 11 or 15 would be particularly suitable for this exercise.)

Later musicals

West Side Story is perhaps the greatest of all musicals, but it remains unique – neither Bernstein nor any other composer seemed able to pursue such total integration of music and drama in later works. It therefore did not directly change the face of the musical. Later musicals such as *Oliver!* (1960, Lionel Bart) and musical films such as *Mary Poppins* (1964, Richard and Robert Sherman) were very popular but – or perhaps because – they perpetuated the nostalgic musical styles of earlier generations rather than developing the type of challenge offered by *West Side Story*.

But slowly musicals did change, some developing separate strands from those that had come together so successfully in *West Side Story*. In 1963 the producer Joan Littlewood staged an entirely new type of musical, *Oh! What a Lovely War*, in which the notion of using a scriptwriter was abandoned in favour of developing the work through improvisation by its actors – just as so much of *West Side Story* arose from the input of its dancers. But Littlewood went further, and also abandoned the idea of specially composed music. Instead the work makes its impact through irrepressibly tuneful but jingoistic songs from the first world war, ironically juxtaposed with spine-chilling factual information about the appalling conditions and casualty rates of the conflict.

In *West Side Story* Bernstein had used music to evoke a strong sense of time and place. Jerry Bock's score for *Fiddler on the Roof* (1964) does likewise in its portrayal of a small Jewish village in Russia in 1905. Not only does it reflect idioms of Jewish music of the period but it also underlines the tensions that arise as a changing world impinges on traditional ways of life. Similarly, John Kander's score for *Cabaret* (1966) draws brilliantly on earlier styles in its portrayal of seedy Berlin lowlife in the Nazi era. Dominated by a recreation of the style of 1930s cabaret music (eg 'Money makes the world go round'), it too evokes Jewish idioms (in 'Meeskite') and includes a chilling portrayal of the Hitler youth movement in the simplicity of 'Tomorrow belongs to me'.

West Side Story also shows how a strong plot (originating in Shakespeare's *Romeo and Juliet*) offers much more dramatic and musical potential than a reliance on the general, often exotic, 'themes' that hold together the string of songs in many earlier musicals. Transformation of drama from a literary to a musical medium had been common in opera for centuries, but it started to be used increasingly in musicals. *Oliver!* gains much of its dramatic strength from being based on *Oliver Twist* by Charles Dickens, *Cabaret* evolved in part from the stories of Christopher Isherwood, and *Fiddler on the Roof* is based on the stories of Sholem Aleichem, one of Yiddish literature's most beloved authors. *Les Misérables* (1985) by Alain Boublil and Claude-Michel Schönberg is based on Victor Hugo's epic novel of the same name. It tracks a saga of social injustice, following the life of Jean Valjean who was imprisoned for 19 years for stealing a loaf of bread.

We saw that Bernstein drew on Latin-American dance rhythms in *West Side Story*, as well as on the styles of cool jazz and big-band jazz. But although the work is centred on youth culture, it does not

You should study some short extracts from other musicals in order to identify different approaches to the genre and make comparisons between them. We have mentioned several musicals in this section, but it may be easier for you to study works that are more readily to hand, or even that you have taken part in.

When studying extracts from musicals you will find that recordings (and scores) of the complete work will be far more useful than collections of 'highlights'. The latter will help you to understand matters such as word-setting, but isolated songs taken out of context are unlikely to reveal much about the integration of music and drama in the work as a whole.

West Side Story and *Cabaret* were produced by Harold Prince, one of the most influential figures in the development of the modern musical. He went on to produce musicals by Stephen Sondheim and Andrew Lloyd Webber as well as many serious operas.

really reflect the pop music of its time. This was left to the rock musical, a genre that owed as much to the concept albums and theatricality of late 1960s pop music as to the traditional musical.

Concept albums and rock opera

The concept album arose out of technological developments in the 1960s. As the pop single (a record with one song on each side) gave way in popularity to the long-playing record (LP), musicians started looking for ways to give coherence to the many separate songs on an LP by linking them to a common theme.

The original album was re-released on CD in 1987 on Parlophone CDP 7 46442 2.

The most detailed scores of the songs in Sergeant Pepper can be found in *The Beatles Complete Scores*, published by Northern Songs (NO90548) and available from Music Sales. It is very expensive, but the 1136 pages include full transcriptions of all of the Beatles' songs. The songs from Sergeant Pepper are also available as sheet music (arranged for piano and voice, with guitar chords) from Music Sales, NO90893.

For a detailed analytical account of the work see *The Beatles: Sgt Pepper's Lonely Hearts Club Band* by Allan Moore, published by Cambridge University Press (1997). ISBN 0-521-57484-6.

One of the most famous concept albums, as they came to be called, was *Sergeant Pepper's Lonely Hearts Club Band* (the Beatles, 1967). It uses the old theatrical device of a performance within a perform-ance to create the impression that it is not the Beatles that we hear but Sgt Pepper's Lonely Hearts Club Band – an imaginary Edwardian concert band which presents a vaudeville of fantasies in styles old and new. The band's name is significant. Their role is to create an illusion for lonely people, but they themselves are lonely and it is the theme of loneliness, and how it is covered up, which links their songs. This device allowed the Beatles to use a much broader range of musical styles than normally found in pop music at this time, in order to evoke a sense of time and place. These styles include ragtime (*When I'm Sixty-Four*), community songs (*With a Little Help From My Friends*) and surreal fairground music that includes a waltz for steam organ (*Being for the Benefit of Mr Kite!*).

To create the illusion the album begins with tuning-up, audience noises and applause. To maintain the illusion, the separate tracks are closely spaced and sometimes overlap – a feature making it deliberately difficult for radio DJs to break up the album's unity by playing isolated tracks. In addition, when the LP was released it sought to involve the listener by including Sergeant Pepper cutouts, a collage of portraits and a printed version of the complete lyrics. This last feature was most unusual at the time and reflects the fact that, unlike the words of most earlier pop songs, the lyrics are often ambiguous and open to interpretation.

The illusion is seemingly brought to an end by a reprise of its opening number, now at a more urgent tempo and with its title-line curtailed to produce poignant repeats of 'Sergeant Pepper's lonely, Sergeant Pepper's lonely, …'. This framing device is then extended into a quite different final number (*A Day in the Life*), which exists like an epilogue outside the context of the show. This at last is clearly the Beatles performing, but it is far from clear that we are back to reality. After a sardonic commentary on the news and an account of humdrum everyday life ('Woke up, got out of bed') the song quickly reverts to dreaming. The final stanza loses all sense of coherence ('Now they know how many holes it takes to fill the Albert Hall; I'd love to turn you on') and so does the concluding music. And so again there is a suspicion that everything thus far has still been part of the illusion. After a final colossal chord a locked playout groove presents sounds from the post-production party and an inaudibly high tone put there at Lennon's request, 'to annoy your dog'. So is this, at last, the return to reality?

The concept album was essentially a studio-based work and one that was often impossible to recreate in live performance. But an even more ambitious pop project appeared from The Who in 1969. The 90-minute long *Tommy* was designed from the outset for live performance and is widely regarded as the first successful 'rock opera'. Indeed, it was played at New York's Metropolitan Opera House in 1970, it was re-recorded with symphony-orchestra backing in 1972, turned into a film in 1975 (with performances from Eric Clapton, Tina Turner and Elton John) and was subsequently staged as a Broadway musical. The work has a much clearer dramatic thread than Sergeant Pepper, and recounts the story of Tommy Walker, a young boy growing up in post-war Britain. The trauma of witnessing his father kill his mother's lover leaves him deaf, dumb and blind. Abused by his relatives, he finds salvation in playing pinball. His success leads to the recovery of his senses and fame, but the latter eventually overwhelms him.

While Pete Townshend was composing *Tommy*, a young composer named Andrew Lloyd Webber (born 1948) was finishing a work for Colet Court school in west London, where his brother Julian was a pupil. Andrew had teamed-up with the lyricist Tim Rice and together they wrote a short 'pop cantata', *Joseph and the Amazing Technicolor Dreamcoat* (1968) that retells the biblical story of Joseph in colloquial modern English. Much of the music reflected the simplified-jazz styles of earlier pieces for children, such as Herbert Chappell's *The Daniel Jazz* (1963) and Michael Hurd's *Jonah-Man Jazz* (1966), both indirect descendents from the jazz-influenced *West Side Story*. But there was more in *Joseph* – particularly a diversity of style that ranged from the parody of Elvis Presley in the 'Song of the King' (marked '1957 Rock time' and supplied with idiomatic 'Bop-shu-wah-doo-wah' responses), through the agitated $\frac{7}{8}$ rhythms of 'Who's the Thief' to simple but memorable ballads such as 'Close every door to me' and 'Any dream will do'.

Building on the success of *Joseph*, Tim Rice and Andrew Lloyd Webber embarked on a far more ambitious project – a full-length rock opera based on the biblical account of Christ's last days on earth, *Jesus Christ Superstar* (1970). It was originally released as a recording because producers were initially too nervous of staging a rock treatment of such a sensitive issue. The album attracted so much acclaim that the work was staged in New York in 1971 (and in London the next year). It was clear that pre-releasing the music generated an enormous appetite for the show itself, and Lloyd Webber habitually followed this pattern in his many later works.

Some of the most successful musical features of *Joseph* resurface in *Superstar*, especially short ostinato figures in asymetric metres, such as those in Example 58. The second of these is sung by the money-changers in the Temple as they harangue the worshippers. After Jesus throws them out he is beseiged by the lame and ill seeking to be cured. They are as out of control as the money-lenders, and Lloyd Webber uses the same rhythm – but notice how the free inversion shown in Example 58(c) ends with a more desperate cry of 'Christ' on a top E. Notice, too, how the entirely syllabic setting and urgent, repetitive rhythms enhance the repetitions and hardness of the entirely monosyllabic text of Examples 58(b) and (c).

The terms 'rock opera' and 'rock musical' are often considered interchangeable, but it is perhaps more useful to think of a rock musical as a theatrical work which, like most musicals, includes sections of spoken dialogue, while a rock opera is constructed from almost continuous music.

Joseph was such a success that the school mounted a second performance in central London. This attracted a favourable review in the national press which led to a further performance of an enlarged version of the work, a recording and publication – thus launching Lloyd Webber's career as one of the best-known writers of modern musicals. *Joseph* was altered and enlarged several more times, eventually becoming a highly successful full-length musical. There have been at least 12 different cast albums of the work.

Example 58   Andrew Lloyd Webber
Jesus Christ Superstar

(a)
Try not   to get   wor - ried,

try not   to turn on   to   prob - lems...

(b)
Roll   on   up   for the price is   right,
Come   on   in   for the best   in   town.

(c)
Will   you   touch, will you mend me Christ?
Won't   you   touch, will you heal   me Christ?

The cabaret style of Potiphar's Song (one of the later additions to *Joseph*) is also reflected in Herod's Song in *Superstar*:

> So you are the Christ, you're the great Jesus Christ,
> Prove to me that you're divine – change my water into wine.

Lloyd Webber sets the mocking insults in ragtime style, with tuba doubling the bass (as in early recordings of jazz), and adds the directions 'razz-ma-tazz' and 'honky-tonk' to the piano part.

References to early rock-and-roll styles are also apparent, such as the syncopated riff over alternating chords of A^7 and D^7 shown in Example 59(a). Sung in three-part harmony to the words 'What's the buzz? Tell me what's a-happening', it captures the spirit of an early rock backing-vocal. Even more closely related to *Joseph* is the oily motif shown in Example 59(b) – compare it with Example 59(c) which comes from the start of 'Who's the thief?' in the earlier work. But whereas in *Joseph* this motif is harmonised by a simple chord of D minor and forms the basis of just a single song, in *Superstar* it is harmonised by a half-diminished 7th chord (D–F–A♭–C) and it forms a recurring motif that helps to unify the work. First heard on lead guitar in the opening bars of the overture, it becomes a motto of unalterable destiny – it is the melody sung when the priests of the temple plot the downfall of Jesus ('This Jesus Must Die') and it is the melody sung by Pilate when Jesus is brought to trial.

Example 59 Andrew Lloyd Webber
Jesus Christ Superstar

There are many other ways in which *Jesus Christ Superstar* is a much more developed work than *Joseph*. *Superstar* is scored for much larger vocal and instrumental resources, the latter including a large orchestra, piano, organ and Moog synthesiser, as well as lead guitar, rhythm guitar, bass guitar and drum kit. The rock-group instruments have important (and often fully notated) parts throughout the work and the use of powerful bass-guitar riffs, often featuring open strings, such as those in Example 60, give the work much of its rock-music character.

The contrasts in *Superstar* are also much more vivid, with rapid mood changes from dark to light and from loud to soft. This was also a feature of *Tommy* and of much progressive rock of the time. Although motivic material is seldom developed, Lloyd Webber makes frequent use of repetition, often with different words sung by different characters, for dramatic effect as we have already seen. Particularly telling is the riff in Example 60(a). It is the bass of the opening song, sung by Judas and thereafter associated with Judas. In the second act we hear it (unaccompanied) 39 times in succession, once for each of the 39 counted lashes of Christ that resulted from Judas' betrayal. The song 'I don't know how to love him' sung in the first act by Mary Magdalene, the repentent sinner, is ironically recalled in the second act in a distorted version sung by the suicidal Judas as he realises the enormity of what he has done. The whole of the Crucifixion scene is darkened by repeated falling semitone figures.

Example 60 Andrew Lloyd Webber
Jesus Christ Superstar

One of the most memorable transformations of material between acts is shown opposite. Example 61(a) is sung by Jesus after he throws the money changers out of the Temple. The low tessitura, quiet dynamic, unfinished phrase and plodding crotchets all speak of his weariness:

Example 61 Andrew Lloyd Webber, *Jesus Christ Superstar*

(a) The Temple

Jesus: Af - ter all I've tried for three years, seems like thir - ty... seems like thir - ty...

(b) Gethsemene

Jesus: I will drink your cup of poi - son, Nail me to your cross and beat me – kill me, take me –

Bass guitar

In Act 2 Jesus is alone in the garden of Gethsemene, addressing God, but full of human doubt:

> I'm not as sure as when we started,
> Then I was inspired, now I'm sad and tired,
> Listen surely I've exceeded expectations
> Tried for three years seems like thirty.

The words recall the memory of his weariness in the Temple but, as Jesus comes to accept the inevitability of his destiny, the simple outline of Example 61(a) blossoms into the most ecstatic and operatic moment of the entire work, shown in Example 61(b). The rhythm is given life and the pitch is transposed up a minor 6th to produce a climax on 'cup' (the word used in the biblical account: 'Father let this cup pass from me'). Pulsating inner parts drive up the tension and the texture is thickened by sustained brass, organ, harp and the rock group. Above the entire edifice a glorious counter-melody on oboe and high unison violins cascades in descending sequences with heart-wrenching appoggiaturas (marked *) on almost every strong beat.

Even here the text is redolent of *Joseph* ('Do what you want to me, hate me and laugh at me') but the musical treatment is totally different, and relies on tried-and-tested techniques that had helped contribute to the success of Puccini's Italian operas in the early 20th century. But their inclusion in a rock opera was unprecedented, and there is no denying that the emotional effectiveness of such romantic moments, particularly in contrast to the many other styles of music within the same work, has contributed to the enormous success of Andrew Lloyd Webber's musicals.

When studying Example 61(b) don't be confused by the rich melodic decoration and instrumentation. Both are impressive but the conventional tonality is clearly defined by simple harmonic progressions: V–I in E♭ major in the first two bars, followed by V–I in the relative minor (C minor) in bars 3–4.

Example 62 Andrew Lloyd Webber 'Superstar' motif

Je - sus Christ ___ Sup - er - star, ___

Private study

1. Show how the 'Superstar' motif (Example 62) is adapted to suit various dramatic situations in *Jesus Christ Superstar*.

2. Discuss the integration of music and drama (or dance) in any musical of your choice by Andrew Lloyd Webber.

If you answer question 2 choose your work carefully. Lloyd Webber's later musicals are very varied in construction. For instance, *Cats* is really a suite of separate numbers, linked more by text than music.

Curlew River

Benjamin Britten (1913–76) achieved worldwide fame in 1945 with *Peter Grimes*, which was hailed as the greatest English opera to be written since the death of Purcell, 250 years earlier. His skill in setting the English language to music can be seen in any of his vocal works, but here we have chosen to concentrate on *Curlew River* (1964) since it will introduce us to a number of totally new perspectives on the relationship between music and drama.

During an extended concert tour of the far east in 1956 Britten had heard gamelan music in Bali and traditional Japanese music in Tokyo. Both profoundly influenced many of his later works. One of the pieces he heard in Tokyo was *Sumida-gawa* (Sumida River), a 15th-century Japanese Nō play by Juro Motomasa. The Japanese Nō tradition is an ancient and highly formal type of musical drama, characterised by extreme restraint. By limiting overtly expressive techniques it aims to intensify the emotional depth of the drama, just as the Japanese haiku aims to distil the essence of poetry through formality and brevity, and the garden of a Zen temple seeks to intensify contemplation through little more than irregular rocks on a lawn of raked sand.

Britten's recording of *Curlew River* (made in 1966) is available on CD from Decca, 421 858-2LM. Among more recent recordings, that on Philips 454 469-2PH is a little more costly, but has been very well reviewed. A 'rehearsal score' (with production notes) is published by Faber Music but it is rather expensive (ISBN 0-571-50002-1).

The libretto of *Curlew River* by William Plomer is based on an English translation of *Sumida-gawa*, but the drama is transferred to the fenlands of medieval East Anglia and given a Christian context. This may well have been suggested by the success of one of Britten's most popular works, *Noye's Fludde* (1958), a musical setting of an ancient mystery play about the biblical story of Noah. Like *Curlew River*, it was first performed in the starkly impressive parish church of Orford on the Suffolk marshes. Indeed, Britten described *Curlew River* as a 'parable for church performance', to indicate that it is not intended for the theatre. It was the first of three such church parables that he wrote.

The work begins with an unaccompanied plainsong hymn sung by a group of monks. Their Abbot announces that they have come to tell of a mystery that occurred beside the Curlew River. The monks assume different roles to act out the story. One plays the part of a madwoman, needing to cross the river to seek her lost child. Another plays the part of a ferryman who, as he takes the party across the river, tells how a year ago to the very day, a dying boy had asked to be buried by a nearby shrine. The madwoman realises this was her son and that her search is over. The ferryman guides her to the tomb and the spirit of the child rises from the grave to tell his mother that they will meet in heaven. The madwoman is purged of her madness by the grace of God and the monks go on their way singing the hymn with which the work started.

Such minimal action is typical of the Nō play, and many other aspects of the production reflect that tradition – even the details of the raised acting area (there is no scenery other than a mast and sail). The principal characters sing through masks so that emotion cannot be conveyed by facial expression, only by ritualistic gestures that require yoga-like muscular control. The opening and ending, in which the monks (and instrumentalists) process through the audience to the performance area, are the only naturalistic parts.

The number five is important in Nõ theatre – there are five types of play, five acting skills and five structural elements. Britten reflects this by writing his work for five soloists, all of whom are male (this is also part of the medieval mystery-play tradition which is reflected in *Curlew River*). The role of the madwoman is sung by a tenor. Britten's use of a small chorus (of just eight singers) to comment upon the action also comes from Nõ theatre.

The accompaniment is scored for an unusual ensemble of flute, horn, viola, double bass, harp, percussion and chamber organ. Individual instruments are often associated with particular characters. For instance the madwoman's opening off-stage phrases are sung in canon with the flute (Example 63, second bar), and the flute later develops the same motif into an elaborate, flutter-tongued cadenza for her actual entry. In the central part of the work the flute represents the curlews with which the woman becomes obsessed, and when she finds her son's grave her soliloquy is accompanied only by a canonic flute part.

Although Britten does not attempt to emulate a Japanese style, several features of Nõ music strongly colour *Curlew River*. Most notable is the use of exaggerated vocal *portamento* (indicated by the diagonal lines in Example 63, bar 1). Also characteristic are the thin textures and often linear style of the music. The percussion instruments (five drums of indefinite pitch, five small bells and a gong) also strongly suggest far-eastern colour.

But most characteristic of all is Britten's use of rhythm. He hardly ever uses time signatures in this work and there is seldom a sense of regular metre. Unmeasured monodic chant plays an important role (as it does in Nõ music) and in places some parts move at a different tempo to others. Such rhythmic flexibility precludes the use of a conductor so the musicians have to work as a small chamber ensemble, listening very carefully to all the parts around them. Conventional barlines are used only when everyone arrives simultaneously at the start of a bar and Britten invented a special 'curlew' sign (⌒) that he used over notes which can be extended or curtailed in order to regain precise ensemble. Another special symbol (⊣‖) is used to indicate a tremolando with a gradual, unmeasured accelerando. When used on a small drum the effect is again very redolent of far-eastern music. Even more characteristic of the far east (and this time of gamelan music) is the use of heterophonic textures in which different versions of the same melody are heard simultaneously – see Example 64(a). In fact true choral polyphony is heard only twice in the work, both times used for key texts, thus creating important points of structural focus.

Intense musical integration is evident throughout *Curlew River* – it is built on constant transformation and recall of musical ideas. The motif shown in the first bar of Example 63 dominates the work and becomes the 'curlew motif'. The contours of the opening plainsong hymn are also often present – compare Examples 64(b) and (c). Immediately after the latter the plainsong is restated and developed in instrumental heterophony. At the end of the work this pattern is mirrored by further verses of the hymn in vocal heterophony, leading to Example 64(d) and then to a return to simple monophonic plainsong, to frame and finish the work.

Example 63 Britten, *Curlew River* Entrance of madwoman

Example 64 Britten, *Curlew River* Prologue and Epilogue

Two years before *Curlew River*, Britten's most substantial choral work received its first performance in Coventry Cathedral. The *War Requiem* (1962) was commissioned for a festival celebrating the opening of an excitingly new building, which replaced the medieval church that had been destroyed by bombs in the second world war. Britten seized the opportunity to write a sacred but decidely non-liturgical work that reflected his own pacifist view of a hatred of war and mass slaughter. To do this, he created a colossal work which amalgamates three planes of music:

✦ soprano soloist, choir and symphony orchestra perform one of the greatest and most dramatic musical settings of the Latin Requiem Mass (the Mass for the Dead)

✦ between the movements of this Mass, and eventually combined with it, tenor and bass soloists supported by a separate chamber orchestra perform a cycle of songs about the horror of war to texts by the war poet, Wilfred Owen

✦ above both of these planes (and also eventually combined with both) a boys' choir supported by organ provides a detached and distant reminder of a mystic world in which neither church ritual nor even warfare matter any longer.

Of the many CDs of the *War Requiem* one of the finest is still the 1969 recording by Giulini, available from BBC Music Legends/ IMG Artists on BBCL 40462.

Boosey and Hawkes have reissued a full score of the *War Requiem* in their series 'The Masterworks Library' at a reasonable price.

A very thorough account of the work can be found in the Cambridge Music Handbook *Britten: War Requiem* by Mervyn Cooke (1996). Cambridge University Press, ISBN: 0-521-44633-3.

The plan of unity through diversity even extended to Britten's intention that the three soloists for the first performance should come from the three countries that suffered the worst loss of lives during the war – Britain, Germany and Russia. He quoted Owen on the title page of the score: 'My subject is War, and the pity of War'. We do not have the space to discuss this work here, but some useful resources are listed in the margin. Widely regarded as one of the greatest choral works of the 20th century, it is substantial and complex, and it offers many opportunities to explore the relationship between words and music in a concert work.

Electro-acoustic music

Bernstein's own 1972 recording of *Mass* is available on CD from Sony Classical, SM2K 63089. A vocal score of the work is published by Schirmer.

The use of modern poetry to comment on a traditional liturgical text is also a feature of Bernstein's *Mass* (1971). Sub-titled 'A theatre piece for singers, players and dancers', it is about a celebration of the Mass in which the congregation starts questioning matters of religion, and eventually the priest himself suffers a crisis of faith. Conceived on a colossal scale, the work requires a pit orchestra of strings and percussion with concert and rock organs, a costumed stage orchestra of woodwind, brass, electric guitars and synthesisers, a large mixed choir, gospel singers, solo singers, a boys' choir and dancers. Sections on prerecorded four-channel tape at first alternate and then combine with the live performance.

African Sanctus is recorded on Philips CD 426 055-2PM and a score is published by Warner/Chappell.

Pre-recorded music is equally essential in *African Sanctus* (1977) by David Fanshawe (born 1942). This unorthodox, cross-cultural setting of the Mass is based on recordings of traditional African music made by the composer on a four-year trip to the continent, and which are heard in counterpoint with music for a live chorus, soprano soloist, piano, guitars and drums. Each of its 13 movements represents a place visited by Fanshawe on his journey (eg Cairo in the Kyrie and northern Uganda in the Sanctus).

Stimmung (1968) was written by the German composer Karlheinz Stockhausen (born 1928). The title can mean either tuning or mood, and both meanings are reflected in the work. It is composed for six vocalists with microphones, and the text consists of names, words, days of the week in German and English, and excerpts from German and Japanese poetry.

It introduces us to a new type of relationship between words and music, because in *Stimmung* words are used as much for their sound as their meaning. The work could well be described as minimalist, since it depends on the transformation of a very limited amount of material over a long period of time. The principal material is the series of overtones on B♭ shown in Example 65, which outlines a major 9th chord. And for the entire 75 minutes no other chord is heard. The singers are required to alter the shapes of their vocal cavities to produce different resonances (and thus different proportions of overtones), gradually moving closer to the exact pitches of Example 65 in successive sections. If this sounds complicated, try singing 'ah–ee– ay–oh–oo' to a continuous note. As your mouth changes shape for each vowel, listen carefully to the changing timbres.

Example 65

The graphic score of *Stimmung* consists of four elements: a formal plan, six pages of syllabic models, six pages of magic names and a page of poetry.

The formal plan maps out 51 sections of unfixed duration that specify which harmonic of B♭ is to be sung, which singer is to lead the section and which sections involve the use of magic names.

The syllabic models are patterns of nonsense syllables, sometimes with words such as the days of the week, sometimes 'hallelujah' and so on. They are notated with international phonetic symbols to indicate the precise sound required and numbers that specify overtones. The rhythm of the syllabic pattern is also indicated. Each model is introduced by one singer and repeated periodically until that model is assimilated by the other singers. Once the leading singer is satisfied that it is fully established the incantation passes to another singer and a new model is introduced, initially overlapping with the previous one.

A superb recording of *Stimmung* by Sing-circle is available on Hyperion CDA66115. The score is published by Universal Edition (UE 14805), but you may find it is easier to follow the work by ear alone.

Each singer has a sheet of 11 'magic names' drawn from various world religions (Isis, Jesus, Allah, Indra, Shiva, Zeus, Mixcoatl and so on). In 29 of the 51 sections at least one of these names (chosen at random) must be introduced by a singer, once a model has been established. After a singer has called a name, it is repeated in the same tempo and with the same articulation as the model until it is fully integrated with the model itself.

There are four poems which are spoken at various intervals. The singer may take a word or syllable from these and treat it in the manner of a magic name.

This bald description of the construction of *Stimmung* cannot do justice to its intimate and deeply meditative quality – it needs to be heard. The continually transforming chant-like texture reflects the enthusiasm for transcendental meditation in the 1960s, but it also looks forward to the minimalist styles of later decades.

Music theatre

The term 'music theatre' is sometimes used in a wide sense to include staged works such as musicals, but usually the term refers to works that involve some sort of dramatic presentation although not necessarily one that is fully staged and acted. One of the most famous music-theatre works in the early 20th century was Schoenberg's *Pierrot Lunaire* (1912), in which the singer delivers the 21 songs in costume and make-up, aided by the use of facial expression and mime.

In 1967 concern about the problems of getting new works of music performed led two British composers, Peter Maxwell Davies and Harrison Birtwistle (both born in 1934), to create a small ensemble for the performance of contemporary music. The Pierrot Players took the first part of their name from the unusual instrumental resources used in *Pierrot Lunaire* (flute, clarinet, violin, cello and piano, to which they added percussion) and chose the second part ('players') to suggest theatre as well as music. In 1969 they gave the world premières of two new music-theatre works by Maxwell Davies, *Eight Songs for a Mad King* (for singer and ensemble) and *Vesalii Icones* (for nude male dancer and ensemble).

Eight Songs for a Mad King is a disturbing and moving portrayal of madness (and thus in this respect it is comparable with *Curlew River*). The king is George III, although it is never really clear whether the singer is meant to be the British monarch or someone under the delusion of being the king. Randolph Stow's text is based on the story that George III sought relief from his dementia by teaching caged birds to sing, and it incorporates sentences recorded as having actually been spoken by the king.

On stage the flute, clarinet, violin and cello players sit inside huge cages, representing the birds with whom the king has extended dialogues (the score for the third song is even laid out like a bird-cage, with vertical as well as horizontal staves). The players have clockwork bird-song devices to operate at various points in the work while the percussionist, who represents the king's keeper, is also required to play various bird-call instruments and a didgeridoo.

In the first song the king believes he is a prisoner of one of his own sentries – 'my kingdom is locks and slithering'. Then, as he walks in the country he envisions strangling ivy turning into pythons. The third song is addressed to the flute, which he sees personified as a young courtier – until he remembers that his courtiers are terrified of him. Then he dreams of relief from his responsibilities and imagines himself on the Thames, which he asks to 'evacuate my people'. The fifth song is addressed to the imaginary Esther, whom he thinks he has married after divorcing the queen – 'they say that some other woman is my wife'. The words of the next song ('I am nervous. I am not ill') are taken from the real king's own monologues. The climax of the work occurs in the seventh song, which we shall discuss in detail later. At the start of the final song the king announces he is dead and then, as sanity painfully returns, realises that he is alive and has still to suffer more. 'He will die howling, howling' are the king's final words as his keeper metaphorically beats him off-stage with leather straps on a bass drum.

An excerpt from *Vesalii Icones* can be found in *Sound Matters* by David Bowman and Bruce Cole, published by Schott.

A recording of *Eight Songs for a Mad King*, conducted by the composer, is available on CD from Unicorn-Kanchana, DKPCD 9052. A score of the work is published by Boosey and Hawkes (HPS 1170).

Various extended instrumental techniques are required from the players. For instance the pianist must sometimes pluck the strings and the clarinettist is required to have sufficient flexibility of embouchure to play chords and wide, sweeping portamento parts that sound almost like a police siren. But the most extreme techniques are reserved for the singer, who needs to be able to perform chords (using vocal harmonics) and have a range of over four octaves in order to produce the yelps, screeches, howls and groans that portray the agony of the king's condition. The part itself freely switches between rhythmic speech, conventional song and the half-way stage of *sprechgesang* (speech-song) in which pitches are more indefinite.

Just as the text quotes the king's own words, Maxwell Davies frequently quotes 18th-century music in the work. This is most obvious in No. 7 ('Country Dance') which begins with an extended parody of 'Comfort ye my people' from the king's favourite work, *Messiah*. It begins with Handel's opening ritornello transformed into a smoochy jazz style with stride-piano bass and swung quavers. The singer enters, first emulating a female vocalist an octave above Handel's original tenor part, then paranoically switching to the bass register an octave below Handel's original. The trill is marked 'in style' but suddenly the king lets forth an enormous whinny 'like a horse'. The phrase ends in despair, an octave lower still with chordal resonances (vocal harmonics) above the very low notes – there is no comfort in this for the mad king:

Example 66   Peter Maxwell Davies, *Eight Songs for a Mad King*, No. 7 (Country Dance)

Four over-inflated chromatic chords next collapse into a foxtrot in 1920s style, above which the king bawls his fractured memories through a tin megaphone. The juxtaposition of styles is as surreal and unnerving as the king's condition, but the whirligig continues. As the percussionist moves from light drum-kit to thunderous bass drum and gong, and the pianist's increasingly complex chords turn into tone clusters, the king becomes hysterical with repeated cries of 'sin! sin!'. Reaching through the bars of the cage he snatches the violin from its player and strums it wildly to the words 'black vice, intolerable vileness in lanes, by ricks, at courts'. The vocal part (marked *ffff* regal) starts with an inversion of the falling 3rd of 'comfort ye' – just as the words have become an inversion of the original text about comfort. This is supported by the piano with a new transformation of Handel's music. Starting in the style of Liszt, the thickly-doubled chords then turn into enormous clusters played with the forearms and the percussion becomes overpowering as the work reaches its climax and the king smashes the violin.

Let us leave the last words to the composer: 'This is not just a killing of a bullfinch – it is a giving-in to insanity, and a ritual murder by the king of a part of himself, after which, at the beginning of the last song, he can announce his own death.'

Minimalist vocal music

The *Song for Athene* by John Tavener (born 1944) that brought the funeral of Princess Diana to its dramatic close in 1997 unwittingly introduced contemporary art music to a larger audience than at any other time in history. It also reminds us how circumstances of time and place can profoundly affect the reception of new music.

The Lamb (1985) is a sacred song for four-part choir by Tavener, which sets to music an 18th-century poem by William Blake. It is truly minimal in that all the music derives from its simple opening phrase of four pitches. This is immediately repeated, but do you notice that the alto part is an exact inversion of the same notes, creating a brief moment of bitonality?

Example 67   John Tavener, *The Lamb*

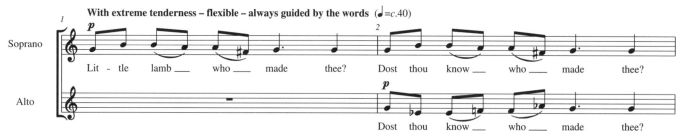

The simultaneous use of a melody and its own mirror image is used to express the rhetorical question asked of the lamb – 'Dost thou know who made thee?' – the only possible answer is shown to be the altos' reflection of the question itself. The next phrase moves forward with entirely syllabic word-setting. Bar 3 is formed from the first four soprano notes above, to which are added the only new pitches from the alto part (Eb, F♮ and Ab) of bar 2. Bar 4 then restates bar 3 in retrograde motion:

Example 68   John Tavener, *The Lamb*

Example 69   John Tavener, *The Lamb*

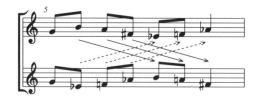

In the next phrase the sopranos repeat the melody of bars 3–4 to new words, accompanied by an exact inversion of the same pitches in the alto part. This permits the interchange of pitches shown in Example 69 – essentially the intensity of a serial-like technique in the context of a tonal familiarity that continues to centre around the unharmonised note of G. Tavener uses both textural and tonal contrast for the last two phrases, but not melodic change. The pitches of bar 1 are presented four times in a homophonic texture in which all four parts are heard for the first time. The harmonisation throws new light on what had previously seemed to be a simple tune in G major, because all the notes are from the aeolian mode on E (like E minor, but with D♮ instead of D♯) giving the music a more wistful quality. The repetitions are not exact – the increasing use of rhythmic augmentation effectively slows the pace of the music for the end of the verse.

A recording and an aural test based on the second verse of this work are included in *Aural Matters* by David Bowman and Paul Terry. A complete recording is available on Collins Classics 1270-2.

After such intensity in only ten bars the second verse is a simple rescoring of the first verse: *tutti* octaves instead of unison trebles, pairs of voices (soprano/tenor and alto/bass) in octaves instead of just trebles and altos, and the final four lines are an exact repeat of the music for the final four lines of the first verse.

Film music

Some of the most dramatic modern music can be heard on film soundtracks. We have outlined the key issues about film music on pages 22–23, but the topic is a larger one than we have space to discuss here. Studying film music can be frustrating since the only scores usually available are simple arrangements of the main themes from the film, and these will tell you little about how the music is used dramatically. Even CDs need to be treated with caution since they often contain specially-arranged excerpts. The best way is to watch the film itself and use your ears to spot how motifs identify characters, how instrumentation and textures create mood, how style conveys a sense of time and place, and so forth. Many of the techniques used in film music are similar to those we have already discussed in the context of other types of music. The resources listed in the margin, although not designed for the OCR specification, contain some helpful material.

A 14-page section on music for film and television is included in *A Student's Guide to AS Music for the Edexcel Specification* by Paul Terry and David Bowman. *Rhinegold Publishing Ltd.* ISBN: 0-946890-90-0. This is based on six extracts that are available in score and on CD in Edexcel's *New Anthology of Music* (published by Peters Edition).

Private study

1. Compare the portrayals of madness in *Eight Songs for a Mad King* and *Curlew River*.

2. Can a rock musical really capture the spirit of modern pop music or is its style always likely to sound years out of date?

3. Watch a film that is famous for its soundtrack (such as *Titanic* or *Planet of the Apes*) and make precise notes on how music illustrates conveys the drama in any one scene that you find particularly effective.

Sample questions

In the exam there will be three questions on your chosen topic, of which you must answer one. Always answer by referring to the composers and precise works you have studied.

Set A

1. Name a work from this period that you feel shows an unusual approach to word-setting and describe the techniques used.

2. In what ways does *West Side Story* differ from most other musicals that came after it?

3. Discuss the use of **either** minimalism **or** electro-acoustic techniques in vocal works of the late 20th century.

Set B

1. Justify the claim that some of the greatest settings of the English language are to be found in the works of Benjamin Britten.

2. Show how **either** film music **or** music theatre has become an important genre in the second half of the 20th century.

3. Outline ways in which composers during the period 1955–2000 have adopted new approaches to the setting of sacred texts. Refer to at least two works in your answer.

Topic 5: 1945 onwards (solo song)

Introduction

This topic spans two contrasting musical traditions:

✦ art songs, mainly intended for performance at song recitals in small concert halls

✦ pop songs, usually intended to be heard on recordings although also sometimes performed live.

Before 1900, art songs were usually performed in the home by accomplished amateurs. For instance, early-17th century lute songs (see pages 50–51) and early-19th century lieder (see pages 87–97) were intended primarily for domestic performance of this kind.

Be sure to read the 'Introduction to the age of technology' on pages 108–109.

In the first half of the 20th century, the rise of broadcasting, recording and cinema created a huge market of listeners who preferred to be entertained by professional musicians, rather than making their own music. The resulting cult of the recording star is seen in various styles of music, and especially in pop music.

The English song tradition

Although Britain produced a succession of great composers in the 15th to 17th centuries, new music in the following 200 years was dominated by visiting and immigrant musicians from Europe rather than by native talent. However, an 'English music revival' began in the early years of the 20th century, most notably in small-scale genres such as the solo song. Within a few decades composers such as Vaughan Williams, Finzi, Ireland and Warlock had created a well-crafted and uniquely modern English song repertoire. The lyrics of these songs were often drawn from the works of English poets such as Shakespeare or Thomas Hardy – and the nostalgic verses of A. E. Housman were a particular favourite, lending themselves to musical settings in which folk-like modality is partnered by yearning late-romantic harmony.

For more on Britten, see pages 124–126.

Benjamin Britten (1913–1976) studied music under Frank Bridge and John Ireland. Although his style was more cosmopolitan than that of his teachers, vocal music played a significant role in Britten's output. Many of his songs are grouped into cycles (sets of related songs) and were composed for particular singers – most notably the tenor, Peter Pears, often with Britten himself as the accompanist at the first performance.

The songs range from light-hearted settings of poems by Britten's friend W. H. Auden (*Cabaret Songs*, 1937–9), through operatic settings of poetry from France (*Les Illuminations*, 1939) and Italy (*Seven Sonnets of Michelangelo*, 1940), to sombre settings of verses by Hardy (*Winter Words*, 1953) and Blake (*Songs and Proverbs of William Blake*, 1965). Most of these cycles are for voice and piano, although *Les Illuminations* and the *Serenade for Tenor, Horn and Strings* (1943) are orchestral song cycles, while *Songs from the Chinese* (1957) has guitar accompaniment and the *Eight Folksong Arrangements* of 1976 are scored for voice and harp.

Two important features of Britten's vocal writing are:

✦ A declamatory style of text setting that mirrors perfectly the rhythms of spoken English. This has often been compared to the style of word-setting used by Purcell nearly 300 years earlier – a composer whom Britten studied and admired.

✦ An ability to create a distinctive and readily identifiable mood for each song that immediately gets to the heart of its poetic meaning.

Both of these points are illustrated in Example 70, in which the leaps of 'the wild cataract' are reflected in cascading horn triplets that increase in excitement as the singer challenges the brass soloist to 'Blow, bugle, blow, set the wild echoes flying'. The direction *senza misura* ('without beat') indicates that the dialogue between the two soloists should be in free time, like a cadenza, rather than being strictly metrical. It is supported by an almost imperceptibly quiet buzz of strings trilling in five-part harmony.

The many recordings of Britten's Serenade include those sung by Ian Bostridge on EMI 556183-2 and by Peter Pears (conducted by the composer) on London 436395-2 and on Decca 425996-2. A miniature score of the work is published by Boosey and Hawkes.

Example 70 Benjamin Britten, *Serenade for Tenor, Horn and Strings: Nocturne* ('The splendour falls on castle walls')

This example illustrates two other common features of Britten's music – melodic ideas based on triadic figures, and a harmonic style that is often clearly tonal (and, in this passage, purely diatonic) although the chords are enriched with added notes and a tonic pedal on E♭.

Each of the texts Britten chose for the songs in the Serenade deals with a different aspect of the night. The fourth is a setting of a grim

15th-century poem from Yorkshire called the 'like-wake dirge' – anonymous verses that were recited during a night-time watch over a dead body.

Britten captures the eerie mood from the outset by setting most of the first verse (bars 1–5 *below*) without accompaniment:

Example 71   Benjamin Britten, *Serenade for Tenor, Horn and Strings: Dirge* ('This ae nighte')

Once again, Britten's melody is triadic – the vocal part is based on a descending chord of G minor, decorated with slithering chromatic semitones (G–A♭–G and D–C♯–D) that bring out the spooky quality of the text. Notice how Britten starts this tune very high in the tenor's range, resulting in an almost unwordly timbre at a quiet dynamic. The melody descends throughout each verse, which is then joined to the next by a ghostly *portamento* (indicated by a diagonal line) as the tenor slides up an octave to regain top G.

Britten reflects the obsessive nature of the text by setting it as an *ostinato* – an 'obstinately' repeating pattern. The opening six bars are heard nine times in succession, once for each verse of the poem. By themselves, they make the G-minor tonality crystal clear. But just before the end of the first verse (at cue 14) the cellos and double basses enter with a new theme, in a lurching rhythm and in an entirely different key. The result is bitonality – two different keys at the same time.

Each of the other accompanying parts enters in turn with this new theme, gradually building-up a fugal texture, and each enters in its own key, resulting in polytonality – the use of several different keys at the same time. The part-writing becomes increasingly dense until the horn joins in the fugal texture for a central climax at the point where the poem warns that the soul of the deceased will be tested by 'purgatory fire'. Finally, parts drop away until verse nine mirrors the opening by ending without any accompaniment other than a few isolated bass notes.

The original recording of *Songs and Proverbs of William Blake* by Fischer-Dieskau, with Britten at the piano, is available on Decca 417428, although it is part of a three CD-set (with Britten's opera *Billy Budd*) and thus rather expensive. A score of the song cycle is published by Faber Music.

Britten's *Songs and Proverbs of William Blake* were written for the baritone Dietrich Fischer-Dieskau in 1965. Britten clearly had the German singer's dark, intense sound in mind when writing this cycle of bleak songs. It consists of seven poems by William Blake, the mystic poet of the late-18th century, each preceded by a linked extract from Blake's Proverbs of Hell.

The *Songs and Proverbs of William Blake* form a continuous cycle, in which each number flows seamlessly into the next. It is one of relatively few works in which Britten made use of some aspects of 12-note technique, although nowhere near as systematically as such serialist composers as Schoenberg (see *right*).

The music for the proverbs acts as a ritornello (a short 'returning' passage) in which 12 pitches are arranged as three cells of four notes each:

◆ D♯ – E – G – D (pitches 1–4)
◆ C – C♯ – F♯ – B (pitches 5–8)
◆ G♯ – A – B♭ – F (pitches 9–12).

The notes in each cell are freely repeated, in varying orders of pitch, before the music moves on to the next cell. Also the 12-note series is at first heard only in the piano accompaniment. The opening of the first proverb, showing the first appearance of the first cell, is given in Example 72(a). Notice how the vocal part (which is marked 'recitative') is simply a monotone in free time – it is not aligned to the tempo of the piano part, although Britten makes use of the 'curlew' sign (explained on page 125) at points where the singer must adjust the length of a note in order to synchronise with the accompaniment. The grace note at the end of each phrase anticipates the pitch of the reciting note for the next phrase.

As the cycle progresses, the vocal part gradually absorbs the note row. In the third song, 'A Poison Tree' all 12 pitches of the piano part in the ritornello are present in the vocal line, although Britten again treats the serial process freely, changing the position of some pitches, as shown on the first stave of Example 72 (b). Look at the second stave of this example and notice how, when this new order is inverted, Britten avoids mathematically precise inversion at the point where the words 'I told it not' are repeated:

Serialism

Serialism developed in the 1920s as a way of giving order to atonal music, in which there is no sense of key to give structure to a piece, as there is in tonal music. Serialism is particularly associated with Schoenberg and his pupils Berg and Webern.

In its simplest form, all 12 pitches in the octave are used in a specific order called a series that forms the basic musical material of the composition. To avoid giving prominence to any particular note, each one is used only once in the series.

This series can be used in its original order (the prime order), or backwards ('retrograde motion'), or in inversion, or in retrograde inversion. All four orderss can be transposed to start on any of the 12 semitones in an octave, giving 48 possible permutations of the basic series.

The notes of the series can also be used simultaneously to form chords – although 12-note music is often seen as primarily a contrapuntal style, in which serial melodies are combined, often in various types of canon.

Example 72 Benjamin Britten, *Songs and Proverbs of William Blake*: (a) Proverb I, (b) 'A Poison Tree'

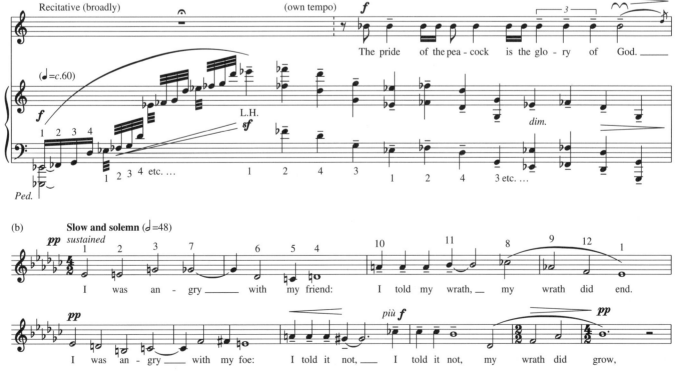

The fourth song is a setting of Blake's famous poem *The Tyger*. Britten treats this as the scherzo of the cycle – a fast and furious song in which the poet's questions tumble over each other in a breathless frenzy. Notice the dissonant chords made from five adjacent pitches in bars 3–5 *below*. These are known as 'tone clusters' and they play a prominent role in the accompaniment to this song. However, Britten has no use for the note row in *The Tyger* – the song is clearly rooted in B major, to which is added the characteristic raised fourth degree (E♯) of the lydian mode.

Example 73   Benjamin Britten, *Songs and Proverbs of William Blake*: 'The Tyger'

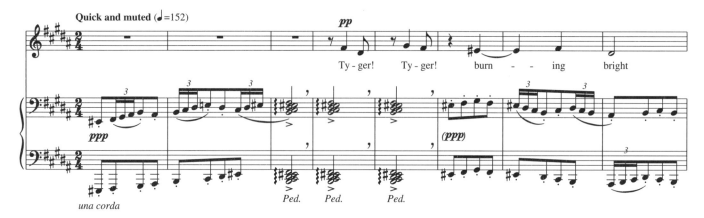

However, Britten later returns to his note row. Near the end of the cycle, in Proverb VII, the full series in its original form occurs both melodically in the vocal part and (by means of the process known as 'verticalisation') harmonically in the piano part – the two versions symbolically combine at the words 'To see the World in a grain of sand'. Notice how, even here, Britten repeats and doubles pitches from the row in his very free interpretation of serialism:

Example 74   Benjamin Britten, *Songs and Proverbs of William Blake*: Proverb VII

Proverb VII

As at the start

To see a World in a Grain of Sand,   And a Heaven in a Wild Flower,   Hold In-fin-i-ty

The first six volumes of Britten's folksong arrangements are published by Boosey and Hawkes. There are many fine recordings, including a bargain-priced double CD from Naxos (8.557220-21), but the best way of getting to know these songs is to sing them yourself.

In addition more than 100 original songs, Britten produced at least 50 arrangements of folksongs (some are perhaps more accurately described as traditional songs). Since they are arrangements of existing material, the style of these songs is tonal and most have extraordinarily inventive piano accompaniments. For example, the third volume (published in 1947) includes:

✦ *The Plough Boy* – a melody by the classical composer William Shield, to which Britten adds a delightfully chugging accompaniment with a very high countermelody in imitation of the boy's cheeky whistling.

- ✦ *Sweet Polly Oliver* – a traditional tune that Britten ingeniously treats in canon.

- ✦ *The Miller of Dee* – a minor-key folksong to which Britten adds a 'perpetual motion' ostinato to suggest the churning of the mill wheels.

- ✦ *The foggy, foggy dew* – a Suffolk folksong to which Britten adds the most delicate of chordal accompaniments in order that the naughtily suggestive lyric can make make its point with utmost clarity.

- ✦ *O Waly, Waly* – a famous folksong from Somerset ('The water is wide I cannot get o'er') that Britten supplies with a sonorous but subtle accompaniment full of poignant diatonic dissonance.

The American song tradition

There are several parallels between the work of Britten and that of the American composer Aaron Copland (1900–1990). Both wrote music for the stage and screen, both wrote new music that had a wide appeal as well as other works that were sometimes perceived as modernistic and difficult, and both were deeply interested in music education. And Copland, like Britten, produced imaginative arrangements of traditional songs, most notably in his two sets of *Old American Songs*. In fact, the connection doesn't end there, as Peter Pears and Benjamin Britten gave the first performance of the first set of Copland's arrangements, at the Aldeburgh Festival in June 1950. The five songs in the set are:

- ✦ *The Boatmen's Dance* (a minstrel song from 1843)

- ✦ *The Dodger* (a campaign song)

- ✦ *Long Time Ago* (a ballad)

- ✦ *Simple Gifts* (a Shaker song) and

- ✦ *I Bought Me a Cat* (a children's song).

Like Britten's song arrangements, they are simple, tonal, diatonic and exploit the sonorities of the piano, particularly making use of pedal points and ostinato-like figures:

Example 75   Traditional, arranged Copland, *The Boatmen's Dance* (bars 6–12)

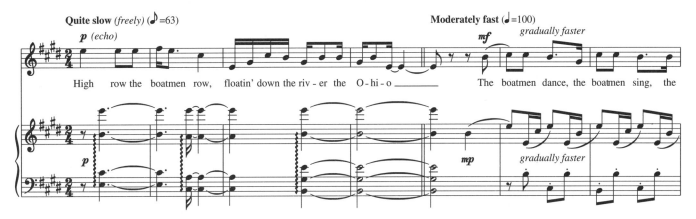

In the United States, the enormous influence of the great popular songwriters of the early 20th century (Irving Berlin, Jerome Kern, George Gershwin and Cole Porter) encouraged singers to include lighter material in their recitals of art songs. It also produced a number of composers, such as Alec Wilder (see page 140) who wrote songs in a 'cross-over' style, drawing heavily on jazz-influenced harmony and the melody-dominated texture of early-20th century popular song.

Although Ned Rorem is best known for his 400 or so songs, he is also an accomplished instrumental composer. In 1976 he won a prestigious Putlitzer Prize for his *Air Music*, which is an orchestral suite.

But one composer stands out in the field of American art song – Ned Rorem (born 1923). In a life devoted to song-writing, he has maintained an austere but lyrical style, rarely affected by such modernist theories as atonality and serialism or significantly influenced by ideas from jazz and popular song. Rorem often uses tonal materials in innovative ways, but much of his music is essentially diatonic and perfectly crafted for the human voice.

Ned Rorem is fascinated by words and has achieved success as a diarist, essayist and reviewer in addition to his work as a composer, although he makes it clear that 'I am a composer who also writes, not a writer who also composes'. However, he has also made it clear that it was not the human voice that attracted him to song writing, but rather the idea of 'poetry as expressed through the voice'. Rorem's influences were Stravinsky and the French composers Debussy, Ravel and Poulenc. His songs are elegant, often understated and sometimes melancholy. Like Britten, he didn't shrink from the prospect of setting to music some of the greatest poetry, including such more modern poets as Auden, Emily Dickenson, Gerald Manley Hopkins and Sylvia Plath.

In 1997 Ned Rorem produced his most ambitious song cycle, *Evidence of Things Not Seen*. It consists of 36 poems by 24 poets and takes the listener on a journey from innocence through experience to solitude and extinction – in essence, the entire span of human existence. It starts with 'Beginnings' – songs about moving forward in life and the 'wistful optimism of love'. The second section, 'Middles', deals with coming of age and the horrors of war. Finally, 'Ends' tackles issues of death – in part inspired by the fate of friends of the composer who had contracted AIDS at a time when it almost invariably led to terminal illness.

Ariel

Ned Rorem wrote *Ariel*, a setting for soprano, clarinet and piano of five poems by Sylvia Plath in 1971. The American poet Sylvia Plath (1932–1963) achieved success at an early age. She wedded the English poet Ted Hughes, but the marriage was unhappy and she tragically committed suicide at the age of 30. Two years later, *Ariel*, a collection of some of her last poems, was published.

Recordings of *Ariel* are available on CD from Phoenix USA (JDT 126) and Orfeo (C620 041A). The score of *Ariel* is published by Boosey and Hawkes.

Ariel was written for one of Rorem's favourite sopranos, Phyllis Curtin. It was first performed by her, with David Glazer (clarinet) and Ryan Edwards (piano), at The Library of Congress in Washington on 26 November 1971.

The last, and most substantial, of the five settings in *Ariel* is of the poem *Lady Lazarus*. The title refers to a woman who has the ability to die and be reborn every decade. Like the proverbial cat, she has nine lives.

Lady Lazarus is an angry, bitter monologue. The first part of the poem dwells on grotesque images such as the spectacle of the woman's worm-eaten flesh being restored to life. In the second part, Lady Lazarus hints that she is the victim of some terrifying demon who seeks to profit from this freakish 'miracle' – and she ends by warning that when Lady Lazarus rises from the ashes, she will consume men as fire consumes oxygen.

Rorem sets the poem with angular melodic lines and driving piano rhythms. He makes full use of extremes of range and requires various extended techniques from the singer, including phrases marked 'half yelled' and, at the end, 'A loud gasp':

Example 76 Ned Rorem, *Ariel*: 'Lady Lazarus' (a) bars 29–31, (b) the final three bars

For much of the 20th century there was a clear division between art music and popular music. However a number of composers, particularly Gershwin, Weill, Bernstein and others working mainly in America, sought to bridge the gap between the two types of music. Alec Wilder (1907–1980) was one of the most successful American composers at blending the lyricism of popular song with the harmonies of jazz and the forms and techniques of European art song. His is a type of 'cross-over' style that takes us much closer to pop and jazz than any of the previous songs we have studied.

Although Wilder's songs have sometimes rejected by jazz fans as lacking in spontaneity, and by art-music critics as devoid of intellectual challenge, his work has appealed to a diverse range of musicians, from Frank Sinatra and the jazz pianist Keith Jarrett to the modern-day counter-tenor, David Daniels. Sinatra was a life-long friend and aupporter, and conducted some of Alec Wilder's instrumental music for recordings made by Columbia – Wilder wrote his last song for Sinatra (*A long night*) in 1980.

Blackberry Winter sung by David Daniels (counter-tenor), accompanied by Craig Ogden (guitar) is available on the CD 'A Quiet Thing' (Virgin Classics 5456002). A score of **25 songs for solo voice** by Alec Wilder is published by Hal Leonard Music.

Blackberry Winter was composed in 1976. It is a perfect miniature consisting of a four-bar introduction followed by the classic type of 32-bar song form (four eight-bar phrases in the form AABA) that had become the mainstay of American popular music in the first half of the 20th century. The fluid rhythms are totally typically of Wilder's style. Notice how descending phrases with narrow intervals reflect the poignant lyric, while repeated intervals of a 4th in the penultimate bar of this example illustrate the frustration of the singer. The 'blackberry winter' of the title is a sudden cold-snap at the start of June in the south of the USA (just after blackberries start to blossom) that briefly interrupts the arrival of summer.

Example 77   Alec Wilder, *Blackberry Winter*: end of the B section (the 'middle eight') plus the start of the final A section

The popularity of 'cross-over' and jazz-fusion styles in the 1960s and 1970s was just one aspect of a reaction against the complexity and dissonance of much modernist art music of the mid-20th century. In the closing decades of the century many composers started to explore how traditional materials, such as diatonic harmony, could be used in entirely new ways.

This type of music is referred to as post-modernism – a term borrowed from the contemporary style of architecture that rejects the cold concrete structures of 1960s' buildings for forms that put the aesthetic and practical needs of people first. In particular, audiences have been attracted by the musical style known as minimalism, in which a small number of musical elements are hypnotically repeated with interlocking rhythms and very slowly changing textures. Early minimalist pieces were often instrumental, but the style has proved adaptable to vocal music – both in songs and in opera.

One of the leading minimalists is the American composer Philip Glass (born 1937). His song cycle *Songs from Liquid Days* dates from 1986 and consists of six substantial songs with accompaniment for instrumental ensemble. Glass asked a number of songwriters from the fields of pop, folk and experimental music to write the lyrics: David Byrne (of Talking Heads), Paul Simon, Suzanne Vega and Laurie Anderson. He also decided that different songs in the cycle should be allocated to different singers, rather than using one voice throughout. The extract *below* shows the repetitive patterns, layered texture and static harmonies typical of much minimalist music.

A CD of *Songs from Liquid Days* is available on Sony Masterworks MK 39564. A score of the work (with accompaniment reduced for piano) is published by Amsco / Music Sales.

In the accompaniment *below* each part has its own repeating rhythm (triplet crotchets, triplet quavers or simple crotchets). These rhythms are superimposed to create what is known as a layered texture.

Example 78   Philip Glass, *Songs from Liquid Days*: 'Freezing', bars 9–16

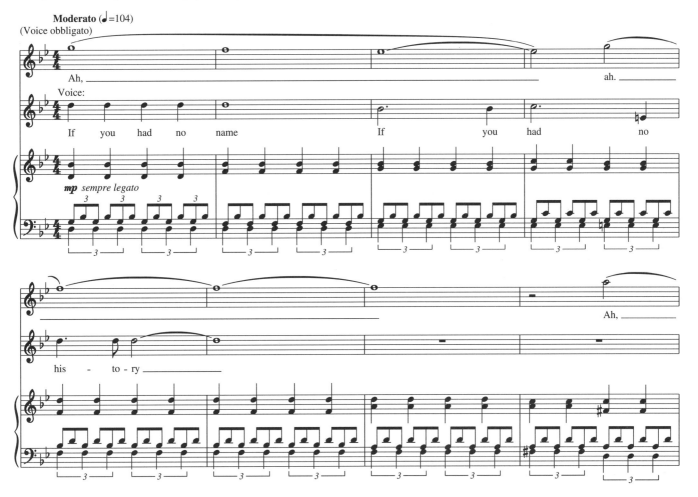

1. Outline some of the ways in which technological advances in the 20th century influenced the development of solo song.

2. Explain what is meant by each of the following: (a) a song cycle, (b) an ostinato, (c) diatonic harmony and (d) serialism.

3. The piano accompaniment in Example 74 (page 136) shows the verticalisation of a note row. What does this mean?

4. What do you think are the most important musical characteristics in the solo songs of Britten?

5. Choose a song by **either** Benjamin Britten **or** Ned Rorem that we have *not* discussed in this chapter and write your own account of the ways in which the music relates to the text.

6. Here is the opening of Stravinsky's final work, a setting of 'The Owl and the Pussy-Cat'. The prime order of the note row on which the song is based is shown by the numbers under the piano part. Explain how the vocal melody (marked 'Canto') relates to the piano part and briefly comment on Stravinsky's use of the row and on his approach to metre and rhythm:

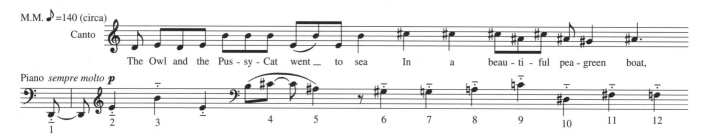

7. Here is another extract from later in the same song. Using the terms retrograde, inversion and transposed, explain how both the vocal melody and the piano part relate to the prime order of the series shown *above*:

Popular song, 1945 to the present day

This is such a large topic that we will have to be rather selective in the areas that we study. Our period starts at the end of the second world war, at a time when amplification had become sufficiently well developed to allow a solo singer, even when gently 'crooning', to be heard over the sound of the large swing bands that had become popular during the war years. The charts of the time were dominated by such American singers as Bing Crosby, Frank Sinatra, Perry Como and Ella Fitzgerald.

However, popular music in America was more diverse than in Britain, partly because the many different radio networks focused on developing regional tastes. Thus country music, blues and gospel developed alongside the mainstream styles of more commercial pop music.

As black singers from the south of the USA moved to industrial cities such as Chicago in search of work, the traditional blues changed from a generally slow and melancholy type of rural music to a harder urban style. Rhythm and blues (R&B), which emerged in the 1940s, later became one of the key influences on rock music. It invested the traditional blues style with the rhythms of jazz and, since it was often used as dance music in the large dance halls of the day, with the relatively loud sounds of drum kit, saxophones and amplified voices and guitars.

Chester Burnett (1910–76) was a black American blues singer, guitarist and harmonica ('mouth organ') player who worked under the name Howlin' Wolf and was famous for keeping alive the impassioned vocal delivery of the Chicago rhythm and blues style. His 1958 recording of *I'm Leaving You* is typical of R&B songs of the 1950s – six repetitions of a 12-bar blues pattern, without modulation, and with the vocal replaced by an instrumental solo in the fourth chorus. There is a two-bar introduction, a two-bar link before the instrumental, and the piece finishes with a coda in which the fade-out indicates that the song was conceived more for recording than for live performance.

The blues influence is apparent not only in the structure of the song, but also in its many blue notes. The jazz influences are in the shuffle rhythm, the improvised guitar lines and the emphasis of 'backbeats' (beats 2 and 4) by the drummer. Howlin' Wolf became extremely influential in shaping British rock 'n' roll in the 1960s and 1970s, the bands that recorded his songs including the Rolling Stones, the Yardbirds, the Grateful Dead, Cream, Little Feet, the Doors and Led Zeppelin.

Rock and roll began when white people started playing rhythm and blues in about 1954, and became instantly popular when Bill Haley's *Rock Around the Clock* was included in the 1955 film, *The Blackboard Jungle*. It combined elements of rhythm and blues with an American country-music style known as rockabilly and the result tended to be more tightly rhythmic than the laid-back jazz-like style of R&B. Rock and roll adopted the instrumentation of rockabilly music, typically consisting of:

✦ a lead-guitar part played on an electric guitar, often with the use of a plectrum and prominent echo effects

✦ a rhythm-guitar part played on an acoustic guitar

✦ a plucked double bass – later to be replaced by the electric bass guitar – often performing a 'walking bass' part in continuous crotchets played with a percussive 'slap' technique

✦ drums, with the bass drum on the downbeats (beats 1 and 3) and the snare drum on the backbeats (beats 2 and 4)

✦ a solo vocal melody, often based on broken-chord figures that derive from the underlying harmony.

Rhythm and blues

'Rhythm and blues' has long been used to refer to the style of black American music that combines elements of jazz and blues and that emerged in the 1940s. However, be aware that more recently the abbreviation 'R&B' has also been used to describe 'Urban' – a combination of soul and hip hop originating in the 1980s.

I'm Leaving You is included on *Moanin' in the Moonlight* – a compilation of Howlin' Wolf tracks that were originally issued on shellac '78' records between 1951 and 1958, and that is now available on CD from Chess/MCA (CHD 5908).

Rock and roll

An extract from Carl Perkins' recording of *Blue Suede Shoes* can be found in *Aural Matters* (Bowman and Terry, published by Schott), pages 87–88. The complete song is also available on a number of bargain-price CDs.

Blue Suede Shoes was recorded in 1955 by the song's composer, Carl Perkins. It uses the harmonies of the 12-bar blues, but like many early rock and roll songs, it extends the pattern to 16 bars (a phrase length much more typical of western song forms) by means of repeating the chord pattern of the first four bars:

$$I^7 - I^7 - I^7 - I^7 - I^7 - I^7 - I^7 - I^7 - IV^7 - IV^7 - I - I - V - IV - I - I$$

The vocal melody moves largely by intervals of a 3rd, following the notes of the underlying chords. The falling minor 3rds at the ends of phrases, marked ⌐‾‾⌐ *below*, are a feature of blues-based styles as, of course, are the blue notes (C♮ and G♮):

Example 79   Carl Lee Perkins, *Blue Suede Shoes*: start of verse 2

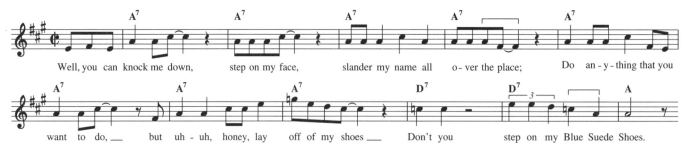

Listen to the recording and notice:

✦ the characteristic 'walking bass' of early rock and roll, formed largely from crotchets that outline the harmonies

✦ the short guitar solos (known as 'licks') that fill the rests at the end of many of the vocal phrases

✦ the 'instrumental' that begins at the end of the extract – this is a verse in which the guitar replaces the singer, giving him a break, just like the saxophone improvisations that alternated with the vocalist in R&B.

A cover is a version of a song that was previously recorded or made popular by another singer.

Just as rhythm and blues was a key influence for the Rolling Stones in the creation of 1960s' British rock music, so rockabilly was an important influence on the Beatles, who recorded covers of several Perkins' songs. Elvis Presley, perhaps the most famous solo pop singer of the 1950s, also recorded a number of rockabilly hits, including a cover of *Blue Suede Shoes* released in March 1956. If you have access to a recording of the Presley version, it make a fascinating comparison – although it didn't prove to be as successful as Perkins' own recording, which was the first song to achieve success in all three of the pop, country, and R&B charts.

Presley was no composer – all of his hits were covers of earlier songs by others or were specially composed by professional song-writers, such as the team of Lieber and Stoller. However, he made an enormous impact as a singer, and could deliver totally convincing performances of a diverse range of solo song – rock and roll, country music, gospel and even sentimental ballads from the 19th-century, such as *It's now or never* – sung to the tune of *O Sole Mio* (the 'cornetto' song!) – and *Love me Tender*, sung to the American traditional melody, *Aura Lee*.

Soft rock

The success of these more sentimental tracks from Presley is a reminder that, alongside the development of rock music, there has long been a taste for more conservative pop songs – a style known as 'middle of the road' (MOR) or 'soft rock'. Even before 1960 the raw edges of rock and roll were being sanded down by the record industry. White singers from northern America, such as Paul Anka, and their British imitators like Cliff Richard, were encouraged to look more in the direction of cute lyrics about high school, cars and puppy love than towards the rebellion of early rock. With this came a more polished musical production, professional arrangements and even symphony orchestra backing.

Typical of the new professionalism is Neil Sedaka, who made his first record in 1956 and who is still performing 50 years on. *Happy Birthday Sweet Sixteen* (1961) has many of the features that brought success in this style – a crisp, up-tempo drum part, vocal harmonies supplied by a backing group, counter-melodies for strings and a final verse that modulates up a semitone for climactic effect.

An extract from *Happy Birthday, Sweet Sixteen* is given on page 89 of *Aural Matters* (Bowman and Terry, published by Schott). The complete song is also available on a number of CD collections.

The form owes nothing to the 12-bar blues, but follows a much more European structure of repeating 16-bar sections, in the pattern AA^1BAA^2. An eight-bar introduction, later modified to form a repeating coda for a final fade, neatly surrounds the entire song. The traditional harmonies use secondary dominants to take the music through a range of related keys, often by means of modulating sequences, with phrases that end in clear cadential patterns. The vocal line is much more scale-based than the triadic vocal writing of earlier rock and roll. Sedaka also made use of the increasingly versatile technology of the day by double-tracking his light tenor voice to form simple harmony parts in 3rds and 6ths.

The Beatles

Until The Beatles' rise to fame in 1962, the UK pop charts had been dominated by American singers or their British imitators. Even The Beatles began by spending five years learning their craft through performing songs by Americans such as Chuck Berry and The Everly Brothers. Significantly, one of their greatest influences was Buddy Holly, who wrote his own songs – rather than Elvis Presley, who did not.

Although the music of The Beatles was dominated by the work of Lennon and McCartney, the concept of a group working creatively together, rather than a solo singer accompanied by a backing group, had an immediate and long-lasting impact. So, too, did their image of carefully designed suits, their gimmick of occasional falsetto notes at climaxes, sung with a shake of their mop-head hair styles, and the paradox of a near-hysterical cult following combined with an innocent charm that appealed to a record-buying generation of mums and dads. All of this was avidly exploited by the rapidly growing medium of television.

The early musical style of The Beatles is well illustrated in their second single, *Please Please Me*, released in January 1963. It uses the (by then) common line-up of electric lead, rhythm and bass guitars, plus drums, to which is added a harmonica ('mouth organ') solo played by John Lennon.

A recording of *Please Please Me* is available on Parlophone CDP 7 46435 2. Transcribed scores of all The Beatles' tracks are available in *The Beatles Complete Scores*, published by Northern Songs (NO90548) and available from Music Sales.

The song is based around the descending stepwise melody shown on the first stave of Example 80 (*overleaf*). This is a 'hook' – a short melodic idea in a pop song, designed to be memorable. This two-bar hook occurs at least once in every section of the song. The numbers in this diagram show the number of bars in each section, and the position of the hook is indicated by shaded boxes:

Intro	Verse 1	Chorus	Verse 2	Chorus	Bridge	Link	Verse 3	Chorus	Coda
4	8	8	8	8	8	2	8	8	5

Instead of a 'fade-out' ending (sometimes called an 'outro') the song concludes with a coda that brings it to a definitive end with two perfect cadences.

In the verses, Lennon's vocal melody is accompanied by a simple but very effective backing vocal from McCartney – just an inverted tonic pedal on E. In contrast, though the chorus consists of an antiphonal dialogue between Lennon on the one hand, and McCartney and George Harrison on the other.

Notice how the falling scale of the verse is balanced by the rising semitones of the chorus, just as the second-beat openings of the verses contrast with the anacrusic openings of the chorus:

Example 80   Lennon and McCartney, *Please Please Me*: (a) start of verse, (b) start of chorus

The harmony is noteworthy, too. Even in early songs like this, The Beatles did not rely on the 'three-chord trick' (harmonisation with just chords I, IV and V), adopted by some less accomplished guitarists. After the static tonic chord at the start of the verses, the vocalist's breathing place in the fourth bar is filled with rapid harmonic movement, including a surprising detour to a bluesy chord of ♭III (G major), while the chorus sees the use of secondary triads in the progression IV–ii–vi–IV–I–IV–V–I. Another harmonic twist occurs at the very end of the song, where chord ♭VI is used as the approach to the final cadance (C–B–E).

The use of unusual chords and unexpected chord progressions became as much a feature of Lennon and McCartney's work as their mastery of memorable musical lines and enthusiam to explore techniques such as modality. Examples include the dorian mode melody of *Eleanor Rigby*, the use of the mixolydian mode in *She Said She Said*, the use of a chorus in the key of the flattened leading note in *Penny Lane*, and the so-called 'double plagal' progression that so assiduously avoids the dominant (I, ♭VII, IV, I) in the final section of *Hey Jude*.

By the mid-1960s The Beatles had made a conscious decision to explore new creative concepts in popular music. Their producer, the classically trained oboist, George Martin, played an important role in this – he scored the delicate string quartet backing in *Yesterday* (1965) and supervised the complex multi-track recording of *Rubber Soul* (1965) – an album devised as a studio production containing material impossible to reproduce in live performance. The restrained slow ballads and use of unusual instruments, such as the sitar in the waltz-time opening of *Norwegian Wood* were the precursors of a range of experimental techniques used in the albums *Revolver* (1966) and *Sgt. Pepper's Lonely Hearts Club Band* (1967).

For more on *Sgt. Pepper's Lonely Hearts Club Band*, see page 120.

The success of The Beatles established a world-wide market for British pop music and many other groups followed their model. For example, the songs written by Ray Davies for the Kinks, such as *Waterloo Sunset* and *Dedicated Follower of Fashion*, generally have a tight verse-and-chorus format, with a strong melodic line and often a suggestion of 'sing-along' music hall style – as do the hits of The Small Faces, such as *Lazy Sunday* and *Itchycoo Park*.

The group Procul Harum (Latin for 'far beyond these things') had a huge hit in the summer of 1967 with *A Whiter Shade of Pale* – a marriage of surreal lyrics with a rather Bach-like accompaniment. The main instrumental line is assigned to an electric organ, offering a much thicker sound than a lead guitar and anticipating the importance of electronic instruments in the following decades. Notice the free rhythm of the melismatic vocal melody, with its poignant appoggiaturas (on-beat dissonances) marked *, floating above the inexorably descending scalic bass:

An extract from *A Whiter Shade of Pale* is included on page 91 of *Aural Matters* (Bowman and Terry, published by Schott). The complete song is also available on a number of CD collections.

Example 81   Reid and Brooker, *A Whiter Shade of Pale*: start of chorus

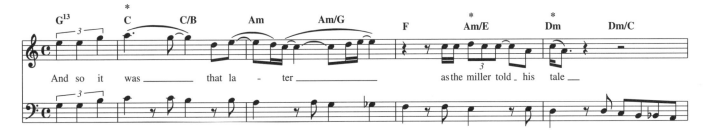

Several other types of pop music co-existed alongside such early 'Britpop' styles. Groups such as The Rolling Stones continued to look back to rock's R&B roots to recapture the raw, rebellious energy of singers such as Chuck Berry, five of whose songs they covered in their first successful year.

In 1960s' America, Soul developed from a combination of gospel singing and R&B rhythmic energy. The vocal style of Soul is very expressive, with high-pitched melody lines, emotionally-charged improvisation and elaborate instrumentation that often includes string and wind sections as well as guitars and drums. Important soul singers include James Brown, Aretha Franklin and Roberta Flack, as well as girl groups such as The Supremes, The Shangri-Las and The Ronettes. Vocal technique plays an important role in Soul – singers may frequently be expected to use falsetto, extended melismas, sighs, sobs or chanting, and to switch easily between pure lyricism and the most earthy tone. Such vocal dexterity also had a great influence on many other types of pop singing.

The folk revival

Historically the term 'folk' was used to describe traditional music, particularly from rural communities, that had been passed on by word of mouth. In the first half of the 20th century a number of musicians helped to preserve such traditions by recording such music and notating it. In America much important conservation work of this kind was undertaken in the 1930s and 1940s by the folk-song collector Alan Lomax, and his assistant, Pete Seeger. Seeger, unlike Lomax, was primarily a performer – his first group, the Almanac Singers (1940) included Woodie Guthrie, who went on to write and record his own material in a modern folk idiom.

Seeger, too, wrote a number of modern folksongs, including *If I had a Hammer* (1949), *Where have all the Flowers Gone?* (1956), *Turn, Turn, Turn* (1962) and *We Shall Overcome* (adapted from a Baptist hymn of 1901). None of these now-famous tunes became popular until the 1960s – and when they did it was mostly in cover versions by other singers, for Seeger's reputation had been damaged when his left-wing views were misrepresented as 'anti-American' during Senator McCarthy's communist purge of the 1950s.

Despite this set-back, the Newport Folk Festival was established on Rhode Island in 1954, and by 1960 had become a major annual event in the folk revival. There Joan Baez established her reputation singing songs from the 'Child Ballads', a famous collection of English and Scottish folksong that had migrated to America with the settlers. Also at Newport, from 1962, could be heard the singer-songwriter Bob Dylan, who was to become a profound influence on The Beatles, The Rolling Stones, David Bowie and many others.

Dylan's early songs, like *Blowin' in the Wind* (1962), followed Seeger's lead in drawing on a number of features of traditional folksong, including diatonic and mainly stepwise melody with much use of repetition and sequence, simple harmony and strophic form (in which the same tune is used for a number of verses):

Example 82   Bob Dylan, *Blowin' in the Wind*: chorus

In 1965 Dylan started using a rock band, rather than the traditional acoustic instruments of folk. Pete Seeger was enraged and Dylan was booed by the audience of the Newport Folk Festival that year. From this point, a divison emerged between such new folk-rock music and what was perceived as a more traditional folk style.

The folk revival movement was not unique to the USA. In Britain, it was led by Peggy Seeger, sister of Pete, and her Scottish husband, Ewan MacColl, and initially was associated with left-wing politics and causes such as the Campaign for Nuclear Disarmament. But by 1969 British folk music was also achieving commercial success with songs such as Ralph McTell's *Streets of London* and the band Fairport Convention, who presented traditional folk material in a totally rock context.

More traditional styles of folk performance were given by the band Steeleye Span. Their 1975 recording of *All Around my Hat* reached the top five in the hit parade – the highest chart placing ever for a traditional song.

An extract from Steeleye Span's recording of *All Around My Hat* (1975) appears in *Aural Matters*, pages 94–95.

A diversity of styles

The years between 1965 and 1975 witnessed a proliferation of different types of pop music – in addition to rock, commercial pop, R&B, folk-rock and traditional folk music, jazz-influenced work (sometimes called 'jazz fusion') appeared from groups such as Steely Dan and Weather Report. Elaborate staging, with light shows, projection and other performance effects, was pioneered by Pink Floyd and led to the spectacular presentation style of 'stadium rock' bands such as Queen. Rock versions of art music were a feature of the work of Emerson, Lake and Palmer – and eventually, the domination of the pop group gave way to the return of solo singers such as Elton John and David Bowie.

One of the most significant influences of this period was the re-discovery of the Afro-American roots of rock, not only through Soul but also through Jamaican styles of pop such as Ska and Reggae. Bob Marley and the Wailers had achieved success in Jamaica in the 1960s, but it was not until Eric Clapton's cover version of Marley's *I Shot the Sheriff* became a hit in 1974 that both Marley and Reggae became widely known outside the West Indies. Eventually, Reggae developed into Dub, in which new versions of pop songs were made by remixing existing recordings, above which half-chanted raps were over-dubbed. In New York, a similar process of rapping over existing music (although in this case, usually disco tracks) led to the development of Hip-Hop.

The development of music technology had a major impact on pop music of the 1980s and resulted in a swing towards instrumental rather than vocal forms. At first this trend was led by led by those virtuosos of the synthesizer, Jean-Michel Jarre, Tomita and Vangelis, who drew on elements of jazz and minimalism in their work. Later, as the technology became more affordable, it led to a proliferation of dance styles such as House, Drum and Bass, and Techno.

Commercial pop continued to thrive in the music of groups such as Abba, Duran Duran, Wham! and Take That. One British group, The Police, had considerable success in developing a somewhat new style of pop, influenced by the hypnotic patterns of both minimalism and reggae. They broke up soon after the release of their most successful song, *Every Breath You Take*, in 1983. However, by then their composer, Gordon Sumner, who was also bass player and lead singer for the group, had begun to develop his own solo career under the stage name of Sting.

Sting's musical background was in jazz and he brought a refreshingly imaginative approach to solo song at a time when the music of many groups was becoming predictably formulaic.

Sting's 1987 album *...Nothing Like the Sun* included contributions from two of the leading pop musicians of the age – Eric Clapton and mark Knopfler, the song-writing guitarist of Dire Straits. The length of the album (54 minutes) was designed for the still relatively new medium of the CD – it is too long for a single vinyl record but two short to span a pair. Many of the songs deal with aspects of alienation and include such subjects as political prisoners in Chile (*They Dance Alone*), terrorisim (*Fragile*) and eccentricity (*An Englishman in New York*). The layered arrangements leave little room for improvisation, but they transcend the quadruple-metre straight-jacket of much sequenced music. For examle, *The Secret Marriage* (adapted from a melody by the German film composer Hanns Eisler) freely alternates between $\frac{3}{4}$ and $\frac{4}{4}$ time, while the futuristic *Straight to my Heart* is set in $\frac{7}{4}$ throughout. Notice the influence of reggae in the modal melody (much of which uses only four notes of the scale), the short repetitive phrases, the syncopated bass part and the static harmony:

An excerpt from *Straight to my Heart* is included in *Aural Matters*, page 97. The complete CD of *...Nothing Like the Sun* is available on Universal CDA6402. Detailed scores of seven of the songs were included in the *Sting Rock Score*, from Music Sales, although at the time of going to press this collection was unfortunately out of print.

Example 83   Sting, *Straight to my Heart*: start of verse 1

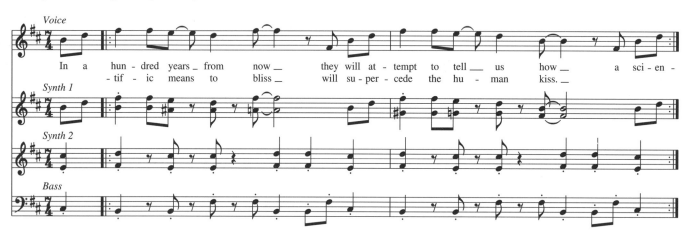

Popular music in the late 1980s continued to be dominated by technology-based dance music on the one hand, or the aggresively distorted guitars and heavy drums of Grunge on the other. But, as has constantly happened in the history of music, a reaction set in – the mid-1990s saw a return to popularity of guitar-led vocal groups of the type that had characterised British pop music of the 1960s.

The music of groups such as Blur, Oasis, Pulp and Suede looked back to that earlier period, often with lyrics that referred to uniquely British topics and concerns, in much the same way that The Beatles had referred to Liverpool landmarks such as Penny Lane, or The Kinks to Waterloo Sunset. And, like those older groups, the musical style of Britpop is characterised by strong melodies and traditional chord progressions.

Blur's album *The Great Escape* is available on Virgin CD 40855. A score (for voice and guitar) is published by MCA Music Limited (AM934780).

Blur's 1994 album *Parklife* consisted of a series of cameos of British life among ordinary people, very much in the style of Ray Davies' songs for The Kinks. It was hugely successful and the following year Blur followed it up with the album *The Great Escape*, which also reached number one in the UK album charts. The songs are based on a theme of urban alienation – in fact, Damon Albarn (the group's principal composer) later revealed that many of the songs are about himself – for instance, the title of the 13th song, *Dan Abnormal*, is an anagram of 'Damon Albarn'.

The third song on *The Great Escape* is entitled *Best Days* – the opening of the first verse shows how solo vocal music has gone almost full circle in its return to the style of 1960s' popular music. Notice the elegantly shaped melodic line and a chord progression (based on a I–vi–ii–V pattern) of a type that was common in the late 1950s and early 1960s:

Example 84   Albarn, Coxon, James and Rowntree, *Best Days*: start of verse 1

Private study

1. Briefly describe the style of popular song likely to be heard immediately after the end of the second world war in 1945, and name one of the well-known singing stars from this time.

2. What are likely to be the main differences between a rock and roll song and a rhythm and blues song?

3. What was distinctive about the music of The Beatles?

4. What is meant by soft rock?

5. Compare Procul Harum's 1967 hit, *A Whiter Shade of Pale*, with the 1969 hit for The Hollies, *He Ain't Heavy ... He's My Brother*. Consider the use of melodic shape, harmony and the role of the bass part in your answer.

6. What are the musical features of Britpop?

Sample questions

In the exam there will be three questions on your chosen topic, of which you must answer one. Always answer by referring to the composers and precise works you have studied.

Set A

1. Why is the work of The Beatles so highly regarded in the field of popular song?

2. Explain what is meant by minimalism and show how it has influenced song writing in the late-20th century.

3. Outline some of the differing approaches to tonality in the song writing of this period.

Set B

1. Justify the claim that some of the greatest settings of the English language are to be found in the works of Benjamin Britten.

2. Discuss the impact of music technology on song writing.

3. Explain what you consider to be effective word-setting in song writing, giving examples from **either** the work of an American writer **or** from songs in a Britpop style.

Synoptic essay

In the final section of the paper in Historical and Analytical Studies there will be five questions of which you must answer one. The word synoptic literally means 'see together' and refers to taking a general overview, in this case pulling together your studies for all six units in AS and A2 music. While the questions are therefore likely to be of a general nature, the examiners will be assessing your ability to make connections between performing, composing and historical studies, to see the relationship between different types of music, and to understand factors which affect continuity and change in musical traditions.

The specification and sample paper indicate the type of topics that may occur. These include discussion of such subjects as the nature of virtuosity in music, matters of performance practice, the concept of national characteristics in music, the ways in which music can express ideas beyond the music itself, the role of music as an outward expression of beliefs or aspirations in society, and the impact of technology upon music.

Plenty of essay-writing practice will provide a good foundation for this section. To help you make a start the first question below draws on some of the issues discussed on pages 108–109. Read those pages and list the points you think are most relevant – note that the question refers specifically to new styles of composition, and does not ask for a general overview of music technology. Further your research by some wider reading and try to find examples to support your points – for instance, what pieces of music might show how Messiaen used early electronic instruments, or what might illustrate how synthesisers were first used? Then assemble your notes into a coherent structure and write them up in essay form. If you find essay writing difficult, remember that points are usually clearer if sentences and paragraphs are short. Try to devote one paragraph to each main point and briefly summarise your conclusions at the end. Try to avoid repeating points and remember that for a good mark the examiners will expect to see plenty of references to relevant pieces of music that support your arguments.

 ## Sample questions

In the exam there will be five questions, of which you must answer one.

1. To what extent have developments in music technology led to new styles of composition in the 20th century?

2. How important is it for a performer to be able to improvise?

3. Discuss some of the ways in which composers of western art music have been influenced by **either** popular music **or** jazz.

4. Describe what is specially distinctive about the music of **either** the United States of America **or** any one European country of your choice.

5. In what ways do you think that studying music history and analysis is relevant to a performer **or** to a composer?